THE HIGHER FAITH

– You were meant to go higher –

The Higher Faith
© Copyright 2024 by Paul Balius
Published by HA'KODESH PUBLISHING

ISBN 978-1-7349097-6-0 (hardcover)
ISBN 978-1-7349097-7-7 (paperback)
ISBN 978-1-7349097-8-4 (epub)

Editorial services by Thomas Womack, *BookOx.com*

Proofreading by Misti Moyer, *MistiMoyer.com*

Design by Monica Thomas for TLC Book Design, *TLCBookDesign.com*

Images from Adobe Stock: mountains © Faith Stock; doves © zolotons; cross © mayillustration; sword with flame © JoelMasson; columns © Alena.

Quotations in chapter 9 from and about Brother Lawrence are from the Robert J. Edmonson translation of Lawrence's *The Practice of the Presence of God* (The Community of Jesus, Inc.; published by Paraclete Press, Brewster, Massachusetts, 1985), pages 92, 102, 85, 62, 66, 83, 85, 105, 66, 97, 70, 87.

Quotations in chapter 12 from Watchman Nee are from *Serve in Spirit* by Watchman Nee (Christian Fellowship Publishers, 2009), pages 11, 29, 36, 115, 99, 119.

Quotations from Oswald Chambers are from *My Utmost for His Highest*, first published in New York by Dodd, Mead & Co. in 1935. Quotations in chapter 14 are from the devotions for Sept. 30, Feb. 2, Feb. 6, May 15, July 15. Quotations in chapter 15 are from the devotions for Aug. 27, June 6. The quotation in chapter 18 is from the devotion for July 14.

Scripture quotations are predominantly from:
The Holy Bible, New King James Version (NKJV) © 1984 by Thomas Nelson, Inc.

Other Scripture quotations are from:

The Amplified Bible (AMP) © 1965, 1987 by Zondervan Publishing House. *The Amplified New Testament* © 1958, 1987 by the Lockman Foundation.

The Amplified Bible, Classic Edition (AMPC) © 1954, 1958, 1962, 1964, 1965, 1987 by the Lockman Foundation.

Contemporary English Version (CEV) © 1995 by American Bible Society.

Complete Jewish Bible (CJB) Copyright © 1998 by David H. Stern. All rights reserved.

Easy-to-Read Version (ERV) Copyright © 2006 by Bible League International.

The Holy Bible, *English Standard Version* (ESV) © 2001 by Crossway Bibles, a division of Good News Publishers. Used by permission. All rights reserved.

The Good News Translation (GNT) © 1992 by American Bible Society.

God's Word (GW) © 1995 by God's Word to the Nations Bible Society.

Holman Christian Standard Bible (HCSB) Copyright © 1999, 2000, 2002, 2003 by Holman Bible Publishers, Nashville, Tennessee. All rights reserved.

International Children's Bible, New Century Version (ICB) © 1986, 1988 by Word Publishing.

The Holy Bible, King James Version (KJV).

New American Standard Bible® (NASB) © 1960, 1977, 1995 by the Lockman Foundation. Used by permission.

The Holy Bible, New International Version (NIV) © 1973, 1978, 1984, 2011 by Biblica, Inc.™ Used by permission. All rights reserved worldwide.

Holy Bible, New Living Translation (NLT) © 1996, 2004 by Tyndale Charitable Trust. Used by permission of Tyndale House Publishers. All rights reserved.

The New Life Version (NLV) © 1969 by Christian Literature International.

The Names of God Bible (NOG) © 2011 by Baker Publishing Group. From *God's Word*® © 1995 God's Word to the Nations. Used by permission of Baker Publishing Group.

The Living Bible (TLB) © 1971. Used by permission of Tyndale House Publishers, Inc. All rights reserved.

The Passion Translation® (TPT) copyright © 2017, 2018 by Passion & Fire Ministries, Inc. Used by permission. All rights reserved. ThePassionTranslation.com.

THE
HIGHER
FAITH

You were meant to go higher

PAUL BALIUS

HA'KODESH PUBLISHING

Contents

You Were Meant to Go Higher

Never underestimate what an extraordinary God can do through an ordinary person.

For we are His workmanship, created in Christ Jesus for good works,
which God prepared beforehand that we should walk in them.
– Ephesians 2:10 NKJV

D ear Christian, God is not done with you yet. So long as you have breath in your lungs, the Lord is drawing you higher. You were meant to go higher. *You were meant for something more.* There's no end to the height of your faith with an infinite God in heaven.

There are some who think they've reached the limit of their faith, and they're right. They've reached a limit of their own making. But make no mistake about this: There's no end to how much we can grow in our faith, and we must keep going toward that infinite level.

There are some who think they cannot grow in their faith because they're not strong enough, and they're right. None of us is strong enough. But Jesus Christ is our strength, and the Holy Spirit helps us grow higher in our faith.

The secret to growing higher in our faith is believing that we can—and trusting in the Lord to help us do so. The degree of willingness in a believer will determine what God can do with them. You don't need any special abilities; you need only a willing heart. Even a child can have a willing heart—you can be sure that you can too.

This book includes four sections, with ten chapters each. The four sections represent the four pillars that support the higher faith in a believer. It would be better to read through this book slowly and gain more from it than to read fast and retain less. Perhaps a chapter a day for forty days would be a workable pace for you.

At the end of each chapter, you'll be asked to write out some things. I encourage you to use a small notebook or journal for this. Don't shortchange yourself and all that God can do for you by not being willing to write a few things down. Be willing to invest a little time now that will reap a harvest into eternity.

The first pillar is the foundation of faith—principles that we must learn and then live, so God can do a work in our lives. We must learn to believe that God can change us, then come to trust that He will. We need to learn what a higher faith really is, on God's terms and not our own. We need to learn what it truly means to be a Christian. We have to believe for more before the more will come.

The second pillar is tearing down the natural. This is a difficult phase in the life of a believer. In this section, you may be tempted to put the book down, but if you dare to go on, you'll find that the greatest treasure of all is buried beneath the natural state of who you are. You cannot grow higher in your faith and remain as you are. There are things in your life that don't belong in heaven, and by the power of heaven, they can be stripped away here on earth.

The third pillar is the building up of the spiritual. You cannot get to pillar three until pillar two has been firmly plowed into your life. Remember that it's more important to have the right spirit in our spiritual life than to have a higher spiritual life. The higher faith doesn't set you above others; rather, it sets you beneath God. Until you get that straight, He won't lift you one inch higher. Spiritual growth is necessary before our faith can go higher.

The fourth pillar is going higher with God. There's no place on earth or heaven better than being nearer to the Lord. If you want to be nearer to Him, you must go higher in your faith. You must believe that He can help you. You must let Him tear down the natural things that don't belong in you. You must let Him build up the spiritual life you were meant to walk in. From there, He can take you higher.

Child of God, the Lord can raise you up to the higher faith. My prayer is that you'll allow Him to do that in your life, then go on to help others in their faith journey. God has so much for you if you would dare to take hold of it. God is not done with you yet! He wants to use you to reach others. Be willing to be a utensil in the hands of God.

Many years ago, I started to hear the Holy Spirit very clearly every day. In this book, words in italics are those that I've heard from the Holy Spirit. I always compare whatever I hear to the Word of God, which is the foundation I stand on. I pray that you, too, will stand on His Word. When you do, you're standing on good ground.

Throughout this book, you'll sometimes see Hebrew names used for the Father, the Son, and the Holy Spirit. There's so much richness when we see how the names used in Scripture describe God in all His majesty. In this book, these Hebrew names will have the English translation next to them. I encourage you to learn some of these names.

For Scripture quotations, I often use the *New King James Version* (NKJV) translation, which was the standard translation used in the prisons where I taught and preached for many years. I'll also draw from several other Scripture translations in this book. Please look up the verses in the translation you prefer to use. The best translation is the one you read. An even better translation is the one you live.

Blessings to you,
Paul Balius

Foundation of Faith

Sometimes, it's a hard truth that gives us the foundation by which we then can stand.

Jesus taught us, "Therefore whoever hears these sayings of Mine, and does them, I will liken him to a wise man who built his house on the rock: and the rain descended, the floods came, and the winds blew and beat on that house; and it did not fall, for it was founded on the rock." – Matthew 7:24-25 NKJV

If you want to have a higher faith, you must first have a strong foundation that you can stand on. You may have been a Christian for a few days or several decades, but until you have this foundation for your faith, your faith will go no higher.

This foundation has less to do with learning everything about the Christian faith and more to do with actually *living* the Christian faith.

We should always be learning more, and at the same time, always be living more in the ways that the Lord is teaching us. If you want to grow in your faith, you must be willing to be changed. You can barely change yourself an inch in a decade, but God can change you a hundred miles in a single moment. Where God is trying to take you, you need more God moments than you need personal effort.

We come into the Christian faith with the wrong idea of what faith really means. We fabricate our own ideas, then try to fit into them the best we can. But the Lord doesn't ask us for our opinion on what faith truly is; rather, He instructs us in His Word and by the Holy Spirit in what it means to live our lives with a simple faith that trusts Him in all things.

Too often we rush through the programs and processes of man, eager to quickly ascend ever higher in our faith and bypass foundational truths that are needed to go higher. We generally fall into one of two extremes: thinking the Lord can't change us, or thinking we don't really need to change all that much. Both are a hindrance to what the Lord wants to do in our life.

We need to be lifelong learners, always willing to learn more so that we can grow more. We need to go slower and develop more spiritually rather than going faster and missing out on all that God has intended for us to learn. Let God take you on this journey and help you build the foundation that will last for all eternity. Never rush an eternal God.

Believe that the Lord can change you, and believe that He can take you higher than you can imagine. Then ask Him to help you each step along the way. *Never give up on God, because God will never give up on you.*

1

God Can Change You

*There's nothing impossible
for God—not even you.*

"For with God nothing will be impossible." – Luke 1:37 NKJV

In however you need to change, God can help you. The only limit to how much Yahweh Ezer (the LORD our helper) can help you is how much you'll let Him. So just let Him.

If you want to grow higher in your faith, you must believe in this truth: God can change you. He can make you into something new. The Lord who created you is the same Lord who can remake you. It doesn't matter where you are now, only that you turn to Him and ask Him to change you, and be willing to let Him do that. If you dare let Him, He will take you just as you are, then change you into all that you can be.

You'd be surprised what God can change in you, if you just let Him. God promised us, "I will give you a new heart and put a new spirit within you. I will take away your heart of stone and give you a heart of flesh. And I will put My Spirit within you and cause you to follow My Laws and be careful to do what I tell you" (Ezekiel 36:26-27 NLV).

Many of us get trapped in a cycle of failures and think we'll never escape them. We long to live righteously but have no idea how to do that. We want to live higher than we do but continue to walk in defeat. Just because you can't see the way out doesn't mean it isn't there. With faith, where there's a will, there's a way, so long as the Lord is helping you.

It is not a question of God's ability to change you, but of your willingness to let Him. "Create in me a clean heart, O God, and renew a right and steadfast spirit within me" (Psalm 51:10 AMP).

In whatever way you're failing the Lord Jesus, He can forgive you. In whatever sin you're in right now, He can rescue you out of it. No matter your weakness, His strength is always enough. The secret to overcoming sin is being overcome by the power of the Holy Spirit within you. Then by His strength, you can get the victory.

With however you need to change, start from where you are. "'Cast away from you all the transgressions which you have committed, and get yourselves a new heart and a new spirit'" (Ezekiel 18:31 NKJV).

I often hear people give their testimony, and it frequently begins like this: "If God can change me, He can change anyone." They then proceed to tell how messed up they were and how Yahweh Hoshiah (the LORD saves) scooped them up and made them into something new. I just love those stories! They really are true. I know they're true because I have the same testimony. And you're no different—He can surely change you.

I spent several years in prison ministry, and the common theme I found in prisons was that most knew they needed a Savior. I didn't have to convince them they needed to be changed. That makes ministry much easier—we can then jump to the part where we talk about how to be changed. But outside of prison, what I find is often different. People act like there's nothing more about them that needs changing. They're wrong. Be willing to admit just how much God still needs to change you.

If you can believe God can change you, He will. Yeshua (Jesus, whose name means "salvation") promised, "If you can believe, all things are possible to him who believes" (Mark 9:23 NKJV).

I remember a time when the Lord was pressing me to change something about myself. I was thinking I wasn't so bad off, so I asked the Lord, "What about the other guy?" The Lord responded to me with, "*You are the other guy.*" I don't care how far along you think you are—God still has a lot of work yet to do in you. As with me, you're also "the other guy."

There was another time when I was telling the Lord I didn't know how He could change a person I knew, someone who seemed beyond His reach. The Lord responded, "*That's what some people used to say about you.*" Friend, when you look at yourself—and at other people— you need to come to the point where you finally believe, "'God can do anything!'" (Luke 1:37 ERV).

Many argue that they've already progressed far in their faith. But by the way they argue, I know they haven't come very far at all. The further you go on with Yahweh Raah (the LORD is my shepherd), the more you find out just how high He is calling you up to. Prideful people are far from God; only the humble are near Him.

You must acknowledge your need to change, then be willing to let the Lord change you. Dare to ask God what needs to be changed in your life. You cannot change yourself, but God can change you. Your choice is to either be willing to let Him help you, or not. Be willing.

God changes those who let Him. "If you choose to love sin, it will become your master.... But if you choose to love and obey God, he will lead you into perfect righteousness" (Romans 6:16 TPT).

Just because you're broken doesn't mean you have to stay that way. It's in our brokenness that Yahweh Mekoddishkem (the LORD who sanctifies) can put us back together. It's when we're crushed that He will form us into what He has intended for us to be all along. The Lord looks for those who are weak, because they are the ones who will let Him be their strength.

The Lord can do more with a broken sinner than with a sturdy saint. "The LORD is close to the brokenhearted; he rescues those whose spirits are crushed. The righteous person faces many troubles, but the LORD comes to the rescue each time" (Psalm 34:18-19 NLT).

We progress in our faith journey and think we'll always ascend higher. But our journey sometimes takes us up mountains, and sometimes we then tumble down. Right when we think we've overcome something, it will turn around and overcome us. But though we fall, we must always get back up.

What matters is not how many times you fall, but how many times you get back up. "For a man who is right with God falls seven times, and rises again, but the sinful fall in time of trouble" (Proverbs 24:16 NLV).

Most of us had imagined a faith journey easier than the one we've been on. We thought God would make our path easy; instead, He gave us trials. We imagined how much more we could do for the Lord if He had made the path easier. We had imagined all the doors He would open, but never considered all the doors He would close.

We thought we would always progress in higher living as we grew in our faith. But, along the way, we had times of failing and never imagined we would struggle as much as we did. But no matter the fall, the Lord is always there to pick us back up again. Sometimes,

El Yeshuatenu (the God of our salvation) allows us to fail so He can show us His mercy and teach us to treat others the same.

Live a life worthy of the mercy God has shown you. "Let your gentle spirit [your graciousness, unselfishness, mercy, tolerance, and patience] be known to all people. The Lord is near" (Philippians 4:5 AMP).

Child of God, don't despair. No matter where you are today, the Lord can take you higher. If the Lord can change you once, be sure He can change you again. There's never a question of whether He will take you back, but only "Will you return to Him?" Never think yourself above falling. And when you fall, be willing to get back up and go to your Father, who is waiting for you.

The path back to the Father begins from where you are right now. "'So he returned home to his father. And while he was still a long way off, his father saw him coming. Filled with love and compassion, he ran to his son, embraced him, and kissed him'" (Luke 15:20 NLT).

We have times of refreshing, and we have times of drought, and each season is there to grow us. We need both sunshine and rain so our lives will bear fruit for the kingdom. We needed the season before, so that the present season which follows will fulfill its purpose.

As the seasons change, so must you. "There is a season (a time appointed) for everything and a time for every delight and event or purpose under heaven" (Ecclesiastes 3:1 AMP).

El Shaddai (God Almighty) can change you. If there's a lack of change in you from God, the problem is with you. It's not that you're too weak, but too strong—in that you haven't yet surrendered all to Him. The promises of God found in His Word say that He can help you. You need to pray and declare these promises over your life right now.

Stop telling God He can't change you and just let Him. "The name of our Lord Jesus Christ and the power of God's Spirit have washed you and made you holy and acceptable to God" (1 Corinthians 6:11 CEV).

Prayer

Lord Jesus, help me to stop trying to fix myself and to just let You change me. Show me anything about me that doesn't belong in heaven, and help me overcome it while I'm still on this earth. Help change me to become who You want me to be.

Challenge

Ask the Lord Jesus to show you what things need to be changed in your life. Write them down in a list. Beneath this list, write out a statement handing them over to the Lord Jesus. Perhaps you could write, "Jesus, I give you this list of things that need to be changed in my life. Help me do that, Lord Jesus—give me the will to change, and the strength to make it happen." Now put this list somewhere where you'll see it every day. Be daring enough to let others see it too. Leave it up until the Lord Jesus is finished with this first list. Then make a new list, and keep going. *Be who God can help you to be.* "For God is working in you, giving you the desire and the power to do what pleases him" (Philippians 2:13 NLT).

Going further

Find that man or woman you trust and will submit to and allow them to hold you accountable. We're far more likely to change when someone knows the specifics of what we're trying to change. If your pride gets in the way, be sure that it's the devil trying to keep you from the victory the Lord Jesus would have you take hold of. Don't let the devil win this round. Let Jesus change you, and let one of His servants help you along the way.

2

Spiritual Potential

God's plans for you are bigger than your dreams and better than you can imagine.

Now to Him who is able to do exceedingly abundantly above all that we ask or think, according to the power that works in us.
–Ephesians 3:20 NKJV

You have the spiritual potential to walk in the higher faith, and with God's help, there's nothing that can stop you.

There resides in you a greater spiritual potential than you have yet to imagine. Elohim (God the strong and mighty one)—the God who created all things—also created you. When He created you, He placed in you the potential to reach heights only He could imagine, and that only He can help you reach.

If God could raise Jesus from the dead, imagine what He can do for you. "Just as Christ was raised from the dead by the glory of the Father, even so we also should walk in newness of life" (Romans 6:4 NKJV).

There's a spiritual potential for your life that can revolutionize the way you live. You could have a life where the fruit of the Holy Spirit would be ripe within you. A life where your heart would be filled with love and hope and your mind set free of all that might frustrate and worry you in this world.

Squandered potential is the tragedy of what could have been. It's unfulfilled emptiness, with fullness sitting idly by.

Your potential isn't the limit of you, but the unlimited power of the Holy Spirit that dwells within you. "You shall receive power when the Holy Spirit has come upon you" (Acts 1:8 NKJV).

You reach your spiritual potential not by your efforts, but by your surrender. Your potential is beyond your ability and can be achieved only by the power of the Holy Spirit within you. The harder you try, the further you'll be from all that God has for you.

Our spiritual potential remains buried beneath any part of our natural self that we refuse to die to. "For those who live according to the flesh set their minds on the things of the flesh, but those who live according to the Spirit, the things of the Spirit" (Romans 8:5 NKJV).

The spiritual life God has for you isn't one of being set on display before others. Rather, it's a life that is humbly set before your Father, who is in heaven. The world will not understand you, but God will. The Lord will always be with you, and your life will be a blessing to the kingdom and to those around you.

Only God can take you higher than yourself. "With Your help I can go against many soldiers. With my God I can jump over a wall" (Psalm 18:29 NLV).

Your spiritual potential is measured not in the gifts God might give you, but in all the ways you've surrendered to Him. The more of yourself you give to Him, the more He gives of Himself to you. The more filled you are with God, the less you can be full of yourself. When you have God, you have everything you need.

It's one thing to know about God, and quite another to be filled with God. "That you may be filled with all the fullness of God" (Ephesians 3:19 ESV).

The spiritual life that Yahweh Machsi (the LORD my refuge) wants you to live is one that's always relying on Him. When you're weak, His strength will fill you; and when you're foolish, you'll gain His wisdom. The more you try to be strong and wise on your own, the less wise and strong you'll be. You plus you equals you. You plus God equals God in you.

In your own strength, you're the limit of you. "Seek the LORD and His strength; seek His face continually" (1 Chronicles 16:11 NASB).

Your spiritual potential is meant to serve others, not elevate you over them. Spiritual heights can be reached only by a natural lowliness within you. The more you kneel down, the higher El Elyon (God Most High) can take you. The lower you are, the higher you'll soon be.

In the kingdom, your stature is determined by how low you kneel. "Humble yourselves [feeling very insignificant] in the presence of the Lord, and He will exalt you [He will lift you up and make your lives significant]" (James 4:10 AMPC).

The spiritual potential for you is nothing less than the fullness of Ruach Ha'Kodesh (the Holy Spirit) within you. You can be so filled that you'll start to overflow to those around you. There'll be an anointing upon you, an anointing within you, and an anointing that touches those who get anywhere near you.

You can't be filled with the Spirit of God and continue as you were before. "The mind-set controlled by the Spirit finds life and peace" (Romans 8:6 TPT).

Never doubt what the Lord can do with you. He can do beyond what you think possible and beyond what you think you may deserve; His grace means He'll do for you that which you don't deserve. It's not a matter of how much you want it, but how much you surrender to Him. Surrendering requires you to stop your efforts.

You'll do more of God's work not by striving more but by surrendering more. Jesus taught, "Yes, I am the vine; you are the branches. Those who remain in me, and I in them, will produce much fruit. For apart from me you can do nothing" (John 15:5 NLT).

Ask Yahweh (I Am, the Self-Existent One) to help you reach your spiritual potential. Pray that He will help you surrender. Know that sometimes you'll fail in your journey, and be confident He'll always pick you back up. You don't have to prove yourself to Him, only wait in humility for Him to show you what He has in store for your life.

You're one prayer away from a new life. The Lord Jesus taught, "For this reason I am telling you, whatever things you ask for in prayer [in accordance with God's will], believe [with confident trust] that you have received them, and they will be given to you" (Mark 11:24 AMP).

In my faith journey, I've considered what are the greatest things God has done for me. I think many of us think that miracles or spiritual gifts are the pinnacle of spiritual potential. We think of prophetic words and visions of heaven as being the highest point of faith we could get to. But these assumptions are wrong.

Our problem is that we think the higher faith is a higher outpouring of what God does through us. But that equation is focused on gaining power that can be seen by men, which is rooted in pride, and God will have none of that. The higher faith, our spiritual potential, is not what God would do through us but what God would do *in* us.

All the rest is what He can do through us once He has prepared us to humbly walk in our calling.

Christ in you is the best version of yourself. "Test yourselves and find out if you really are true to your faith. If you pass the test, you will discover that Christ is living in you. But if Christ isn't living in you, you have failed" (2 Corinthians 13:5 CEV).

Your spiritual potential is to have such a great confidence in the Lord and His sovereign care over your life that nothing will shake you. The Lord can replace your anxiousness with His peace and your frustrations with His love. You can have a prayer life in which you trust the Lord with every problem and leave every issue with Him as you experience a worry-free life. You can have such love for others that it cannot be lessened, even when they hurt you.

Your spiritual potential is not to be something more before men but to be humbly bowed down before Yahweh Qadosh (the Holy One). You can overcome obstacles because you can trust that He will help you. You can live a life you never dreamed possible, the life God planned for you. When you start living out what God has for you, the life you had before will seem so distant.

Nothing is impossible in your dreams, and that's why God will sometimes meet you there. "'For God may speak in one way, or in another, yet man does not perceive it. In a dream, in a vision of the night, when deep sleep falls upon men, while slumbering on their beds, then He opens the ears of men, and seals their instruction'" (Job 33:14-16 NKJV).

You have the spiritual potential to help others find their way to Christ. It's not your position in the church that God cares about as much as your role in the kingdom. You have the potential to touch lives for God in ways nobody else can. You have the potential for a life that's a ministry to everyone you meet. Your spiritual potential is to be a violin in the hands of the Master, with the Lord playing His song to a hurt and dying world through your life.

You can become who God intends for you to become. You can accomplish more by His plans than by yours. You have the spiritual potential to be a godly vessel, prepared by Him and used for His glory to the benefit of the kingdom. Don't set your goals by the limits of man, but by His plans that He has for you.

Prayer

Yeshua HaMashiach (Jesus the Messiah), help me reach the spiritual potential You have for me. Help me overcome all the natural hindrances of anxiousness, frustrations, pride, and selfishness, so I'm set free to serve You in Your kingdom.

Challenge

Ask the Lord to tell you the areas of your life in which He wants to take you higher. Ask Him to show you what anxieties and frustrations He no longer wants you to carry. Ask Him to show you how you need to love people deeper. Ask Him to give you names of people He wants you to minister to. Write these things down. Then, below this list, write out this verse: "I can do all things through Christ who strengthens me" (Philippians 4:13 NKJV). Keep this list where you can see it often, and watch as He helps you work through these things. *The problem is never that you're not strong enough, but that you're not weak enough. Natural strength is the hindrance to spiritual power.* The Lord told Paul, "My grace is sufficient for you, for My strength is made perfect in weakness" (2 Corinthians 12:9 NKJV).

Going further

When God directed Nehemiah to build the wall, He helped him with provisions and protection, but Nehemiah and the people had to lift every stone. God will do His part, but we still must do ours. Reaching your spiritual potential will happen only with His help, but you must do your part. Nehemiah built the wall one stone at a time. You'll reach your spiritual potential one step at a time. Let the Lord lead you into each step. Then keep track of your progress in a journal. Don't try to do everything at once, but ask God to help you with one thing today. Staying on the right path is more important than traveling fast. Be patient as God forms you, and be diligent to exercise all that He's doing inside you.

3

Meant for the Higher Faith

The higher faith isn't you taking hold of God,
but God taking hold of you.

"For I am the LORD your God who takes hold of your right hand and says to you, do not fear; I will help you." – Isaiah 41:13 NIV

You were meant for the higher faith, and the Lord wants to take you by the hand and pull you up there. Let Yahweh Ezer (the LORD our helper) help you to become all that you were meant to be.

There's a faith higher than the faith you have right now. This faith is stored up in heaven and can be poured down into your life. God has a purpose and a plan for your life, and you must walk in a higher faith in order to live out all that He has for you.

The reason so many do not walk in a higher faith is that either they think they're not able, or they think they already are. The first is easy to overcome; they need to simply surrender to Him who is able. The second is rarely overcome, because there's no defensive wall greater than that of self-deception. "For if anyone thinks he is something when he is really nothing, he is fooling himself" (Galatians 6:3 CJB).

Too often, we settle for far less than we were meant to have. We reach the first step and think we can go no higher. We've climbed a lowly hill and think ourselves high up on a mountain. The Lord Jesus wants to take you higher. You have to climb to the first summit, and from there, you'll see the next one rising higher. You'll never reach the end, but you'll have all eternity to keep going. Jesus can raise you up—not by your strength, but by your weakness.

You won't get the higher faith until you stop settling for anything less. We have too many settled Christians. "Not that I have already attained, or am already perfected; but I press on, that I may lay hold of that for which Christ Jesus has also laid hold of me" (Philippians 3:12 NKJV).

I used to think that the higher faith was only for those who were talented and popular. I thought it was only for those chosen few who had higher positions in the church or in some ministry, and who stood taller than everyone else. I believed that these select people somehow had a higher strength to be more holy than the rest of us. I thought they walked in a greater holiness because of some special strength they possessed within themselves.

I never thought I could reach a higher faith. I can sometimes be disciplined, but in many areas, I just flounder as if I have no strength at all. No matter how hard I tried, I just kept failing. I always felt so weak in myself and never thought I could overcome and walk in holiness. On my own power, I felt powerless. I thought I would have to be satisfied with a meager faith and a lower standing of where I could get to in my faith journey.

I was right about one thing: I would never have the strength to be holy in my own power. I was wrong about something else: People who appear to be "all that" in the church rarely are. But this is where I learned that none of that matters on the path of walking in the higher faith. The more things you can do on your own, the more of a hindrance you are to God, who alone can help you walk in the higher faith. The higher faith has to do with what the Lord can accomplish, not what you can do. It's not what you appear to be before men, but who you are before God that really matters.

If you want a higher faith, you must first go low. "Live in harmony with one another; do not be haughty [conceited, self-important, exclusive], but associate with humble people [those with a realistic self-view]. Do not overestimate yourself" (Romans 12:16 AMP).

The higher faith isn't found in the limelight of popularity but in the lonely places where it's just you and El Roi (the God who sees me). The higher faith isn't found standing before crowds but in the secret place, all alone with your Father. Your highest place in faith is not where people can see you but where only your Father sees you. If you want to get nearer to God, you must spend time all alone with Him. Intimacy is found only in privacy.

If Jesus needed time alone with the Father, how much more do we? "So He Himself [Jesus] often withdrew into the wilderness and prayed" (Luke 5:16 NKJV).

Get alone with Yahweh Magen (the Lord is my shield) and meet with Him in your secret place. If you don't have a secret place, make one. Whether it's a closet, a back room, a car, or a bench seat outside, make it your secret place to be with the Father. Go to this place often.

Let Adonai (the Lord) prepare you for what He has had for you all along. No one who walks in the higher faith ever regrets getting there. It's the place God has chosen for you before time began. God has a plan for you, if you will only walk in it.

The call to holiness isn't to shame us where we fail, but to call us higher to where we should be. This call is by "the power of God, who has saved us and called us with a holy calling, not according to our works, but according to His own purpose and grace which was given to us in Christ Jesus before time began" (2 Timothy 1:8-9 NKJV).

You were meant for something higher. Your life has a greater purpose. Your faith is supposed to grow. Your faith can go higher. God has more for you than you can handle on your own, but He will give you only what you're ready to receive. He isn't waiting for you to be higher but to be lower. Once you're low, He will take you higher.

If Christians would seek a higher faith as much as they do a higher position, they'd be giants in the kingdom. From the song of Mary: "He has done mighty deeds with His arm; He has scattered those who were proud in the thoughts of their hearts. He has brought down rulers from their thrones, and has exalted those who were humble" (Luke 1:51-52 NASB).

So long as you try to attain the higher faith on your own, He cannot give it to you, because it's a gift and cannot be taken as a prize. It's your pride that makes you think you can grow your own faith, and it's your pride that stands in the way of you receiving it.

If you want a higher faith, you must have a lower opinion of yourself. Yeshua (Jesus, which means "salvation") taught, "Remember this: everyone with a lofty opinion of who he is and who seeks to raise himself up will be humbled before all. And everyone with a modest opinion of who he is and chooses to humble himself will be raised up before all" (Luke 14:11 TPT).

Once you realize your faith grows by Jesus Christ working in you—and letting Him do that is all you need to do—the journey will begin. Reaching a higher faith can never be done when trying to raise yourself above others. Kingdom truths reveal prideful motives.

The higher faith is not you exalted in the church, but Christ exalted in you. "I have been crucified with Christ: and I myself no longer live, but Christ lives in me" (Galatians 2:20 TLB).

The reason so few Christians reach a higher faith isn't that they can't, but that they won't. They may say they can't, but the truth is that they don't really want to. You'll never take hold of the things of heaven so long as you refuse to let go of the things in this world.

You can't go on with God and hold on to the way things were before. "Put away the old person you used to be. Have nothing to do with your old sinful life. It was sinful because of being fooled into following bad desires. Let your minds and hearts be made new" (Ephesians 4:22-23 NLV).

The higher faith is found not in a title or a degree, but in a simple childlike trust. Intellect will not get you closer to God; only a simple faith will. Religious titles will not get you closer to God; only a humble heart will. You cannot always see the higher faith in a person, but those with a higher faith will see El Elyon (God Most High).

Seek to be pure, not popular. Jesus taught, "Blessed are those whose thoughts are pure. They will see God" (Matthew 5:8 GW).

There was a moment many years ago in which the Lord gave me a word that changed the course of my life. It was so clear and so simple, and it altered my faith journey ever since. He told me, *You were meant for something more.* At that very moment, I knew He was telling this not to me but to other people I was to minister to. It was the message I was meant to encourage others with. It was the message the Lord wanted believers to believe for their lives: *You were meant for something more.*

If you believe God wants you to go higher in your faith—and that He's standing ready to take you there—this will change your life. Once you embrace the simple truth that you were meant for the higher faith, for the "something more," you can begin to reach for it.

You won't grasp it on your own power; rather, He will help you every step of the way, if you will only believe.

Prayer

Abba ("dear Father" in Aramaic), I know that You want me to walk in the higher faith, and I trust that You will help me get there. I pray that You would pour into me Your Spirit, that I could get to the places only You can help me get to.

Challenge

Consider how you may have used the wrong measure with those who you thought had a higher faith. Ask the Lord to bring to your mind three people who have a genuine higher faith—not people with high positions or who are popular, but people you know in your life who live a simple faith and walk at a higher level with God. Write down some of the characteristics in these people that you believe are pleasing to God. Take this list and pray that God will help you grow in these same characteristics. If these people are still living, let them know how their life has blessed you. God blesses those who bless others. "Those who live to bless others will have blessings heaped upon them, and the one who pours out his life to pour out blessings will be saturated with favor" (Proverbs 11:25 TPT).

Going further

Consider how you start each day. Every morning, put away all the distractions and spend time with the Lord. Whether it be reading the Word, going through a devotion, or spending time in prayer—let the beginning of your day be with the Lord. If necessary, start waking up earlier so you can spend more time with Him. I can guarantee that if you make this your daily practice, it will change the trajectory of your life. *If you want to improve your life, then start.* "If you do what the LORD wants, he will make certain each step you take is sure. The LORD will hold your hand, and if you stumble, you still won't fall" (Psalm 37:23-24 CEV).

4

The Willingness of a Saint

The leading of the Lord is reserved for those who are willing to follow.

For all who are allowing themselves to be led by the Spirit of God are sons of God. – Romans 8:14 AMP

Walking in the higher faith is for those who are willing to let God help them do it. Those who go farthest depend the most on Yahweh Raah (the LORD is my shepherd) to help them get there.

Are you willing to go to heaven by the blood of Christ, and not of anything you can do? It seems that the hardest thing we can ever do is nothing. By our pride, we think that surely we must contribute something in order to gain something. But heaven will have none of that.

You cannot earn your way to heaven, because the only currency God will accept is the blood of His Son Jesus. "He is so rich in kindness and grace that he purchased our freedom with the blood of his Son and forgave our sins" (Ephesians 1:7 NLT).

Are you willing to trust the Lord with that problem you're holding on to? We say we trust the Lord, but the firmness of our grip on our problems proves that we don't trust Him completely. We want the Lord to help us, but we're not willing to give Him our problems to do with as He pleases.

It's not your strength to stand but your willingness to kneel that God is looking for. Jesus said, "You search the Scriptures, for in them you think you have eternal life; and these are they which testify of Me. But you are not willing to come to Me that you may have life" (John 5:39-40 NKJV).

Are you willing to let the Spirit of God lead you each day? We ask for God to show us the way, then jump ahead of Him in whatever we want to do. And then, when by our own fault we end up in a difficult place, we ask Him why He allowed it. He will lead you only when you willingly follow Him.

You can be guided only if you're willing to follow. Jesus taught, "If you want to be my disciple, follow me and you will go where I am going. And if you truly follow me as my disciple, the Father will shower his favor upon your life" (John 12:26 TPT).

Are you willing to wait for God's timing on that thing you're praying for? We pray, then wonder why He isn't moving. Perhaps He is waiting for us to be changed. Consider that God has a purpose in your every trial, and He won't end the trial until His purpose has been fulfilled. Pray for what you need, and let God decide on the timing.

The more you believe in something, the longer you're willing to wait for it. "Rest in the Lord and be willing to wait for Him" (Psalm 37:7 NLV).

Are you willing to deny yourself and hand over to your Lord and Savior your right to yourself? Yeshua (Jesus) made it clear that we must give up our lives before His life will reign in us. We try to negotiate this deal, trying to keep some portion of our lives in our own hands, but the Lord will not bargain with you on what it takes to go higher in your faith.

Church is not a hook to hang your hat on, but a cross to lay your life on. "'I have been crucified with Christ; it is no longer I who live, but Christ lives in me'" (Galatians 2:20 NKJV).

Are you willing to crucify your flesh and be raised to a new life as a new creature? We look around and try to find some other poor fellow whose sin seems far worse than our own, so we can feel more comfortable about ourselves. But the Lord is calling you to a higher standard than that.

The Holy Spirit will change you as much as you're willing to let Him. "Surrender yourselves to God to be his sacred, living sacrifices.... Be inwardly transformed by the Holy Spirit through a total reformation of how you think. This will empower you to discern God's will as you live a beautiful life, satisfying and perfect in his eyes" (Romans 12:1-2 TPT).

Are you willing to love the unlovable and be a servant to those around you? We're not called to love only those who are easy to love, but to love even our enemies. We're not called to seek to be served but to serve the least and the lowest of those around us.

When you pray for your enemies, God just might make them your friends. Jesus taught, "But to you who are willing to listen, I say, love your enemies! Do good to those who hate you. Bless those who curse you. Pray for those who hurt you" (Luke 6:27-28 NLT).

Are you willing to believe that El Shaddai (God Almighty) can do anything? We pray for so little and believe for even less. We make excuses for why God doesn't answer our prayers, and we're convinced that our faith is higher than it really is. Child of God, just believe like a believer in a God who can do anything.

A higher faith means you believe more and doubt less. "[The man told Jesus,] 'Please have pity and help us if you can!' Jesus replied, 'Why do you say "if you can"? Anything is possible for someone who has faith!' At once the boy's father shouted, 'I do have faith! Please help me to have even more'" (Mark 9:22-24 CEV).

Are you willing to pray selflessly, pouring out for those around you? Be the intercessor the world needs and serve the kingdom, even in isolation and unnoticed, where only El Roi (the God who sees me) is watching you. Be the one who dares to go into the throne room of heaven, standing in the gap and pleading with God to have mercy on others.

Let God find you in the gap for your family, for your friends, for your church, for your city, for your nation. The LORD said, "I sought for a man among them who would make a wall, and stand in the gap before Me on behalf of the land, that I should not destroy it; but I found no one" (Ezekiel 22:30 NKJV).

Many years ago, the Lord called me into the prison ministry, where for several years, I taught and preached at several prisons. It was an impossible calling because of the sensory condition I have, a subset of autism where many of my senses are broken. Everyday sensory input is distorted so that what most people find normal can be extraordinarily painful for me. But when God calls us to something, it's not based on our own ability, but His.

This calling into the prison ministry ended up being my lesson in willingness. Would I be willing to do what He was calling me to do, even if it meant extraordinary pain for me? Would I trust Him to help me speak in front of large groups, even if, by His design, I was a loner who tripped over my own words before I could even say them? Would I be willing to endure the pain while serving Him, knowing it was He who allowed me to be so broken?

God changes the willing. "Let God transform you" (Romans 12:2 NLT).

Before preaching a service in prison, I would fast for a day beforehand. Right before the service, I would fall down on the ground and plead with Yahweh Yireh (the Lord will provide) to help me. I felt so completely inadequate. I wanted Him to know I was willing to serve Him in whatever way He was calling me to serve, but I was willing to do so only when I could rely entirely on Him. I feel sorry for people who think they're adequate; they're surely wrong.

Until you're willing to let God help you, asking for His help won't get you anywhere. "I will lift up my eyes to the hills—from whence comes my help? My help comes from the Lord, who made heaven and earth" (Psalm 121:1-2 NKJV).

I never got over the fact that God could not have chosen anyone worse than me to serve Him in the prisons. I was a social flop, hopelessly shy, with very little natural charm. I was neither educated nor skilled in preaching. I had no confidence in myself that I could do anything in my own power. But I was willing to be a utensil in the hands of God. In the ministry, we need willing utensils more than we need self-made men and women.

The higher faith is limited, not to those who are able, but to those who are willing. "'If you have a willing heart to let me help you, and if you will obey me, you will feast on the blessings of an abundant harvest'" (Isaiah 1:19 TPT).

What I discovered was that in my willingness to do anything for the Lord, He provided me with everything I needed. Sometimes, before the service began, Ruach Ha'Kodesh (the Holy Spirit) would tell me to put aside my planned message. I am a planner by design, and I used to panic at having to speak without a written script. But I was willing to do whatever the Lord was telling me to do. Still, in all honesty, what

He asked of me was unsettling for me, and took my breath away each time He did this.

I soon learned that when the Lord told me to put down my message, a greater move of the Holy Spirit would take place at that service. This did not happen because of anything I said or did, but only because I was willing to place my life in His hands and get out of His way. After a few times, it became a wonderful feeling of excitement, just waiting to see what the Lord would do. He never failed to bless me with such amazing experiences.

There were several services where the Lord showed me who would be saved during that day's altar call. It was often the last person I would ever expect to get saved, but the Lord nailed it every time. After a while, I grew in my confidence that I was hearing the Holy Spirit, and I knew that whatever He told me would happen would surely come to pass. He never failed me—and friend, He will never fail you.

Your willingness opens up a life filled with adventure in which all you can do is sit back in awe and adoration for all that the Lord will do. Your willingness will be the door you open so God can work through you. It's not to your glory that He uses you, but to your blessing, as you see what He can do through you.

To hear the Holy Spirit, you must be willing to wait until He speaks to you. Jesus promised us, "When the Spirit of Truth comes, he will guide you into all the truth.... He will also announce to you the events of the future" (John 16:13 CJB).

Friend, what are you willing to do for El Elyon (God Most High)? How much are you willing to suffer for Him? What lowly, unappealing service for the Lord are you willing to do? If you're willing to do the small things, you'll be surprised at what great things the Lord can do through them. Be willing to let your faith cost you something. It will always be worth it.

Most Christians are willing to do anything for God unless it costs them something. "Nothing is as wonderful as knowing Christ Jesus my Lord.

I have given up everything else and count it all as garbage. All I want is Christ" (Philippians 3:8 CEV).

Be willing to be a nobody before all, so that Jesus is the Somebody working through you. Be willing to serve God just as you are. Be willing to let the Holy Spirit have the right of way in your life, then watch what will happen from there. You'll be greatly blessed by all that God can do through you, if only you're willing to let Him.

Prayer

Holy Spirit, help me have the anointing in my life as I serve the Lord Jesus in whatever He is calling me to do. Show me where I'm not willing, and help me change my heart and my attitude so I can live in surrendered willingness to the Lord Jesus Christ in everything I do.

Challenge

Be honest with God. Tell Him where you haven't been willing to be changed by Him. Write it down. When you write down what you're thinking, it makes it clear where you're standing. Don't be embarrassed to list ways in which you're not willing. We all have areas of our lives we're holding on to. The more honest you are about this, the sooner God can get to work in you to help you change your mind and your heart to let go once and for all.

Going further

One of the greatest truths about growing in our faith is that God will help us. He wants us to grow, and He wants us to rely upon Him. He can even help us be willing. *It's the devil that tells you to try harder.* "God is working in you to make you willing and able to obey him" (Philippians

2:13 CEV). Believe this word from God that He can change the course of your willingness toward His purposes in heaven. Then, from the list you wrote on the challenge above, pick one item that you haven't been willing to change, and give that to God right now. Once you've truly given it to Him, keep going down the list. Write out a transfer of ownership, giving yourself to God. The world says it's easier said than done, but when God is helping you, it's easier done than said.

5

Faith in Motion

*Growing in faith isn't you doing more,
but the Lord doing more in you.*

Now may the God of peace—who brought up from the dead
our Lord Jesus...may he equip you with all you need for doing
his will. May he produce in you, through the power of
Jesus Christ, every good thing that is pleasing to him."
– Hebrews 13:20-21 NLT

To get to a higher faith, there must be motion in your
faith journey. Reaching a higher place requires
upward momentum.

Faith isn't supposed to be still but moving. Faith isn't you being a stationary museum piece made of stone to show off before others, but something meant to be active and growing. A growing faith means you will look different now than you did a year ago. If you don't see growth, your faith isn't growing. Faith should be alive, not dead.

You cannot grow in your faith and remain as you are. "And we all, with unveiled face, beholding the glory of the Lord, are being transformed into the same image from one degree of glory to another. For this comes from the Lord who is the Spirit" (2 Corinthians 3:18 ESV).

We're meant to grow in our faith each day, because there's a height we're meant to go toward. We can never reach the top, but we must never stop growing as high as Yahweh (I Am, the Self-Existent One) will take us.

Not even the mountains can say no to a man or a woman who has faith. Jesus proclaimed, "You could say to this mountain, 'Be lifted up and be thrown into the sea' and it will be done. Everything you pray for with the fullness of faith you will receive!" (Matthew 21:21-22 TPT).

As a young Christian, I wanted to have a higher faith. I wanted to be more holy. I wanted to live higher than I was. I thought the path was to study more, memorize Scripture, and understand doctrines. I thought it meant serving more, giving more, doing more, and getting ever stronger within myself. Then I discovered how all these things were centered around me and what I could do. I soon learned that I couldn't do very much on my own.

My faith wasn't growing; only my works were growing. Faith isn't the same thing as works. Faith produces works, but works do not produce faith. I had to learn that for faith to grow, I had to shrink. My natural self is the enemy of growth in the spiritual life. For faith to grow, Jesus needed to reign more in my life. The higher faith is having less of self and more of Him.

If you want to go on with God, you must stop living for yourself. Jesus taught, "If anyone wishes to follow Me [as My disciple], he must deny himself [set aside selfish interests]" (Matthew 16:24 AMP).

Faith isn't about what we learn or do but about what we believe. We can learn that the Lord can give sight to the blind and heal all diseases, but do we believe He can do it? We can serve the Lord until we're blue in the face, but do we have faith He can accomplish more in our prayers than in our efforts? When our faith is growing, we'll believe more today than we ever did before. And the more our faith grows, the less we'll doubt the Lord in what He can do.

I remember a time when my father called me and told me that my mother was in the hospital, diagnosed with congestive heart failure. I immediately left work, drove down to the hospital, and went to her room. While I was in her room, a Spirit-filled chaplain came in, and she was covered with a deep anointing of Ruach Ha'Kodesh (the Holy Spirit) upon her. When you're sensitive to the Holy Spirit, you'll sense others who are filled with the Holy Spirit.

Nobody is filled by a fraction of the Holy Spirit, but by the fullness of God. "Therefore do not be unwise, but understand what the will of the Lord is.... Be filled with the Spirit" (Ephesians 5:17-18 NKJV).

The chaplain and I got on either side of my mother while my father was at the end of the bed. The chaplain started praying and declaring healing over my mother. Oh, how I love a prayer of faith! I could feel the presence of Yahweh Rapha (the LORD who heals). The Holy Spirit was moving in that room. This chaplain believed that her prayers were answered before she even said them. That is the higher faith! I remember to this day how this chaplain encouraged me to pray higher.

That was many years ago, and my mother has reached the age of ninety as I'm writing this. She was healed on that very day. The doctors couldn't explain it. Her heart doctor afterward didn't see any sign that she ever had a problem.

Child of God, what person in your life needs to have a prayer of faith that believes God can do anything? He may not always heal, but He always can, and it's with that level of faith that we should be praying.

When you're praying by heaven's rules, impossible is the goal line. "For with God nothing is ever impossible and no word from God shall be without power or impossible of fulfillment" (Luke 1:37 AMPC).

Recently, as I was driving, the Holy Spirit poured more words into me. Here they are, with some added verses (since I always want to confirm what I hear with the Word):

It's not enough to see the gaps you need to fill; you need to fill them. It's not enough to know where you're wrong; you need to be made right. It's not enough to be inspired to be something more; you need to do it. "You are living a brand new kind of life that is continually learning more and more of what is right, and trying constantly to be more and more like Christ who created this new life within you" (Colossians 3:10 TLB).

Learning a doctrine is good; living it is better. You're better off living one doctrine than knowing ten and not doing any of them. "But don't just listen to God's word. You must do what it says. Otherwise, you are only fooling yourselves" (James 1:22 NLT).

Be willing to let God change your life, and He will. Learn to change. If we're not changing, then what's the point? What are we doing? "And I am certain that God, who began the good work within you, will continue his work until it is finally finished on the day when Christ Jesus returns" (Philippians 1:6 NLT).

What would Yeshua HaMashiach (Jesus the Messiah) tell you right now about your faith? Would He say it's growing each day, and you're on the right track? Ask the Lord how you're doing, then let Him help you go higher. Don't fear a hard word from the Lord but a soft word from the devil.

Your faith is a journey, and the path is never straight and easy. There are hills and valleys and many obstacles along the way. You'll trip and fall at times, but you must always get right back up and keep going. The hard times are the lessons meant to teach you.

Adversity is a harsh teacher that gives a cruel lesson, making you a better student in the end. "You know you learn to endure by having your faith tested. But you must learn to endure everything, so you will be completely mature and not lacking in anything" (James 1:3-4 CEV).

You cannot learn to have more faith, nor can it be gained through any program. Faith is a gift from God, and it's given to those willing to receive it. A greater faith can be received only in humility and dependence on God, who gives it when we're ready.

Faith is not a prize but a gift. You cannot earn faith, but only receive it. "God has dealt to each one a measure of faith" (Romans 12:3 NKJV).

The more faith God pours into a man or woman, the more that faith will emanate from their lives. Those with a greater faith have a lower posture before others because they realize how low they truly are in comparison to El Olam (the eternal God).

The higher faith is not looking godly before man, but simply kneeling before a mighty God. Anyone can be near to God, but only a few will. The Lord told Isaiah, "But on this one will I look: On him who is poor and of a contrite spirit, and who trembles at My word" (Isaiah 66:2 NKJV).

When faith fills you, it pours out from you onto those around you. Your faith will lift the faith of others as they witness what a greater faith looks like. If you want to teach about the higher faith, you must live it. It is best taught by example.

Faith stirs up faith. Peter had faith that Tabitha could be raised from the dead, and his faith stirred up faith in others. "Then he [Peter] gave her his hand and lifted her up...he presented her alive. And it became known throughout all Joppa, and many believed on the Lord" (Acts 9:41-42 NKJV).

A growing faith produces fruit, the fruit that proves your faith. Your faith isn't meant to lift only you higher, but to lift others higher as well. Bow low before El Elyon (God Most High) so He can lift you, and from there you can help others on their faith journey.

Jesus never said you would discern others by their gifts, but by their fruits. Jesus taught, "A good tree cannot bear bad fruit, nor can a bad tree bear good fruit.... Therefore by their fruits you will know them" (Matthew 7:18,20 NKJV).

Faith produces miracles. The height of your faith is the height you pray to with confidence that God can do it. Your faith is meant to be more than a trinket or an admirable trait seen by others. It's meant to be a conduit for the Lord to heal the sick, give hope to the lost, and bring restoration to the broken. A faith moving in the right direction believes more every day.

I don't need to prove that my prayers can bring healing; I need only believe that His power can. "If you have faith when you pray for sick people, they will get well. The Lord will heal them" (James 5:15 CEV).

Prayer

Abba ("dear Father" in Aramaic), help me have a growing faith.
Help me have a faith in motion, so that as time progresses,
my faith reaches ever higher. Show me, Lord,
where I've grown stale, and help me overcome every
obstacle in my way, especially myself.

Challenge

When you come across a situation that requires prayer, stop and pray right where you are. Never delay, or you might be too late, or you'll forget altogether. Whenever possible, pray out loud so that others around you will know you're inviting God to help in the situation. Don't try to sound religious; just be yourself, speaking with words you normally use. Don't rely on the words you choose as the reason for heavenly power, because you are never the source of the power. The only thing you can offer is your faith, and then it will be by the power of God alone that your prayers can be answered. Pray like that.

Going further

As you look back on your faith journey, you'll have people along the way who stand out by inspiring you in your faith, causing you to reach ever higher for the things of heaven. As you go along in your faith, seek to live a life that inspires others. The more you give your life to God, the more He will use your life to inspire others. It's not with great effort that we can inspire others, but in a humble surrender to our Father. *If you want to change people around you, live a life that inspires them to do so.* "Be an example to show the believers how they should live. Show them with your words, with the way you live, with your love, with your faith, and with your pure life" (1 Timothy 4:12 ICB).

6

The Measure of a Christian

*Our success for the kingdom is measured
not by how much we've gathered,
but by how much we've poured out.*

God is always fair. He will remember how you helped his people in the past and how you are still helping them. You belong to God, and he won't forget the love you have shown his people. – Hebrews 6:10 CEV

El Deah (the God of knowledge) doesn't use the measurements of man to measure the height of our faith, and neither should we. Look to the Word of God as your measure.

There's no greater measure of our Christian faith than in how we treat each other. How we are with others reflects how much Christ reigns in us. If you want to know the degree that someone loves the Father, simply watch how they treat His children.

The greater you love someone, the more your actions will prove it. "My children, our love should not be only words and talk. Our love must be true love. And we should show that love by what we do" (1 John 3:18 ICB).

While I was in prison ministry, I was blessed to meet many wonderful believers, and we've remained friends long after they were released. One such man is Jesus Lira (known as Chuy). He's a special man with an incredible faith and a servant's heart. When I met him in prison, he was an usher at the church there and was always so kind to me. For years, I visited with him at church on Sundays or at one of the classes or seminars I taught or helped with. I wish more Christians were as kind and respectful as he is. After he was released, he invited me to join him at a ministry he was serving in the Skid Row homeless area of Los Angeles.

The ministry there is called Jesus Knows My Name Ministry. It was founded by Jennifer Chou. She chose that name because of what a homeless man told her one day as he stood in the food line. Robert was a military veteran and had lived on Skid Row for some twenty years. Jennifer walked up to him and greeted him by his name. Robert was completely floored that she remembered his name. She told him, "Jesus knows your name." That inspired the banner name for her ministry. Skid Row is filled with souls with as many stories as there are people.

The more you pour out, the fuller you will be. "Do not forget to do good and to help one another, because these are the sacrifices that please God" (Hebrews 13:16 GNT).

Jennifer went on to expand her ministry there and started a street church called the Church Without Walls. The church service is held every Sunday morning in a parking lot that an auto repair shop owner lets her use. Jennifer knows many of the people on Skid Row who attend these services regularly. She calls them all her friends. She doesn't preach the higher faith; she lives it.

It's not enough that we learn about the love of God; we must live it. "The message that you have heard from the beginning is to love each other" (1 John 3:11 NOG).

I've found that the people who made the greatest impact on my life were those who believed in what I could be. That is how Jesus Lira and Jennifer Chou treat every human being they meet. They don't see people where they are, but as what they can be—then they encourage them to get there. Who is that person in your life who would benefit greatly by you encouraging them in all they could be?

Teach only what you know, preach what you live, and never think of yourself above another. "Don't be conceited, sure of your own wisdom" (Proverbs 3:7 TLB).

Over the years, I used to visit and preach a service, or bring someone else who would preach. I've been so honored just this year to start preaching there on Skid Row once a month. I take my Bernese Mountain Dog named Samson with me. I find that dogs are such a wonderful example of how we should love everybody just as they are. It's interesting to me that the measure Jesus used for our faith was in how we treat the poor, the sick, and the imprisoned—people who can do nothing for us, but who need us the most. Jesus uses that test to see what we will do for Him. When we help the least, we're serving Him the most.

Don't get so focused on the prophetic that you miss the practical. Jesus taught, "I was naked and you clothed Me; I was sick and you visited Me; I was in prison and you came to Me" (Matthew 25:36 NKJV).

Our measure as Christians isn't in how much we know or in some title we have. It's not how much we have served or what committee we've been on. It's not how much we believe in El Elyon (God Most

High) or claim to walk in His giftings. The measure is in how we treat others.

Show grace to other people, knowing we're all in this together. "Therefore, as God's chosen people, holy and dearly loved, clothe yourselves with feelings of compassion and with kindness, humility, gentleness and patience" (Colossians 3:12 CJB).

It's not enough that we know the Word of God; it's that we live it. It's not what we do in front of men, but what we do when nobody's watching. It's not just what we do for others, but how we make them feel. It's not what we've done *for* others but *to* others.

To the degree you're not loving toward others, God isn't in your life. "Beloved friends, let us love one another; because love is from God; and everyone who loves has God as his Father and knows God" (1 John 4:7 CJB).

The measure of a Christian isn't in our Sunday attendance but in how we treat people throughout the week. It's not whether we've done something great before men, but whether we've done something small before El Roi (the God who sees me).

If only we were as sensitive to how we treat others as we are to how they treat us. Jesus taught, "In everything you do, be careful to treat others in the same way you'd want them to treat you, for that is the essence of all the teachings of the Law and the Prophets" (Matthew 7:12 TPT).

The measure of a Christian isn't in people looking up to us, but in our never looking down on them. It's not in how we're seen in the church, but in how we see other people who need our help. The measure is in how we treat every person we come across, especially the least and the lowest.

A smile doesn't cost you a thing, yet it's priceless to the soul who receives it. "Finally, all of you be of one mind, having compassion for one another; love as brothers, be tenderhearted, be courteous" (1 Peter 3:8 NKJV).

Another high mark that Jesus calls us to is having love for our enemies. I recently saw a saying: "The test of Christianity is not loving

Jesus; it's loving Judas." All too often, we justify how poorly we treat people by how poorly they've treated us. But the higher faith must operate on a higher principle, and that principle is to love even our enemies. Our best will be revealed in how we treat the worst.

I can always tell the degree that Christ reigns in a saint by the way they speak to someone they disagree with. "'By this all will know that you are My disciples, if you have love for one another'" (John 13:35 NKJV).

I've found that Yahweh Mekoddishkem (the LORD who sanctifies you) arranges some of the most irritating people to be in my life. He will find people who, for one reason or another, think themselves justified to treat me terribly. They'll talk down to me, work against me, and lie to me, all the while justifying themselves for how they treat me. Sometimes, to be honest, I wish I could step into my flesh and fight back at the level they're coming at me. I want to act like I'm not saved all the way. Thank God for His Holy Spirit that both convicts me and restrains me.

We don't have to agree with each other to love each other. Jesus taught, "This is My commandment, that you love one another as I have loved you" (John 15:12 NKJV).

When we're treated poorly by others, it's a chance for our faith to be tested and fine-tuned. The Lord will use difficult people to grow the sweetest of saints who learn to forgive at the speed they're offended. People living the higher faith will take the higher road and not allow themselves to be pulled down into the nonsense of the day. Growing higher in faith is not a one-and-done step but a daily ongoing exercise of staying in prayer and releasing all your frustration to Yahweh Magen (the LORD is my shield).

In the world, people put each other down, but as Christians, we should lift each other up. "Therefore, encourage one another and build one another up" (1 Thessalonians 5:11 NASB).

It's interesting to me that Yeshua HaMashiach (Jesus the Messiah) tells us to love our enemies, and yet we can barely keep from hating those who are merely irritating. These are the very people you need to ask God to show you how to love them. When we pray for those who are against us, it's hard to be so mad at them. Ask God to work in your heart. You cannot go higher in your faith so long as you have a wrong attitude toward others, even those who are against you. God is using the irritating people in your life to raise you to a higher faith.

We'll be judged by how we treat others, not by how they treat us. "But why do you judge your brother? Or why do you show contempt for your brother? For we shall all stand before the judgment seat of Christ" (Romans 14:10 NKJV).

The measure of a Christian is in how well we treat others regardless of how we've been treated by them. It's how nicely we treat the ones who don't deserve it that reflect the grace of El Hanan (the gracious God) within us. If we want to preach a merciful Christ, we need His life reigning in us so that we're showing mercy to others.

Don't let how you treat others be dependent upon how they treat you. "Don't repay evil for evil. Don't snap back at those who say unkind things about you. Instead, pray for God's help for them, for we are to be kind to others, and God will bless us for it" (1 Peter 3:9 TLB).

If you want to mature in your faith, you must grow in your compassion and kindness for others. If you want to change the world, start with yourself. The mark of mature believers is in the kindness they express to others.

Live like it's your last day, and watch how kind you are to people. "Be kind to each other, tenderhearted, forgiving one another, just as God through Christ has forgiven you" (Ephesians 4:32 NLT).

Prayer

The Word of God says that "the love of God has been poured out in our hearts by the Holy Spirit who was given to us" (Romans 5:5 NKJV). Holy Spirit, I pray that you would pour a double portion of this love into my heart, so I can love others as the Father wants me to.

Challenge

Bring to your mind one person in your life who is irritating you more than anyone else. Get into prayer with the Lord and bring up this person's name as you sit in His presence. Ask the Lord to help you forgive this person, then pray that the Lord will bless them with whatever they might need. Don't bring up in your prayer anything they've done wrong or any correction you think they may need. Rather, ask the Lord to change you and set you free from all your frustration.

Going further

The relationships you have with others will determine how high you can go in your faith. If you remain in your flesh and become bitter, your faith will flounder, and your life will become a burden to yourself and others. If you let go of the things of the flesh and choose to grow in your spirit, your faith will flourish, and your life will be a blessing to you and to those around you. *It takes greater strength to let go than to hold on.* "'Forget about the wrong things people do to you. You must not try to get even. Love your neighbor as you love yourself. I am the Lord'" (Leviticus 19:18 ICB).

7

The Will of God

Until you surrender your will, you won't be in His.

Jesus prayed, "Father, if You are willing, remove this cup from Me; yet not My will, but Yours be done."
—Luke 22:42 NASB

The path to the higher faith is found in the will of God. The Lord wants to take you higher, but you can get there only in His will.

Every Christian should be ever mindful of the general will of God. We often worry about what to do in specific situations, but the general will of God stands high above them all. We may need to seek His specific will on some things, but we can always be led by His general will in everything we do.

It's a decision of our will to step into His will, and the choice forever matters. "You need to persevere so that when you have done the will of God, you will receive what he has promised" (Hebrews 10:36 NIV).

Whether it be in prayer, in words, or in action—the Lord wants you to remain in His will. His will is not the loss of freedom but the gain of freedom from every form of bondage in the world. When we surrender to His will, we'll have victory in our lives and the freedom to live as He intended. It's our own stubborn will that imprisons us, keeping us from living in the freedom we were meant to experience.

You can do more surrendered to the will of God than by your own willpower. "Bondservants, be obedient to those who are your masters according to the flesh, with fear and trembling, in sincerity of heart, as to Christ; not with eyeservice, as men-pleasers, but as bondservants of Christ, doing the will of God from the heart, with goodwill doing service, as to the Lord, and not to men" (Ephesians 6:5-7 NKJV).

If you want to know the will of El Chay (the living God), you must read the Word of God. In every book and every chapter of the Bible, His will is forever revealed. You cannot know His will unless you read Holy Scripture and ask the Lord to show His will to you. The Word is our guide, and the Holy Spirit helps us understand it.

It's not enough that you read Scripture; you must then live it. The Word is living, and the Holy Spirit can bring it alive in you. The highest faith is not the one who knows the most but the one who lives the most. You must be in the Word in order for the Word to be in you.

The will of God is in the Word of God. "But whoever keeps His word, truly the love of God is perfected in him. By this we know that we are in Him" (1 John 2:5 NKJV).

When you're praying in the will of God, your prayers have greater power. When you pray for what God wants, you're opening a door through which He can then move. Anyone can pray from their own will, but the true servant of Yahweh Tsidkenu (the LORD our righteousness) will always seek to pray in His will.

It's not about accomplishing more, but being more in the will of God. "Rejoice always, pray continually, give thanks in all circumstances; for this is God's will for you in Christ Jesus" (1 Thessalonians 5:16-18 NIV).

When you're making choices in God's will, this pleases your Father in heaven. Choices made in the will of God can often make our lives more difficult. God's will may not be the easy path, but it's always the right path. Seek His will, and let the cards fall where they may. Eternal outcomes trump temporal consequences when you're in His will.

Better to live one day in the will of God than a thousand going your own way. "And do not be conformed to this world, but be transformed by the renewing of your mind, that you may prove what is that good and acceptable and perfect will of God" (Romans 12:2 NKJV).

Too often we have our own will made up, then we say it's what God wants. But He isn't impressed by our false claims. We think we can "name it and claim it," and we act as though He approves, but He never gave us that right. God names it, and if we obey Him, then we can claim it. Ask El Hanan (the gracious God) what His will is, and be willing to accept His answer.

It's far easier to get into the will of God than to try getting God into your will. "Now this is the confidence that we have in Him, that if we ask anything according to His will, He hears us" (1 John 5:14 NKJV).

Some people lift up their poverty or their suffering, then parade them about as proof that they're in God's will. Conversely, others will show their success or their good health as proof of being in His will.

They're all wrong, because God's will is unique for each of us. Let God lead you in your life and stop trying to prove to others that you're in His will. If *He* knows you're in His will, that's enough.

Seek to be in the will of God, and let Him worry about the rest. "'What you should want most is God's kingdom and doing what he wants you to do. Then he will give you all these other things you need'" (Matthew 6:33 ERV).

To be in the will of Yahweh Qadosh (the Holy One) is to bring heaven down to earth. The more you're in His will now, the less you must change when you get to heaven. Stop trying to get away with as much as you can and still get to heaven; instead, try to live as high as you can and still remain here on earth.

Believe for more, then pray for more—that the will of God would be done on earth. Jesus taught us to pray for God's will, saying, "In this manner, therefore, pray: ...Your will be done on earth as it is in heaven" (Matthew 6:9-10 NKJV).

We need to learn to walk, to operate, and to live in the general will of God. This is exactly where God will test you. Read Holy Scripture. What does it tell you? Meditate on Scripture and consider the words from God. Jesus said that if you love Him, you'll obey His commands. His commands represent the general will of God. When you're in the general will of God, you're expressing your love to the Lord Jesus Christ.

Obedience is the result of our loving Him, not the cause of Him loving us. Jesus said, "If you love Me, keep My commandments" (John 14:15 NKJV).

When you're in the general will of God, you can then find the specific will of God. God's specific will is in the midst of God's general will. So long as you're outside the general will of God, you cannot find His specific will. The general will of God is like the property a house is built on, and Yahweh Machsi (the LORD my refuge) wants you to stay within the boundaries of the property. Within the boundaries is the house, and inside the house, you can find His specific will. You won't find the house or a specific room within unless you're first within the boundaries of the property.

Many circumstances come before us in which we want to know His specific will. The test is to see if we'll live out our faith in each circumstance while staying in His general will. Sometimes we fail our tests, and think ourselves worse off for the experience. But in the classroom of God, He's always teaching us a lesson through our failures. If we learn from our failures, the lesson is successful. When you go outside God's general will, learn from it.

If you don't live what you learn, what's the point of learning? "But prove yourselves doers of the word [actively and continually obeying God's precepts], and not merely listeners [who hear the word but fail to internalize its meaning], deluding yourselves [by unsound reasoning contrary to the truth]" (James 1:22 AMP).

There are times when we must pray to know the specific will of God about a particular situation. For some decisions, we should seek His specific will before going one step further—before getting married, for example, or making any other major change in our life, and especially in influencing the lives of others. And don't dare become a leader in ministry without having His specific will for that revealed to you. Let the Lord lead you on such things; don't move until He tells you to.

At other times, God will give you His specific will without you even asking. He will come and tell you, "Do this." When He does that—when He provides you with His specific will—it's rarely the easy path. It's usually the narrow path that will be hard. But it's the right path, and you need to take it.

God sometimes makes the path difficult to test your resolve. "'The LORD your God is testing you to find out whether you love the LORD your God with all your heart and with all your soul'" (Deuteronomy 13:3 NASB).

God won't make you comfortable on the wrong path. God won't give you peace when you're going the wrong way. Just because you're serving Him doesn't mean you're doing what He wants you to do. The test isn't what you're doing, but whether you're in His will.

There's a difference between being busy and being in God's will. "Therefore, pay careful attention to how you conduct your life—live wisely, not unwisely. Use your time well, for these are evil days. So don't be foolish, but try to understand what the will of the Lord is" (Ephesians 5:15-17 CJB).

Be willing to wait for your answer. But beware of your stubborn heart that waits only for the answer you want to hear. If you don't want to accept His answer, why did you ask the question? Be willing to accept His will for your life, even if it hurts. You can be sure that God will make something out of your pain, and you'll never suffer needlessly.

Prayer

Yeshua HaMashiach (Jesus the Messiah), help me live according to Your example for us all. You stayed in the perfect will of Your Father, and I pray you will help me do that in my life. Only by Your help can I ever hope to get into the will of God and remain there.

Challenge

As you read the Word of God, take note of specific things that proclaim the general will of God that you should walk in. As your list grows, include these things in your prayers and ask the Lord to help you get into the general will of God in everything you've written out. Be willing to tell others your reason for doing this: that you seek to be in His will by His power working in you. Be sure that if you ask God to help you get into His will, your prayer is in His will.

Going further

Identify one thing in your life right now in which you need to seek the specific will of God. For example, this could be with a relationship, a job, a purchase, or a change in your ministry. Be willing to set it down at the foot of the cross and let Jesus guide you in what you should do. Until you've laid it down as a sacrifice before the Lord, you're still trying to manage the course of where you want things to go. Tell the Lord exactly how you feel, but be willing to do whatever He asks you to do. Be willing to wait for His answer. Commit to do what He tells you to do before He even tells you. *Get counsel from man, but be led only by the Holy Spirit.* "Teach me to do your will, for you are my God. May your gracious Spirit lead me" (Psalm 143:10 NLT).

8

Inspired

*The more you're inspired by God,
the more you'll inspire others
to do the same.*

God speaks in different ways, and we don't always
recognize his voice. —Job 33:14 CEV

To go higher in your faith, you must act upon
the inspirations of the Holy Spirit.
The Spirit of God will inspire you in a thousand
ways—if you will only recognize them.

You can be inspired by the Spirit of God. He can inspire you with what to say or what to do. He can inspire you on a decision to make, given a set of choices that stand before you. The Holy Spirit can inspire you in what direction to take every single day of your life. The Spirit of God is always willing to lead you—but are you willing to follow Him?

You can't be led by the Spirit of God unless you listen to the Spirit of God. "For all who are being led by the Spirit of God, these are sons and daughters of God" (Romans 8:14 NASB).

To be inspired, you must first believe that you can be. There's a higher faith that's available only when you start with a little faith. You must exercise that little faith to grow to something bigger. Even if you believe only a little, that's enough. The principle of the mustard seed shows us that big things come from small things.

Pray first for the faith that your next prayer will have legs to stand on. "A man cannot please God unless he has faith. Anyone who comes to God must believe that He is. That one must also know that God gives what is promised to the one who keeps on looking for Him" (Hebrews 11:6 NLV).

To be inspired for big things, we must first be willing to be inspired in little things. I started out being inspired on things to write. Every day, I received a small inspiration. You, too, need to seek in what small ways God longs to inspire you. Let Ruach Ha'Kodesh (the Holy Spirit) reach you.

The most significant thing you can do is in doing every small thing God calls you to do. "So we keep on praying for you, asking our God to enable you to live a life worthy of his call. May he give you the power to accomplish all the good things your faith prompts you to do" (2 Thessalonians 1:11 NLT).

Getting inspired isn't attained by your efforts, because the source of the inspiration isn't you. The Lord will inspire you—through His efforts, the inspiration will come. There's no textbook you can read or program you can follow to accomplish what only God can do. Let El Shaddai (God Almighty) choose how He will inspire you.

If you want to be inspired by God, you must put down the materials of man. Jesus promised, "But the Helper, the Holy Spirit whom the Father will send in My name, He will teach you all things, and remind you of all that I said to you" (John 14:26 NASB).

While we cannot cause inspiration, we can be in a place where we're more likely to receive it. You need to get under the anointing to be prepared for the inspiration. We often think that anointing oil is only symbolic, but it's more than that; properly applied, it carries the anointing from heaven.

He cannot anoint your head if you aren't drawing near to Him, kneeling before Him. "And he poured some of the anointing oil on Aaron's head and anointed him, to consecrate him" (Leviticus 8:12 NKJV).

Get by yourself and anoint yourself with an anointing oil set apart for this purpose. Quiet your mouth and quiet your mind so the Lord can whisper to you when you're ready. We get into prayer to reach God, and in our prayer, God can reach us. Don't rush the Lord on His timing. Don't box the Holy Spirit in regarding how He would talk to you or what He might say.

Don't wait to be inspired; pray to be inspired. Paul wrote, "Always pray by the power of the Spirit.... Pray that I will be given the message to speak and that I may fearlessly explain the mystery about the good news" (Ephesians 6:18-19 CEV).

Be willing to let the inspiration be born out of nothing from you, and delivered only by the Father. Don't go to the Father with your list and expect that He'll be willing to choose only from your options. The very nature of inspiration is that it never came from you. Ask for an answer to a question you have no predetermined answers for.

Clever thinking hinders divine inspiration. "'For it will not be just you speaking, but the Spirit of your heavenly Father speaking through you'" (Matthew 10:20 CJB).

Beware the inspiration that agrees with your flesh. Know that the deception of your mind can develop a counterfeit for the voice of the Holy Spirit that sounds right to our selfish pride but never came from Him. Don't let your flesh rule your spiritual life, because this will taint your spiritual life with darkness. The more an inspiration agrees with your flesh, the more scrutiny you must place upon it.

If ever your flesh agrees, beware. "For the flesh lusts against the Spirit, and the Spirit against the flesh; and these are contrary to one another.... But if you are led by the Spirit, you are not under the law" (Galatians 5:17-18 NKJV).

Don't worry about what man says when El Deah (the God of knowledge) is talking. The most brilliant men on earth, including the leaders of God's people in their day, were complicit in the deaths of the prophets and, later, of the Lord Jesus Christ. Popular opinion cannot sway the oracles of God or the inspiration He gives to your heart.

So long as you're controlled by the opinions of man, the Lord cannot do much through you. Jesus preached the truth, popular or not. "From that time many of His disciples went back and walked with Him no more" (John 6:66 NKJV).

An inspired writer never has to worry about writer's block. The source of inspiration is a never-ending fountain. All we must do is humbly place ourselves before the Lord. We need not worry about what will come next. Our consideration should be, "Am I willing to receive it? Because if not, it will go to someone else."

If God has called you to do something, do it. "'For if you remain completely silent at this time, relief and deliverance will arise for the Jews from another place, but you and your father's house will perish. Yet who knows whether you have come to the kingdom for such a time as this?'" (Esther 4:14 NKJV).

The Lord Jesus has taken me through the classroom of inspiration, and He has taught me to trust in Him *first* before He will then inspire. This classroom is not only for a season, but for a lifetime, and the

Lord Jesus is always teaching. The journey isn't always an ascension, but is filled with hills and valleys and many obstacles along the way. Lose the idea that your faith journey will be fast and easy. That idea is grounded in fleshly thinking. Settle in, Christian—because the ride will be long and certainly bumpy.

Mountaintops inspire, but the valleys below are where a saint is shaped for the real work of God. Never imagine an easy Christian life, but never doubt that the Lord will always be with you. "Yea, though I walk through the valley of the shadow of death, I will fear no evil; for You are with me; Your rod and Your staff, they comfort me" (Psalm 23:4 NKJV).

I've learned that living by the inspiration of Yahweh Yireh (the Lord will provide) is for each day and not reserved for an occasional setting. You're either living with the Lord Jesus or only visiting Him from time to time. And when your life is with Jesus, He will guide your life, because you cannot help but be changed by His presence. I seek His inspiration at every turn, because at every turn, I am with Him. Your life should have no compartments where the Lord Jesus Christ should not be welcome. Any such areas will surely not experience His blessing.

I seek His inspiration as deeply today as I did years ago. We shouldn't get so comfortable on the couches of our faith that we don't fall on the floor when we plead with Yahweh Raah (the Lord is my shepherd) to lead us. If we're not pleading with the Lord, our prayers are surely too small. When God called me to minister in prisons, I knew I couldn't do it without Him, and I relied upon Him to give me words to say. After many years of ministry in prisons, the Lord called me out to write, and I felt exactly the same way—I couldn't do it without Him. The principle is this: We can be inspired by God only to the degree that we realize how much we need His inspiration.

If you want to be inspired by God, you must wait for Him. "Lead me in Your truth and teach me, for You are the God of my salvation; on You I wait all the day" (Psalm 25:5 NKJV).

For many years now, I wake up every morning and hear a word from the Holy Spirit. I can receive it in a moment, or I can strive for an hour and receive it the moment after I am done striving. The same is true for the blogs I've written weekly for many years; I never know what I'll write until the Lord inspires me. The same is true also for the books I write. My first book was completed, but the Holy Spirit had me put it down and inspired me with a new book to write instead. I didn't have much time before it was due for editing, but with God helping me, how could I fail? We can trust the inspiration of the Lord because He will never lead us the wrong way.

You can talk yourself into anything, so listen to God in order to do the right thing. "Your own ears will hear him. Right behind you a voice will say, 'This is the way you should go,' whether to the right or to the left" (Isaiah 30:21 NLT).

I rely on the inspiration of Yahweh Ezer (the LORD our helper) when I'm ministering to another person or prophesying over their life. In my natural self, I feel so unable and so unqualified to offer anything that may be helpful. But when I simply ask the Lord Jesus to help me give a word and to inspire me with what to say, the words always flow. I don't talk about this to my own credit. The Lord just uses me as His utensil; I'm only a fork or a spoon, and there's no glory in that. I'm but the pen when I write, and I'm but the donkey through which God might decide to speak through. Here's a truth: God won't pour out through you so long as you're seeking the glory from it.

Don't try to impress others with who you are, but inspire them with who they can become. The apostle Paul wrote, "I planted, Apollos watered, but God gave the increase. So then neither he who plants is anything, nor he who waters, but God who gives the increase" (1 Corinthians 3:6-7 NKJV).

When you're ready to be inspired by God, He will inspire you. In whatever God puts before you, He can surely give you all you need to serve Him. When your heart is rightly serving Him, He'll give you the right things to say and do. Your anxiety over what to do disappears as you allow Him to inspire you along the way. It's not that the way will be easy, but every step along the way will be wonderfully inspired. Rebuke the thought that you're not worthy of being inspired. His inspirations are based not on your worth, but on His.

Jesus will use you to the extent you're willing to let Him. Yeshua (Jesus) taught, "I am the vine; you are the branches. If you remain in me and I in you, you will bear much fruit; apart from me you can do nothing" (John 15:5 NIV).

Prayer

Holy Spirit, inspire me with what to do and what to say,
so that my life can be an instrument in the hands of the Master.
Help me see more clearly and hear with greater clarity all
that You want to tell me, so my life is useful to You.

Challenge

Start journaling all the many ways that the Spirit of God is inspiring you. Whether it be with His voice or through His Word, in your dreams, or by the mouth of another, write down what the Lord is using to inspire you. Then be willing to act upon the inspiration, to do what He is leading you to do. If you're unsure of the inspiration, keep praying about it, asking the Lord to make it clearer. If you don't think you're being inspired, pray to the Lord to start inspiring you today.

Going further

If you want deeper revelations, you must become more sensitive to the inspirations of the Holy Spirit. Throughout your day, pray to the Lord Jesus about everything that comes before you, asking Him for the inspiration on what to do. The inspired life is a life of continual inspiration from the Lord Jesus Christ in everything you're doing. He won't always answer right away, and sometimes not at all, but when you need to be led you can be sure that the Holy Spirit will certainly do it. *You'll never be lacking when you're drawing from the resources of heaven. Never allow the limits of man to be the high mark of your life.* "The young lions lack and suffer hunger; but those who seek the LORD shall not lack any good thing" (Psalm 34:10 NKJV).

9

The Practice of the Presence of God

You can be as near to God as you want to be.

Come close to God and He will come close to you.
—James 4:8 NASB

If you want to go higher in your faith,
you must get nearer to the Lord.

Thispter's chapter's title is also the title of a book first published in 1692 that contains conversations and letters between an obscure French monk named Brother Lawrence and a few acquaintances of his. Brother Lawrence never wanted his writings published, but we're highly blessed that they were. Born in 1614, he was given the name Nicolas Herman, but was renamed Brother Lawrence years later when he became a monk.

Brother Lawrence was a simple man who was injured in war as a soldier. For the rest of his life, he served other monks at a monastery in Paris. In his simple life, he lived in the presence of Yahweh Shammah (the LORD is there) each day. He wrote, "I applied myself to practicing the presence of God, whom I always considered to be so close to me that He could be found in the depths of my heart."

My friend, this is the life God has for you and for me. To live a simple life in His presence is the highest place we can ever hope to be. Throughout his life, Brother Lawrence grew higher in his faith each day. He once said, "One is not a saint all of a sudden."

Spiritual growth isn't having more mountaintop experiences. Spiritual growth is having a constant presence of God in the smallest details of your life. "How precious also are Your thoughts to me, O God! How great is the sum of them! If I should count them, they would be more in number than the sand" (Psalm 139:17-18 NKJV).

We often think that to live a great life for God, we must live a big life before others. Such thoughts must be tossed out of our mind. The man or woman of God who wants to live a great life for Him will rarely be known to anyone. The greatest moments we can have with the Lord are when we're all alone with Him. We'll be rewarded in the secret place with God, because it's only there that we're just ourselves with Him. Make it your goal in life to spend more time in isolation with Yahweh Hoseenu (the LORD our maker), who gave you your life. Brother Lawrence wrote, "There is no manner of life in the world more sweet or more delicious than continual conversation with God."

I hear people say they don't feel God's presence. The problem is simple—they don't spend time with Him. You must get into His presence to feel His presence. "Let's come into his presence with thanksgiving; let's shout for joy to him with songs of praise" (Psalm 95:2 CJB).

Brother Lawrence explains the simple way in which we, too, can live in the presence of God. He said, "We must establish ourselves in the presence of God by continually conversing with Him." Don't make your faith complicated. It's the simple faith that reaches the depths of all that God has for us. Stop chasing miracles and gifts, and just seek God. Talk with Him.

Those who pray much will be filled much by the presence of God. "'And you will seek Me and find Me, when you search for Me with all your heart'" (Jeremiah 29:13 NKJV).

The more scripted the prayer, the less your words will move God. He is not moved by your well-crafted speeches but by your raw, open heart that trusts Him with how you're really feeling. If you don't trust Him with your feelings, you don't trust Him at all. Learn to tell Him your every thought, and you'll find your thoughts will soon be changing.

Prayer is your time with God, that divine place where we sit in His presence. Yeshua HaMashiach (Jesus the Messiah) taught "that men always ought to pray" (Luke 18:1 NKJV).

Brother Lawrence said, "We must behave very simply with God, and speak frankly to Him, asking Him for help in the things as they happen." Friend, if we simply talk to God on everything that's before us, our lives will be radically changed. Pray aloud that the demons will tremble at your conversations with God. Pray always that you'll never walk this life alone. There's not one thing you do that God is not interested in. Let God into every aspect of your life, and your life will be blessed by doing so.

Desire to be so hidden in God's presence that trouble can't even find you. "You shall hide them in the secret place of Your presence from the plots of man; You shall keep them secretly in a pavilion from the strife of tongues" (Psalm 31:20 NKJV).

Brother Lawrence wrote, "We must always continue to labor, since in the life of the spirit, not to advance is to fall back. But those who have the wind of the Holy Spirit sail even while they sleep." He also wrote, "To become truly spiritual the heart must be empty of all other things, since God desires to be its only Master." Friend, this Spirit-filled life can be yours today, just as it was for Brother Lawrence more than three hundred years ago. Spiritual truths don't change over time, so you'd be blessed to live as Brother Lawrence did.

The presence of God never depends upon the efforts of man. "That He would grant you, according to the riches of His glory, to be strengthened with might through His Spirit in the inner man...that you may be filled with all the fullness of God" (Ephesians 3:16,19 NKJV).

We're only as far from God as we want to be. The distance is measured by the degree to which we want to do things our own way. We think our way is best, as if God doesn't know better. Child of God, He always knows better. Let go of the idea that you have everything figured out and that you know exactly what to do. Give everything to God, and you've placed all things in the right hands.

When you realize you cannot live one minute apart from God, in that moment His presence will remain forevermore in you. "For a day in Your courts is better than a thousand. I would rather be a doorkeeper in the house of my God than dwell in the tents of wickedness" (Psalm 84:10 NKJV).

These words from Brother Lawrence pierced my heart: "Do not leave Him by Himself." Friend, if you only knew—if you only understood—that El Rachum (the God of compassion and mercy) longs to have you in His presence. Make it your daily aim to allow your heavenly Father to fill your day more and more. You don't have to be perfect; you only have to want to be with Him each moment.

If you want eternal joy, get into the presence of the only One who can give it to you. "You will show me the path of life; in Your presence is fullness of joy; at Your right hand are pleasures forevermore" (Psalm 16:11 NKJV).

You can tell those who are closest to God, because they talk to Him as their friend. "So the Lord spoke to Moses face to face, as a man speaks to his friend" (Exodus 33:11 NKJV).

I encourage you to read *The Practice of the Presence of God* by Brother Lawrence. It can be bought inexpensively or found for free online. But don't just read the book; live it. Here is the secret of living this most blessed life: *Don't seek to live your faith to be seen by men but by God.* "The eyes of the Lord are on the righteous, and His ears are open to their cry" (Psalm 34:15 NKJV).

Knowing that I'm easily influenced, I have to be careful about who I spend time with or whose materials I read or watch. It's a great joy for me when I meet someone who has such a positive influence on me, whether I meet them in person or through the words they've left as their legacy. Brother Lawrence is one of those special souls I'm so blessed to have been influenced by.

One area of influence that Brother Lawrence had on me was in dealing with sin. He had such a beautiful perspective on how to deal with sin. He didn't agonize over it or let it consume him; he simply confessed it and moved on with his life. He trusted that Yahweh Hesed (the Lord of faithful love) would forgive him. He just opened his heart, knowing how merciful God truly is. He then asked God to help him live the way he should.

Confess a thing once, and you're clean. Confess a thing twice, and you're doubting God's ability to forgive you. "But if we confess our sins, God will forgive us. We can trust God to do this. He always does what is right. He will make us clean from all the wrong things we have done" (1 John 1:9 ERV).

Once we realize just how much God loves us and is ready to forgive us, we'll bring Him our every sin and leave it with Him, knowing we are wonderfully forgiven. I learned that once I confess a sin, it's over. The devil wants us to carry our guilt, but God has already buried our sins in the sea. It's written about Brother Lawrence that whenever he failed, "he did nothing but admit his fault and say to God... 'It is up to You to prevent me from falling and to correct what is not good.' Afterward, he did not trouble himself at all about his fault."

Something else about Brother Lawrence that had a beautiful influence on me was the peace he found by letting go of his every frustration. There were many things to frustrate him—there's an abundance of frustrations on this earth for us all. But he would simply take every frustration and give it to God. Most importantly, he *left* it with God. He lived a life unburdened by frustrations because he trusted God with everything.

It's hard to be frustrated about things you've given to the Lord. "Pour out all your worries and stress upon him and leave them there, for he always tenderly cares for you" (1 Peter 5:7 TPT).

With every frustration I have, I'm reminded that I can give them all to Yahweh Tsuri (the LORD is my rock). I only have to carry what I refuse to set down. I used to think I'd have less frustration in my life if people around me were simply less frustrating. But people aren't going to stop being who they are. The way to less frustration in our life is to put the frustrations down faster than you can pick them up. Give God your frustrations, and He will surely give you His peace. Brother Lawrence wrote, "I do not know what God holds for me; I am in such great peace that I am not afraid of anything."

For me, the greatest influence of all from Brother Lawrence was learning how not to worry. Brother Lawrence lived every moment in the presence of God, so he knew he had nothing to worry about—because Yahweh Shalom (the LORD is peace) could help him with everything. When a worrisome thought came into his mind, he simply handed it over to the Lord in prayer, and he knew it was in good hands. It's hard to worry when you're in the presence of God. Brother Lawrence realized this, and that's why he stayed close to God.

We worry too much because we pray too little. "Don't worry about anything; instead, pray about everything; tell God your needs, and don't forget to thank him for his answers. If you do this, you will experience God's peace, which is far more wonderful than the human mind can understand. His peace will keep your thoughts and your hearts quiet and at rest as you trust in Christ Jesus" (Philippians 4:6-7 TLB).

For years, I lived the life of a worrisome soul. I worried about my job, my health, my marriage, my reputation, my salvation, and the list kept going. But when I drew near to God and trusted Him, the worries began to go away. The closer I get to God, the more I realize just how much He has me. When your faith believes God is with you and can always help you, your life will show it. It's said that Brother Lawrence "worried about nothing and feared nothing, asking nothing of God but only that he might not offend Him."

I've learned that the higher faith brings great freedom. We were meant to bask in the glory of God, to be forgiven through and through, to be free from frustration, and to live worry-free every day. The way to do this is to remain in the presence of God.

Prayer

Lord Jesus, help me learn from the life of Brother Lawrence. Help me live in Your presence, remaining near to You in every moment of every day. Help me trust You with every confession, every frustration, and every worry. Help me experience the peace that only You can give.

Challenge

Start scheduling times in the day for making a purposeful effort to get into the presence of God. Set an alarm on your phone and determine a place for meeting alone with God. Get anointing oil and anoint yourself as an act of consecrating yourself from the world, giving yourself over to the Lord and all He wants you to be. Develop this habit over many weeks, and you'll see a difference in the way you live. This purposeful habit will change the course of your life. Brother Lawrence wrote, "God does not allow a soul that He wishes to be entirely His to have any other consolation but Himself."

Going further

Start journaling about your days and what you spend time talking with the Lord about. Make this a welcome time to be in His presence. Note the failures as well as the successes, including the times when your mouth was running loose instead of remaining patient in prayer. When you fail, simply bring it to the Lord and give it to Him. Be honest in your failures, and God will be faithful in His power to change you. *Be honest with where you're failing, then let God help you overcome.* "For You light my lamp; the Lord my God illumines my darkness. For by You I can run at a troop of warriors; and by my God I can leap over a wall" (Psalm 18:28-29 NASB).

10

The Deeper Faith

Faith is like a tree; the deeper the roots, the stronger it will stand.

"For he shall be like a tree planted by the waters, which spreads out its roots by the river, and will not fear when heat comes; but its leaf will be green, and will not be anxious in the year of drought, nor will cease from yielding fruit." – Jeremiah 17:8 NKJV

The higher faith comes from a deeper life spent alone in the dark places with El Olam (the eternal God). Roots are in dark places and never seen, but they determine the height of the tree.

Too many Christians live a shallow faith with little depth in their knowledge of God. I'm not talking about intellectual knowledge, because many people are willing to study about God. No, I'm talking about those willing to spend time alone with God to truly know *Him*, not just about Him.

Knowing about Jesus is not the same as knowing Jesus. Our Lord taught, "I am the Good Shepherd, and I know [without any doubt those who are] My own and My own know Me [and have a deep, personal relationship with Me]" (John 10:14 AMP).

We think that to have a deeper faith, we must have a higher position within the church. But our position in the church has nothing to do with our position before God. People are more willing to serve the Lord before men than they are to serve Him in obscurity. Your position in ministry is seen before men, but your position in Christ is known only to El Roi (the God who sees me).

Christians are more willing to serve Christ than to surrender to Him. Jesus said, "If you truly want to follow me, you should at once completely reject and disown your own life. And you must be willing to share my cross and experience it as your own, as you continually surrender to my ways" (Matthew 16:24 TPT).

We think a deeper faith knows the deepest secrets of heaven. We think a deeper faith operates in the deeper gifts by which a person becomes popular before men. But the deepest faith has nothing to do with secrets and gifts; it works only in a heart laid bare before El Yeshuati (the God of my salvation). If we chase after the things of God, we may catch a few, but if we chase after God Himself, He'll let us catch *Him*, and we'll have infinitely more than we could ever imagine or hope for.

Don't rely on yourself for what only God can do. "You will make known to me the way of life; in Your presence is fullness of joy; in Your right hand there are pleasures forever" (Psalm 16:11 NASB).

We think that the deeper our faith, the easier our life will be, as Yeshua HaMashiach (Jesus the Messiah) leads us. But deeper faith comes with deeper suffering, because it's in suffering that the Lord takes us even deeper. Scripture proclaims that most of the Father's greatest servants suffered more than others. Only the carnal Christian church teaches that we should never suffer. Suffering is the path Christ Jesus uses to help us grow the most in our faith.

Tribulation is the currency that either buys character or is squandered into bitterness. Never waste suffering, so that you can "glory in tribulations, knowing that tribulation produces perseverance; and perseverance, character; and character, hope" (Romans 5:3-4 NKJV). *If it was easy, you wouldn't grow.*

We think that deeper faith will mean we'll rise above our weaknesses. But deeper faith realizes how utterly weak we truly are and simply falls in submission to the Father. Our highest moments will be when we fall the lowest before the Lord, who will help us when we're willing. We need to embrace our weaknesses so we'll embrace His strength.

What other people see as your weakness is actually your strength. Jesus said, "'My power is greatest when you are weak'" (2 Corinthians 12:9 GNT).

The deeper faith is a lower standing before men and before Yahweh Hashopet (the LORD our judge). The lower you kneel, the higher your faith, and the further you can go onward with the Lord. Humility is not an acquired attribute of those with deeper faith, but a prerequisite. Until you humble yourself lower, He cannot take you higher, because you'd only fall.

There are two qualifications for being a mighty servant of God. The first is that you're not qualified. The second is that you agree with the first. By this standard, everyone has the first, and few have the second. "'He has brought down rulers from their thrones but has lifted up the humble'" (Luke 1:52 NIV).

Deeper faith is attainable by all but sought by only a few. Many go to church, but few truly are the church. Many will pray to God, but only a few will have a life of prayer. Many say they want a deeper faith, but only a few really do. Deeper faith will cost you the right to yourself. This cost will turn away the masses, but will be willingly paid by the remnant. The higher faith isn't limited to the few, but only the few choose it.

Once you give up the right to yourself, Christ can use you. Jesus taught, "If any of you want to be my followers, you must forget about yourself. You must take up your cross every day and follow me" (Luke 9:23 CEV).

If you want a deeper faith, you must live in the Word and live in prayer. You cannot go deeper until you're ready to be real. So long as you care two cents about what man thinks of you, God can't help you go any deeper. Until you get alone with God, your faith will not deepen. There's a difference between being alone with God and just being alone. Until you acknowledge His presence, you won't experience His presence.

The most productive time of your day is when you're praying. "Now glory be to God, who by his mighty power at work within us is able to do far more than we would ever dare to ask or even dream of—infinitely beyond our highest prayers, desires, thoughts, or hopes" (Ephesians 3:20 TLB).

You can go deeper in your faith. You can have a faith that lifts you out of the frustrations and emptiness of this world, and up into the perfect joy and absolute fulfillment found only in heaven. Be willing to pour out the dead sand in your life so that Jesus can pour in the living water. Be willing to pay the price of yourself to gain abundance in Christ. You'll never go wrong going deeper with the Lord Jesus.

You won't grow higher in your faith unless you're rooted deeper in the Word. "Some people are like seeds on rocky soil. They welcome the word with joy whenever they hear it, but they don't develop any roots.

They believe for a while, but when their faith is tested, they abandon it" (Luke 8:13 NOG).

If you want to go deeper with Yahweh Sabaoth (the Lord of angelic armies), you must spend time alone with Him. I was greatly blessed to be born with a health condition that forces me to be alone most of the time. For people with this condition, the sensory system doesn't process sensory stimuli correctly. Many sights, sounds, and touches that normal people are indifferent to can be unbearable for me. Being around other people often is the hardest thing for me. Because of this, I spend a great deal of time alone with God. I used to think what I had was a curse until I realized how much it pushed me nearer to the Lord.

When God made you a loner, He was keeping you to Himself. "The Lord is the One Who goes before you. He will be with you. He will be faithful to you and will not leave you alone. Do not be afraid or troubled" (Deuteronomy 31:8 NLV).

Perhaps you too have some reason for spending a lot of time alone. We all have something, and I pray that whatever you've been through, the Lord will show you a way to draw closer to Himself. Don't squander the circumstances of your aloneness, but be determined to spend that alone time with the Lord. Sometimes we can become bitter about the reasons we're alone so much. But God has a plan for everything we're going through. Don't squander the chance to be alone with Yahweh Shammah (the Lord is there).

If God made you a loner, perhaps it was so you could spend more time with Him. Jesus said, "You will leave me all alone. Yet I am not alone, for my Father is with me" (John 16:32 NIV).

Many of us are experts at being busy while accomplishing very little. We can spend our time and have nothing to show for it. Consider all you're doing every day—how much of it could you stop doing, and nothing of value would be lost? Now take that time and repurpose it for eternal value and spend time with the Lord. You'll accomplish more spending an hour with God than you could accomplish in a hundred years of wasted time.

Solitude produces what fellowship cannot. "But when you pray, go away by yourself, all alone, and shut the door behind you and pray to your Father secretly, and your Father, who knows your secrets, will reward you" (Matthew 6:6 TLB).

If you're not spending time alone with God, get alone with Him now. Only there can you hope to burrow down deeply, making roots that will build up your faith forever. The time you spend now will pay dividends forever as your faith grows ever higher each day. Christians who spend time alone with God make faithful people in the kingdom for the Father and His purposes.

The greatest harvest begins in a barren field. The highest trees began as seeds that nobody ever saw. The sweetest fruit comes from those trees with the deepest roots. "The surviving remnant of the house of Judah will again take root downward and bear fruit upward" (Isaiah 37:31 HCSB).

Prayer

Father God, I want to go deeper in my relationship with You.
I want to spend more time with You, telling You the things that
are deep in my heart, then being silent before You so I hear
and know the deep things You've stored up for me.

Challenge

We spend time doing that which we're committed to doing. Be sure that the time you spend with God reflects your commitment to Him. Don't worry about all the things you have going on; just trust Him with everything, and you'll find that He blesses every moment you spend with Him. Find times when you can spend time with Him during the day, such as while commuting to work or walking your dog. God isn't holed up in your prayer closet, so look for opportunities to spend time with Him wherever you are throughout each day. Make a list of the times and places you'll commit to meeting with Him, then do it.

Going further

Make it a point in your prayer time with God to share something deep inside your soul. Tell Him about past hurts or current frustrations. Share with Him your deepest secrets of anxiousness and fears that have a firm grip on you. Tell Him about your temptations and how they draw you in, and how hard a time you have resisting them. Journal your talks, and perhaps include subject headings, so you can easily look back later and see how much deeper your walk with God has become. You can go as deep with God as you want to. *There are some secrets that you share only with the Lord; only He can be trusted with them.* "Trust in him at all times, O people; pour out your heart before him; God is a refuge for us" (Psalm 62:8 ESV).

Tearing Down the Natural

The things that are tearing you apart are often what God is using to build you up.

We gladly suffer, because we know that suffering helps us to endure. And endurance builds character, which gives us a hope that will never disappoint us. All of this happens because God has given us the Holy Spirit, who fills our hearts with his love. – Romans 5:3-5 CEV

This second pillar is the hardest part of our faith journey. Nobody gets a free pass from the hard lessons that are necessary to grow us to a higher faith with God. Yet very few want to go down this path, and even fewer dare to teach that it's something we must do. The idea is wildly unpopular that we must suffer for our faith. But that's exactly what we must do.

You may feel like putting this book down as you read through the chapters in this section. Hard truths are never easy to take hold of.

I encourage you to muscle through this section, for those who endure the wilderness have a greater promise at the end. God makes His best saints in the worst of circumstances, so it's to your advantage to let Him decide what's necessary for you to endure.

If you dare to go on into this section, you'll discover that there's a wonderful treasure buried beneath that natural flesh which surrounds you. The tearing away of the natural is the revelation of the spiritual that's contained within. Gaining this spiritual treasure is more valuable than anything it could ever cost. The Lord has intended for you and for me to walk in this spiritual life in which we can do far more than anything we could ever do in our natural self.

To grow higher in your faith requires that you must change. Change sometimes hurts, and we must let it hurt where it needs to. The Lord is like a sculptor, using the hammer and chisel of our circumstances to break away all the debris that doesn't belong to the final statue of who we were meant to be. The parts that must go are the natural things that resist all that the Lord is doing. The Lord must tear away those pieces that don't belong in heaven.

Reject the fleshly teaching of our day that life will always be easy and take hold of the truth from heaven that life will sometimes be very hard. Thank God in the good times and trust Him in the bad, knowing He is shaping you for all eternity. There's no pain He'll withhold from you if it helps you become who you were meant to be.

11

The Great Surrender

Man measures you by what you have.
God measures you by what you surrender.

Jesus said to all of his followers, "If you truly desire to be my disciple, you must disown your life completely, embrace my 'cross' as your own, and surrender to my ways" –Luke 9:23 TPT

You won't get the victory to grow higher in your faith until you've first surrendered. The victory must belong to Yahweh Chereb (the LORD the sword), and the surrender must be of your own free will.

When I first came to faith, I was filled with the hope of my newfound life with Christ. I was eager to jump in and learn everything I could about this Christian walk, which filled my life with such hope and purpose. I remember thinking I wanted to write down everything in Scripture I needed to do in order to please the Lord and live as He wants me to. It didn't take me long to figure out that I'd keep falling on my face no matter how hard I tried. I became convinced it was just me—that I was just too weak, too far gone, and unable to live as God wanted me to.

The great struggle we have in the Christian faith is that we think it's a great struggle. It's not a great struggle; it's a great surrender. "For by grace you have been saved through faith, and that not of yourselves; it is the gift of God" (Ephesians 2:8 NKJV).

Failing is part of our education in our faith journey with the Lord. Until we reach the end of our striving, we'll remain in that striving. And we won't make it very far on our own strength. That doesn't mean we should stop trying to be good, but that we start leaning on the Lord and on all He can do for us. The Lord allows us to get to the end of ourselves until we finally reach out for Him to be our strength. The harder we resist, the more He must put us through trials until we finally surrender.

The Lord Jesus reigns over those areas of your life in which you've surrendered to Him. The greater your surrendering, the greater the Lord reigns in you. "My old self has been crucified with Christ. It is no longer I who live, but Christ lives in me" (Galatians 2:20 NLT).

Our problem is that we're taught from our youth to buckle down and just try harder. In the world, it's what we can do that determines what we can achieve. All Christians start out in this worldly mode of self-determination, and for most Christians, that's where they stay. No matter how much the Lord tries to lovingly discipline them, they're convinced it's the devil who's making their lives so hard. With hardened hearts and blinded eyes, they remain in a state of rebellion accepted by and even promoted by other Christians who are living the same way.

God's ability to use you has more to do with your surrendering than His conquering. "'Choose for yourselves this day whom you will serve.... But as for me and my house, we will serve the LORD'" (Joshua 24:15 NKJV).

Blessed is that Christian who will crumble before El Gibhor (the mighty God) and fall to their knees in utter despair over what they can never do in their own power. I didn't reach this point nearly as soon as I should have, and I think most who get there would say the same. We must once and for all admit that we can never live the higher faith apart from the Lord. Victory in our lives can be achieved only by the Lord and His power working within us.

You'll do your best for God when you let Him do His best through you. "Yes, God is working in you to help you want to do what pleases him. Then he gives you the power to do it" (Philippians 2:13 ICB).

Not long after I came to faith, I started serving. I couldn't do enough! I was determined to excel in all that I did for the Lord. I kept pressing in to serve Him with all my might, but very little of His. I was convinced that God reaches down from heaven and calls us to serve Him through the natural strength and talents we were born with. That makes sense on the world's terms, and so that's what I did. I was able to accomplish quite a lot with my own power. But I was the limit of myself.

Christians are always more willing to serve than to surrender, and that's why so little gets done. "If anyone ministers [serves], let him do it as with the ability which God supplies, that in all things God may be glorified through Jesus Christ" (1 Peter 4:11 NKJV).

After many years of serving, I finally figured out that I was on the wrong path. It looked good to people, but it wasn't pleasing to the Lord. The problem was that I was serving with only my own abilities. Also, I was held tightly by the opinions of other people. Until we fully surrender to God, we're held captive by our own pride and the ever-changing approval of others. God didn't want me to be more by man's standards, but to be less before others so that He could be more within me.

Never measure your faith by what you do; seek only to be surrendered to the Lord. "Always work enthusiastically for the Lord, for you know that nothing you do for the Lord is ever useless" (1 Corinthians 15:58 NLT).

In my zeal to walk in a higher faith on my terms, I wasn't walking any higher. In my desire to be seen with gifts, there were no gifts the Lord would give me. We're so blessed that El Roi (the God who sees me) can see right through us, and create the circumstances through which He can begin to change us. You can make it a lot easier on yourself if you don't make it so hard for Him to change you.

Growing spiritually has to do with yielding ground, not gaining ground. It's not gaining power, but relinquishing power—relinquishing your right to yourself. Jesus said, "Any of you who does not forsake (renounce, surrender claim to, give up, say good-bye to) all that he has cannot be My disciple" (Luke 14:33 AMPC).

In the world, everyone is trying to keep things together. In the kingdom, the Lord is shaking things up. When He gets hold of you and shows you what you've not yet surrendered, thank Him for the lesson, and realize that in the end, you'll be greatly blessed once you've surrendered all.

The struggle we're in often reveals what we've yet to surrender. Jesus taught us, "Come to Me, all you who labor and are heavy laden, and I will give you rest" (Matthew 11:28 NKJV).

Surrendering to Yahweh (I Am, the Self-Existent One) is not a one-and-done experience but an ongoing process of surrendering one parcel of your life to the Lord at a time. The Lord in His wisdom will use different trials to get you to surrender each unique part of your life over to Him until nothing remains that you can call "mine."

The evidence of a life that has surrendered all is a life that has nothing left to lose. Be the Joshua in this generation who can say, "Nevertheless my brethren who went up with me made the heart of the people melt, but I wholly followed the LORD my God" (Joshua 14:8 NKJV).

We all like to think we're more surrendered to Yeshua HaMashiach (Jesus the Messiah) than we really are. We justify our stubbornness and minimize our wayward behavior. But you cannot fool the Lord; He sees right through you. What others may even praise you for, the Lord is trying to break you away from. What you may call good self-discipline is nothing more than your stubborn and rebellious refusal to finally give up and let Adonai (the Lord) reign in your life.

People think it takes a strong will to walk the higher life. They're wrong. A strong will is the greatest obstacle. It takes a surrendered will to step into His will. The Lord Jesus modeled this when He prayed to the Father, "Not My will, but Yours, be done" (Luke 22:42 NKJV).

I've been greatly blessed in my failures, because in these, the Lord has been able to teach me the most. I'd rather be a nobody in the courts of heaven than a somebody who the Lord doesn't approve of. I'm quite certain that even in my mistakes, the Lord has used me. Never regret your mistakes; learn from them. To serve the Lord better, you need only surrender to Him more. Let the cost of your failures be worth something by using them to surrender more to your El Rachum (the God of compassion and mercy), who is mercifully waiting to help you.

God won't bless any part of your life that you've not yet surrendered to Him. "'For whoever desires to save his life will lose it, but whoever loses his life for My sake and the gospel's will save it. For what will it profit a man if he gains the whole world, and loses his own soul?'" (Mark 8:35-36 NKJV).

We have such a biased view of surrendering from our natural life that we struggle to surrender in our spiritual life. The world says surrender is defeat, but in God's kingdom, surrender is the path to victory. But we must remember who we're surrendering to. The Lord is waiting patiently for you not to be more, but to be less—less of yourself reigning in you. When once you start to surrender to Him, you'll discover the true victory you've always longed for.

Jesus is calling you not to a bigger life, but to a higher life. Your calling is to be more, not do more. If you want to be more, you must become less before He can be more in you. Stop getting in His way. "I can do all things because Christ gives me the strength" (Philippians 4:13 NLV).

Prayer

Lord Jesus, help me surrender my life to You, one parcel at a time, so I can be set free of myself and find true freedom in You. Help me see the natural force at work within me, and give me the will and the strength to overcome it. Help me live the surrendered life.

Challenge

Write down a list of any things or areas in your life that you've not yet fully surrendered to God. It just might be everything in your life. List the top ten if there are too many. Find one thing on that list and underline it. Pray to the Lord to help you surrender that one thing. Once you finally surrender the first thing, move on to the next, then keep going. Dare to keep this list posted where others can see it. When the Lord helps you surrender everything on this first list, make a new one and keep going.

Going further

Just as soon as you start to surrender, you'll find that it's the hardest thing in the world to let go, even just a little. We hold on fiercely to things. We're taught from a young age that it's up to us to earn accomplishments in our life. But then we meet the Lord, and He turns everything upside down. We have to learn to let go and surrender to Him so that His strength will reign in us. For everything in your life that you've not yet surrendered to Him, determine in your will that you'll do so. The moment you do, you'll find how much freedom there is and how stubborn you were before you finally surrendered. Wake up each morning and tell the Lord what you'll surrender that day, then do it. Stop putting off what you don't think you can ever do, and let the Lord help you do it today. *The more surrendered you are, the less striving you will do.* "Commit everything you do to the Lord. Trust him to help you do it, and he will" (Psalm 37:5 TLB).

12

Spiritual Breakthrough

There's no such thing as a self-made man or woman in the kingdom of God.

"And the vessel that he made of clay was marred in the hand of the potter; so he made it again into another vessel, as it seemed good to the potter to make." – Jeremiah 18:4 NKJV

The higher faith is born out of broken vessels. The Lord must break down the clay vessel to form it into something new.

S everal years ago, I read a book called *Serve in Spirit* written by Watchman Nee. Mr. Nee was born in China in 1903, became a Christian in 1920, and went on to impart some of the most anointed words in the Christian faith that have stood the test of time. The main point of this book, *Serve in Spirit*, is that the Lord must break down your natural outer man so that your inner spirit can be set free, and your spiritual life can blossom. Mr. Nee wrote, "The greatest problem in service is the outward man, which inhibits the exercise of the spirit."

If you want a breakthrough, you need to be prepared for something to be broken. Those who've been broken down the most are being shaped the most into all God would have them be. "'For whom the LORD loves He chastens, and scourges every son whom He receives'" (Hebrews 12:6 NKJV).

We think that to grow spiritually, there must be an effort on our part, and then God will bless us. But the opposite is true. We grow in the Spirit as our natural is broken away, and the blessing from God is that He arranges the breaking we need.

Sometimes, He has to break you to make you into something new. "Come, and let us return to the LORD; for He has torn, but He will heal us; He has stricken, but He will bind us up" (Hosea 6:1 NKJV).

There are more Christians who desire a spiritual breakthrough than there are Christians willing to be broken so the breakthrough will come. Many Christians reject the idea that any trials they go through are meant by God to change them. Mr. Nee taught, "This breaking of the outward to release the spirit is not just a truth to be recognized and a theological doctrine to be understood. It is a work done in man by God in order to make a man a useful vessel after he is broken."

A sculptor uses a hammer and chisel to break away those things that don't belong to the finished masterpiece. God is the sculptor, and your circumstances are His hammer and chisel. Everything that stands between you and Him is what He is removing. Jesus taught, "Every branch that bears fruit He prunes, that it may bear more fruit" (John 15:2 NKJV).

We must lose the worldly idea that Yahweh (I Am, the Self-Existent One) is here to make our lives easier, and that by living an easy life we will somehow become more spiritual. The teaching of carnal Christianity coddles the believer into thinking their life should be easy. Carnal teachers laugh at the idea that God might make things difficult for us. But all they get for it is a natural life and nothing of the Spirit. They may have natural wealth, but they're spiritually bankrupt. Name one prophet from the Bible who had an easy life.

Until we're broken and yielded unto God, we're just another zealous soul working counter to the kingdom of God. Paul confessed that in his non-Christian past he "persecuted the church of God beyond measure and tried to destroy it....being more exceedingly zealous" (Galatians 1:13-14 NKJV)—then Jesus broke Paul.

Fleshly pride rules in the hearts and minds of so many in our churches. From the popular people in the church to the leaders up front, we can see the pride of man hindering the Spirit of God. The flesh must be crucified before the Spirit reigns in a man or a woman. Pride in a person limits what's possible for that person's spiritual life. Pride runs counter to the principles of the kingdom.

The cost of the heavenly life is your earthly life. "Those who belong to Christ Jesus have nailed the passions and desires of their sinful nature to his cross and crucified them there" (Galatians 5:24 NLT).

We must learn that to serve the Lord rightly, we must first be changed by the Lord inwardly to make us ready to receive spiritual instruction. We like to think we can learn and grow apart from the trials, but we cannot, and that's why Yahweh Qadosh (the Holy One) allows them. If we want to reach the broken, we must first be the broken. The measure of our usefulness to God is the measure of our brokenness before Him. Nee spoke to this when he said, "Those who are broken more and pass through more have more to give."

You will not have the power of the Holy Spirit unless the power of the Holy Spirit has you. "For if you live according to the flesh you will die; but if by the Spirit you put to death the deeds of the body, you will live" (Romans 8:13 NKJV).

When we understand the plans of Yeshua HaMashiach (Jesus the Messiah) and the purposes of pain, we can embrace all that He is doing around us. Our suffering can create bitterness inside with anger toward God, or it can produce a brokenness inside with a longing for Him. We need not ever pray for a trial, because they come without our asking. But let us pray that in the midst of the trial, the Lord will shape us for His purposes. Mr. Nee knew the heart of man when he said, "Even though I have a heart to give myself to the Lord Jesus, yet there remains in me the reluctance of going all the way." Be honest with your assessment of your own heart.

The Lord has a purpose for your pain. "Jesus replied, 'You don't understand now what I am doing, but someday you will'" (John 13:7 NLT).

I don't know what El Shaddai (God Almighty) is putting you through, but I pray that you'll see how much He loves you. The Lord is making you into something new. Be pliable in His hands. Never forget that He loves you so much, and know that He is always with you. Mr. Nee knew what it takes to change a man or a woman when he said, "The outward man is being broken step by step. Each breaking is more advanced than the previous breaking. The Lord is breaking up the outward man till we are truly broken. He works until we let go of ourselves."

The Lord will break you to change you, if that's what it takes. "'Can I not do with you as this potter?' says the LORD. 'Look, as the clay is in the potter's hand, so are you in My hand'" (Jeremiah 18:6 NKJV).

For many, this is a difficult topic to embrace, because of the depth of pain and sorrow they've experienced in their life. One of the most difficult truths in all of Christianity is that Yahweh Sabaoth (the LORD of angelic armies) is sovereign, and as such, He has allowed whatever suffering you've gone through. In our natural thinking, we cannot understand why He would do that. But if we go deeper and allow God to show us, we'll find that in all our circumstances He was working out His plan in our lives. The process is never easy.

We all suffer. The worst suffering is that which is hidden—pain that cuts deep into the soul but isn't visible to other people. This pain, it seems, produces tears that only you have seen and only you have felt. But the Lord sees your every tear. "You keep track of all my sorrows. You have collected all my tears in your bottle. You have recorded each one in your book" (Psalm 56:8 NLT).

No matter what you're going through or have been through, Yahweh Ezer (the LORD our helper) can use it to help you, to shape you, to make you into something new. He will tear away the outer man around you, knead you back into a lump of clay, then plop you down on His potter's wheel and shape you to be that spiritual man or woman you were always meant to be.

Don't despise the season you're in, but only ask God what He wants you do in it. "To everything there is a season, a time for every purpose under heaven...a time to break down, and a time to build up" (Ecclesiastes 3:1,3 NKJV).

We don't like suffering, but we can take solace in the fact that there's a purpose behind it. There's always value in the cost of suffering and all that it does for our lives. Through this suffering we can find the "'treasures hidden in the darkness'" (Isaiah 45:3 NLT). Never underestimate the cost of your faith, and what it will take to go higher. But never forget that the gains of the Lord will always outweigh the cost you must pay, and your life will be a blessing to the kingdom.

Your deepest hurt will be where God does His greatest work to make you useful for the kingdom. "Consider it nothing but joy, my brothers and sisters, whenever you fall into various trials. Be assured that the testing of your faith [through experience] produces endurance [leading to spiritual maturity, and inner peace]. And let endurance have its perfect result and do a thorough work, so that you may be perfect and completely developed [in your faith], lacking in nothing" (James 1:2-4 AMP).

Mr. Nee taught, "Only after our outward man is broken are we able to continue unceasingly in the presence of God." In 1952, Watchman Nee was imprisoned in China because of his faith. He would never see freedom again here on earth; he died in prison in 1972. We're greatly blessed to have his teaching on this invaluable truth that God is at work breaking away the outer man to release our inner spirit.

We seek God the most in our troubles, then wonder why He allows them. God has said, "I will abandon my people until they have suffered enough for their sins and come looking for me. Perhaps in their suffering they will try to find me" (Hosea 5:15 GNT).

It is sad to think that after Watchman Nee taught on this breaking down of the outer man, he was thrown into a cruel prison for twenty years, where he ended up dying. But I trust that while he was there, Yahweh Shammah (the LORD is there) was with him and helped him walk in the higher faith in the midst of all he was going through.

Prayer

Father God, as hard as it is to pray this, I pray that You'll do whatever it takes to change me. I pray that I will see Your hand even in my troubles, and that I'll know You're with me. Help me not to complain to You, and instead to pray that Your plans will be accomplished in all that I'm going through.

Challenge

Write down some of the hardest things you're going through right now. You don't have to get into details, but just write down a word or two that brings to your mind those trials you're experiencing. Then bring each of those to the Lord and ask Him how He is using this trial to shape you into something new. During this prayer time, don't ask for the trial to be removed; ask only that He would show you all that He's doing. Surrender yourself to His ways, no matter how hard it seems to do so. But please, if someone is hurting you or abusing you, get help. We're not meant to get through things on our own.

Going further

Write down a list of trials that you've gone through in your life, and how they helped to shape your character and make you into who you are today. List each trial, then list the things the trial ended up doing for you. Throughout your day, keep this list near so you can read it aloud and encourage yourself. Let the list remind you of how God is working in your life. Use it also as an encouragement to others in all they're going through. *Tell others what God has done for you to encourage them about what He can do for them.* After Jesus freed a man from demons, He told him, "Go home to your friends, and tell them what great things the Lord has done for you, and how He has had compassion on you" (Mark 5:19 NKJV).

13

Into the Wilderness

You have to go through the wilderness to get to the promise. There's not an easy way, because the easy way would never change you.

"And you shall remember that the LORD your God led you all the way these forty years in the wilderness, to humble you and test you, to know what was in your heart, whether you would keep His commandments or not." – Deuteronomy 8:2 NKJV

If you want to go higher in your faith, you'll have to get there through the wilderness. There are no easy shortcuts to the higher faith.

S ometimes, where El Elyon (God Most High) leads us makes sense; at other times, we have no other option but to trust Him. As we keep going further with the Lord, we'll find there are times when He will send us into the wilderness. For each of us, the wilderness is unique as to the particular circumstances we're placed in. But the commonality for us all is that the wilderness is a difficult place that's hard to get through.

You wouldn't learn the lesson if He gave you the answers before the test was over. The testing in the wilderness prepares you for the promise at the end. It was the Lord "'who fed you in the wilderness...that He might humble you and that He might test you, to do you good in the end'" (Deuteronomy 8:16 NKJV).

We don't have to understand His plan to be in His plan. It's more important to be in the will of God than to understand all that He's doing. Part of our training is to learn to trust Him even when things don't make sense. If He didn't test our faith, our faith wouldn't grow. If we want higher faith, there will be difficult lessons for us along the way.

God makes His best saints in the worst of circumstances. "Yes, you will suffer for a short time. But after that, God will make everything right. He will make you strong. He will support you and keep you from falling. He is the God who gives all grace. He chose you to share in his glory in Christ. That glory will continue forever" (1 Peter 5:10 ERV).

For many years now, the Lord Jesus has led me in how to serve Him. Along the way, He started pouring into me words through Ruach Ha'Kodesh (the Holy Spirit) every morning. This started over a decade ago, and it has persisted day after day, year after year, every morning, as sure as the sunrise. From these words, I started to form the writing ministry that the Lord called me to. When God supplies, the provisions never run out.

If the Lord has given you a vision, He will make a way. "'For God speaks again and again, though people do not recognize it. He speaks in dreams, in visions of the night, when deep sleep falls on people as they lie in their beds. He whispers in their ears and terrifies them with warnings'" (Job 33:14-16 NLT).

This outpouring from the Holy Spirit never stopped, no matter what was going on around me. But several years ago, there was one day when the Lord held back for half a day. I had been especially crushed by a situation that left me wondering why God was allowing me to go through it. But early in the afternoon, I got a word from Him and was blessed with the lesson He had for me. After this, I continued hearing from the Holy Spirit every morning, and every day, I was blessed to hear His voice. Most often, it's with a word of correction for my life, but what joy when that correction is coming from the Lord.

You know you're hearing God when you're getting corrected. The Lord Jesus said, "I correct and punish the people I love. So show that nothing is more important to you than living right. Change your hearts and lives" (Revelation 3:19 ERV).

About a month before I started to write this book, I went into the hospital for lower back surgery. I had prayed for years to be healed. Then one day, Yahweh Rapha (the LORD who heals) gave me a wonderful doctor. I believed that even with the surgery, I wouldn't miss a beat in hearing from the Holy Spirit and posting it online. I had my backpack ready with my Bible, devotions, and laptop for after the surgery. The surgery went well, and they put me in my room. But my body was struggling. I was on a high dosage of pain medication, and I couldn't eat. I barely slept, and my mind was numb. All I could do was lie there and be miserable.

Don't be bitter about the trials God is using to make you better. "'Do not harden your hearts, as in the rebellion, as in the day of trial in the wilderness'" (Psalm 95:8 NKJV).

I lay in my hospital bed for four days. I wasn't getting better, so they weren't releasing me. I wasn't able to read the Word, and I certainly couldn't write. My prayers seemed stifled, and I felt so distant from the Lord. The very worst part was that I stopped hearing from the Holy

Spirit. For the first time in ten years, there was a deafening silence from God. It was as if my best friend had suddenly left me without a word or a reason. We need to be honest with how we feel. Still, my faith was strong, and my hope remained. But I felt so alone.

You don't have to understand God to trust God. "'Though He slay me, yet will I trust Him'" (Job 13:15 NKJV).

Later, they released me to go home. For many days at home, I was the same—still numb in my mind, unable to read the Word, having little prayer, and hearing nothing from the Holy Spirit. I was still on heavy doses of pain medicine. For several days, this persisted, and the pain was getting worse each day. I felt as if God had thrown me into the wilderness and left me to be on my own. I was wondering if my writing ministry was nearing an end.

In whatever you're facing, trust that God will help you through it. "The LORD also will be a refuge for the oppressed, a refuge in times of trouble. And those who know Your name will put their trust in You; for You, LORD, have not forsaken those who seek You" (Psalm 9:9-10 NKJV).

After a few weeks, I started to feel better. I got back into my patterns of praying throughout the day, spending time each morning on a devotion, journaling every morning and night, and getting deep into the Word every day. I started praying more deeply and more intimately again. But still, there was nothing from the Holy Spirit. After more than a week of this, I wrote a letter to the Lord, wanting to know what He wanted me to do. Dare to write out your prayers to Yahweh Go'el (the LORD our redeemer).

Though God may be silent for a time, yet He still hears your every cry. "'In my distress I called upon the LORD, and cried out to my God; He heard my voice from His temple, and my cry entered His ears'" (2 Samuel 22:7 NKJV).

I had written to Him these words: "I want to be Your vessel. I want to be useful to the kingdom. But I want to be in Your will more than doing what I want to do." I was ready to give up hearing the Holy Spirit and writing, if that was what God wanted for me.

The Lord measures our service more by what we're willing to give up than by what we're willing to do. Christians are more willing to serve by their own plans than by falling into His plans. If we want to grow higher in our faith, we must be willing to throw our own plans to the wind and wait for the Lord to lead us.

You have to give yourself over to Him before He'll pour out through you. Jesus taught, "For it is not you who speak, but the Spirit of your Father who speaks in you" (Matthew 10:20 NKJV).

I then anointed myself with oil and laid in bed for a long time, praying for His leading in what He would have me do. I was still in a great deal of pain, so lying in bed was about all I could do. After a long time in prayer, waiting for the Lord, the Holy Spirit began to pour words into me. The river flowed again. I realized sometime later that this happened after twenty-one days of silence. You're most blessed to be faithful even when He is silent. Having to wait always tests the heart and reveals what's really inside.

Sometimes, God makes us wait to see if we will. "Therefore the LORD waits to be gracious to you, and therefore he exalts himself to show mercy to you. For the LORD is a God of justice; blessed are all those who wait for him" (Isaiah 30:18 ESV).

When Yahweh (I AM, the Self-Existent One) puts us in the wilderness, it's not meant to ruin us but to build us into all that we were meant to be. The wilderness is always a test. The test is not to prove to God what's in our heart, for you can be sure He already knows. The test is to reveal to *us* what's in our heart—good or bad, lightness or darkness. We need to know the depths of our soul, so we can learn how much we need to be changed. Whether it be for twenty-one days or twenty-one years, don't squander your time in the wilderness and what it can do for you.

If you didn't have the trials, you wouldn't know what you were made of. We need to be "rejoicing in hope, patient in tribulation, continuing steadfastly in prayer" (Romans 12:12 NKJV).

If you really want to know a person, go through a trial with them. In the good times, we can mask the soul and make others believe we're something else. But the hard times are the rough tools that rip away the masks we normally wear; these afflictions will reveal the man or woman we really are. When Yahweh Mekoddishkem (the LORD who sanctifies you) does this, it's not to shame you but to make you into something so much better. The devil wants to use the trial to knock you down, but the Lord is using the trial to call you upward. That call is loudest when He is silent and waiting for you to truly trust Him.

When God is silent, He is teaching you to trust Him. "People, always put your trust in God! Tell him all your problems. God is our place of safety" (Psalm 62:8 ERV).

Child of God, if you're in the wilderness right now, take heart, for the Lord your God is with you. There's nothing He wouldn't do to help you, so just keep praying that He will. We serve a merciful Lord, and we can trust in Him at all times. Don't try to understand everything, but only trust Him more in the midst of what you don't understand. The more you trust Him, the more He'll pour His peace into you.

So long as your peace depends on your circumstances, you're in trouble. "'These things I have spoken to you, that in Me you may have peace. In the world you will have tribulation; but be of good cheer, I have overcome the world'" (John 16:33 NKJV).

Prayer

Yeshua HaMashiach (Jesus the Messiah), I may go into the wilderness, but yet You are with me. I may not hear You for a time, but You hear my every prayer. I may not understand why I'm going through the trials right now, but someday I'll know; until then, I choose to trust You along the way.

Challenge

Write about whatever wilderness you might be in right now. If you're not in one, write about one you've been in recently. List the ways you think God has used or will use such a season to change you. If you cannot think of anything He might want to change in you, ask the Lord to show you. As you grow in your ability to look for how God is changing you in the wilderness, you'll spend less time agonizing over your situation and more time trusting God to help you through it.

Going further

Learning to trust God in the wilderness will help you grow in your faith the most. Whatever wilderness you may be in right now, choose to trust the Lord with what He is allowing you to go through. Pray to Him about all the things you're trusting Him with. Commit in your heart to trust Him more, and He will bless you for it in the end. Pray out loud, expressing your confidence that the Lord is helping you, so that even the demons know that God has you. *You can either worry about it or trust God with it.* "When I am afraid, I will put my trust in You. In God, whose word I praise, in God I have put my trust; I shall not be afraid. What can mere mortals do to me?" (Psalm 56:3-4 NASB).

14

Broken Bread and Poured-Out Wine

A sculptor uses the hardest tools to make the greatest impact. The Lord does the same with your circumstances.

But now, O Lord, You are our Father; we are the clay, and You our potter; and all we are the work of Your hand. – Isaiah 64:8 NKJV

The higher faith is found after you've agreed with El Yeshuati (the God of my salvation) that the higher faith will cost you something. Salvation is free, but the higher faith comes at a great price.

Too often, Christianity is peddled no differently than the many products we see for sale around us in the world. The marketing programs are nearly the same; they speak of all the great benefits and how nice our life would be if we became Christians. Certainly we'll find purpose and meaning as Christians; I never argue with that. But the problem I have with much of the marketing hype is that it hides God's truth; it hides the fact that our faith journey will not be easy; nevertheless, that journey will most certainly be worth any cost we pay.

The day your ministry becomes a business, it's no longer a ministry. "For unlike so many, we are not peddlers of God's Word who water down the message. We are those sent from God with pure motives, who speak in the sight of God from our union with Christ" (2 Corinthians 2:17 TPT).

One of my favorite Christian teachers of all time is Oswald Chambers. He died at the young age of forty-three in 1917, but we are greatly blessed that his wife, Gertrude "Biddy" Hobbs Chambers, recorded much of his talks in shorthand. Biddy is short for Beloved Disciple, or B. D., the nickname Oswald had given her. Many years after Oswald Chambers went to heaven, Biddy Chambers put together the classic devotional titled *My Utmost for His Highest* from her husband's anointed teachings. This timeless devotional is shockingly powerful and must be read prayerfully many times to begin understanding the profound spiritual truths held between its covers.

Oswald Chambers spoke on how God prepares us to serve Him by making us "broken bread and poured-out wine." He went on to say, "Yet God can never make us into wine if we object to the fingers He chooses to use to crush us." God chooses the people and circumstances to crush us, and it's up to us to let Him do that. This crushing is the classroom of adversity in which God will prepare us to serve Him.

You have to crush the grape to make the wine. "And not only this, but [with joy] let us exult in our sufferings and rejoice in our hardships, knowing that hardship (distress, pressure, trouble) produces patient endurance; and endurance, proven character (spiritual maturity); and proven character, hope and confident assurance [of eternal salvation]" (Romans 5:3-4 AMP).

In the midst of the Lord shaping us, we usually pray that God will remove our difficulties instead of asking that God will use them to change us. What we think is destroying us is actually building us into the person God can use. Lose the idea that the Father will make your life easy. Be sure that El Deah (the God of knowledge) knows what He is doing. Let Him break you like bread. Let Him crush you so He can pour you out like wine.

When God has you on your knees, it's there that He can change you. "My brothers and sisters, you will have many kinds of trouble. But this gives you a reason to be very happy. You know that when your faith is tested, you learn to be patient in suffering. If you let that patience work in you, the end result will be good. You will be mature and complete. You will be all that God wants you to be" (James 1:2-4 ERV).

Early on in my faith, the Lord whispered deep into my heart that I would someday write for His kingdom. I was most pleased with that word because I love to spend time alone. The reason I'm a loner is the thorn in the flesh that God has chosen for me to have. As I've mentioned, I was born with a cruel sensory condition, and it often makes life impossible. The pain from it pierces my soul, a burden that has weighed me down throughout my life. Sometimes, the thorns from God pierce us deeply.

You won't produce a harvest until you've first been broken by the plow. "'I said, "Plant the good seeds of righteousness, and you will harvest a crop of love. Plow up the hard ground of your hearts, for now is the time to seek the LORD, that he may come and shower righteousness upon you"'" (Hosea 10:12 NLT).

Before I started to write for Yahweh Go'el (the LORD our redeemer), He saw fit to have me serve for many years inside prisons. I was so angry that He asked me to do something that He knew would be so incredibly painful for me, given the condition He allowed me to have. But after being hard-pressed by Him and receiving His promise to help me, I began teaching and preaching inside prisons. It was a blessing for sure, but there were hardships I couldn't even describe. I learned long ago that normal people simply cannot understand my health condition, so it's better to carry this burden alone. The worst pain is misunderstood pain.

You must first be broken, so He can form you into something new. "And the vessel that he was making from clay was spoiled in the hand of the potter; so he made it over, reworking it into another vessel as it seemed good to the potter to make it" (Jeremiah 18:4 AMPC).

Sometimes, I wonder how Yahweh (I Am, the Self-Existent One) can make something good come from the bad that He puts me through. During such times, His silence is worse than His rebuke. When God places us in the winepress, the process is never easy. You can't have the bread until it's first broken. You can't have the wine without first crushing the grape.

There are bad days, and then there are impossibly terrible days. I remember one such day when I hit bottom and felt like I couldn't go any lower. The pain from my sensory input reached such a level that I just couldn't take it anymore. The worst part for me is that nobody can even see the injuries, because they cut deep into the hidden parts of the soul. There I was, at the end of myself, wondering what God was doing. I loved God, but I was wondering if He loved me. In my anger, I told Him, "Why do You make me suffer so much? Why don't You just kill me? I am done with You."

The foundation of our faith is not in how we feel toward God, but in how God feels toward us. "This is real love—not that we loved God, but that he loved us and sent his Son as a sacrifice to take away our sins" (1 John 4:10 NLT).

For the rest of that day, I didn't talk to the Lord. I was so numb and so hurt. I didn't understand why He continued to allow me to suffer so much even though I was serving Him. I didn't see one good thing that came about from all that I was going through. I shut the Lord out for the rest of the day. You step into a dark place when you step away from the light of the Lord.

You may look knocked down to men, yet be exactly where God can use you. "We are persecuted by others, but God has not forsaken us. We may be knocked down, but not out" (2 Corinthians 4:9 TPT).

That night, I returned to the Lord. I realized then just how much He loved me. Though I had rejected Him, He had never rejected me. Though I turned away from Him, He welcomed me back with open arms. He had broken me, then crushed me by the condition He gave me and the circumstances He put me in. But I'm most confident that because of this, He was able to accomplish more through me. Chambers said, "Stay right with God and let Him do as He likes, and you will find that He is producing the kind of bread and wine that will benefit His other children."

Sometimes you have to hit rock bottom to get your footing. Yeshua (Jesus) taught, "Therefore whoever hears these sayings of Mine, and does them, I will liken him to a wise man who built his house on the rock: and the rain descended, the floods came, and the winds blew and beat on that house; and it did not fall, for it was founded on the rock" (Matthew 7:24-25 NKJV).

The closer you get to El Hakkadosh (the Holy God), the more you realize how He uses your suffering for His purposes. The devilish idea that God is certain to make us rich and comfortable is born out of the pit of hell, then made ripe in the flesh of man. Chambers taught, "God makes us as broken bread and poured-out wine to please Himself."

If you want to reach the broken, be the broken. "The LORD is near to those who have a broken heart, and saves such as have a contrite [crushed] spirit" (Psalm 34:18 NKJV).

We must cast out of our mind the fleshly thought that we could serve the Father better in our comfort than in our suffering. Let the Father use the classroom of your difficult circumstances to prepare you to serve His children. The more you want to serve Him, the harder His lesson will be. Don't complain about what He is putting you through, but yield yourself to the hands of the Potter. Let your suffering be worth something for His kingdom.

You preach a powerful message when you show grace to those who mistreat you. "Let your speech always be with grace, seasoned with salt, that you may know how you ought to answer each one" (Colossians 4:6 NKJV).

Are you willing to be broken bread and poured-out wine for the benefit of the kingdom? I don't know what you're going through, but El Roi (the God who sees me) does. My prayer is that you'll trust our Father in how He is preparing you for kingdom work. He'll be your comfort, but the comfort often comes only after He allows you to suffer. Just as with the prophets and saints of old, our path is not easy, but the kingdom is worth suffering for. As Chambers wrote: "Tell God you are ready to be poured out as an offering, and God will prove Himself to be all you ever dreamed He could be."

He has broken your heart that He might flow through it onto others. "The sacrifices of God are a broken spirit, a broken and a contrite heart— These, O God, You will not despise" (Psalm 51:17 NKJV).

Chambers spoke these words: "We are here to submit to His will so that He may work through us what He wants. Once we realize this, He will make us broken bread and poured-out wine with which to feed and nourish others." Child of God, let the Father do with you as He will. Then your life will be a blessing to His other children. Let Him make you His "broken bread and poured-out wine."

Prayer

Father God, help me accept the times and methods You use to make me broken bread and poured-out wine for Your kingdom. Help me see the value my suffering can bring in helping others come to know You and trust You.

Challenge

If you've never read the devotional book *My Utmost for His Highest* by Oswald Chambers, consider getting it and see how much he can teach you and bless you. Devotions are a great way to absorb much, because you take in only a little each day. You can search and get this devotional for free online, but I suggest buying a printed book that you can hold in your own two hands.

Going further

Chambers said, "Quit praying about yourself and spend your life for the sake of others as the bondservant of Jesus. That is the true meaning of being broken bread and poured-out wine in real life." Write down a statement about your willingness to be broken bread and poured-out wine for the Father and His kingdom. If you're not yet ready, then say so, but ask the Father to help you in this area. If you're ready, ask the Lord to show you how He wants to use you when the time comes for you to go through something. You don't have to be afraid of what God will allow; He will surely help you every step of the way. *Brokenness is the path for being made into something new.* "For the Lord corrects and disciplines everyone whom He loves, and He punishes, even scourges, every son whom He accepts and welcomes to His heart and cherishes" (Hebrews 12:6 AMPC).

15

Sanctified by God

Salvation is free, but sanctification will cost you everything.

But in a great house there are not only vessels of gold and silver, but also of wood and clay, some for honor and some for dishonor. Therefore if anyone cleanses himself from the latter, he will be a vessel for honor, sanctified and useful for the Master, prepared for every good work. – 2 Timothy 2:20-21 NKJV

If you want a higher faith, you'll have to be changed. Sanctification is the process of cleansing you of all that doesn't belong in heaven.

You can be saved and still not yield to your sanctification—and you'll have plenty of company, since this
is where most Christians remain. But Yahweh Tsidkenu
(the Lord our righteousness) doesn't want you to remain
as you are, but to be changed into something new. *You cannot have a
flatlined faith journey and expect to ever walk in a higher faith.* You were
meant to walk in a higher faith.

We're saved in a moment, but we'll be sanctified across a lifetime.

The nearer you want to be to God, the greater you'll have to be sanctified.
"Now may the God of peace Himself sanctify you completely; and
may your whole spirit, soul, and body be preserved blameless at the
coming of our Lord Jesus Christ" (1 Thessalonians 5:23 NKJV).

Sanctification is meant to make you holy. Being holy is more
than being good on man's terms; it means being perfectly righteous
on God's terms. This holiness is so much higher than we could ever
achieve on our own power. And that's why the Lord gave us the Holy
Spirit to help us on this journey. Being holy is the destination, and
sanctification is the path to get there.

*Salvation gets you into heaven, but sanctification determines your posi-
tion once you get there.* "'To everyone who overcomes—who to the very
end keeps on doing things that please me—I will give power over the
nations'" (Revelation 2:26 TLB).

Too often, Christians imagine sanctification as a process where they
get better and better as a person, and thus become more acceptable
to God. But they're wrong. That's a self-serving and self-promoting
attitude that pleases the flesh and lifts up our pride. We're acceptable
to God through Christ, and not through anything we can do. Sanctification makes us more like Yeshua HaMashiach (Jesus the Messiah); it
does not replace what He alone did for us.

*Everyone can be sanctified, but only some will yield in such a way that
they will be.*

Never settle for anything less than the life God has meant for you to live. Be the man or woman God has ordained for you to be. "'Before I formed you in the womb I knew you; before you were born I sanctified you'" (Jeremiah 1:5 NKJV).

When I came to faith, I imagined something entirely different from all it turned out to be. I imagined a fairy-tale story in which the Lord stepped in and answered my every prayer to make my life easier. I thought that with every step on this pathway, the Lord would help me avoid troubles and find happiness in whatever I was doing. But this wasn't my experience, and I soon learned that the Lord had something far different in mind.

Sanctification is the process of changing you from an earthly natural man or woman to a heavenly spiritual man or woman. Sanctification moves you from the old you to who you were meant to be.

My faith journey started with reading the Word. Throughout all the years that I've believed, I've never stopped reading the Word. One thing that I've learned along the way is that in the Bible, God never made it easy for anybody. Why should I think it would be any different for me? It isn't easy for me, but I can be comforted by the fact that God promises me His help even when I'm going through hard times.

The Word sanctifies. The Lord Jesus said, "Sanctify them by Your truth. Your word is truth" (John 17:17 NKJV).

Sanctification of a saint is where the natural life is overcome by the spiritual life, where the man or woman is overcome by God.

Sanctification isn't something you do, but what Ruach Ha'Kodesh (the Holy Spirit) does to you. The only thing you can do is either surrender or resist. Everyone saved will be sanctified, but only to the degree that they surrender. If you resist the Lord, He will wait until you're ready. If you submit to the Lord, He'll begin to reign in you more and more.

It's not the miracles through you that make you different, but the miracle that God does in you. That miracle is the sanctification done in you by the

Holy Spirit. "God from the beginning chose you for salvation through sanctification by the Spirit" (2 Thessalonians 2:13 NKJV).

Your sanctification won't be an easy process. There are areas of your life you won't want to surrender. Many of us imagine that the worst part about us is what God wants to change the most. Certainly, God wants to change those parts. We don't object to changing them because we know they don't belong in our life to begin with. But God sees so much deeper than what's only on the surface.

Sanctification is the process whereby the right to your life is surrendered over to Christ, parcel by parcel. The process is complete only when there remains no ground in your life upon which you can stand and say, "Mine." "Or do you not know that...you are not your own? For you were bought at a price; therefore glorify God in your body and in your spirit, which are God's" (1 Corinthians 6:19-20 NKJV).

The hardest level of sanctification is when we must face ourselves for who we really are. Yahweh Mekoddishkem (the LORD who sanctifies you) must grab us by the back of the neck and hold us up squirming before the mirror of the Holy Spirit. We'll be shocked by what we see. In that mirror, if we dare to open our eyes, we'll see the depth of our own corruption. Even in the good things we do, we lack anything remotely close to the holiness God desires. We start to see that even our desire to be holy is tainted by the filthiness of pride and self-promotion.

It's good to live for Jesus. But the higher calling is that you die for Him. As long as you value your own life more than His, you're not worthy of Him. As Jesus said, "He who does not take his cross and follow after Me is not worthy of Me. He who finds his life will lose it, and he who loses his life for My sake will find it" (Matthew 10:38-39 NKJV).

Christians say they want to hear the Lord speaking to them. But what they really want is for God to tell them how wonderful they are and for people around them to be impressed by the great things they do. They often give themselves a title, then choose what ministry they want, and thank God for their calling—which, in fact, He never gave them. We like to think it's other people who are like the Pharisees, and we're so much better. This very thinking is what we need to be delivered from. We are the Pharisees.

Your first great deliverance is from the bondage of sin. Your second great deliverance is from the bondage of self. The first comes from the blood of Christ alone. The second comes by the power of the Holy Spirit alone. Both require surrendering yourself so that you receive the gift of salvation, then the gift of sanctification. "For God's grace, which brings deliverance, has appeared to all people. It teaches us to renounce godlessness and worldly pleasures, and to live self-controlled, upright and godly lives now, in this age" (Titus 2:11-12 CJB).

We embrace the mediocrity of self, thinking that it's everything—when it's nothing. The greater sanctification isn't from the world but from yourself.

There's no greater deliverance you need than to be delivered from yourself. Yet our self tries to convince us we don't need deliverance. If, however, you dare to listen to the Holy Spirit, you'll get a different story. Lose the idea that God will pat you on the back and tell you how great you're doing. Instead, get ready for Him to slap you upside the head and kick you in the rear. Child of God, your heavenly Father will hurt you, if that's what it takes to change you.

You cannot belong to God and still be prostituting yourself to the world. Sanctification separates the man or woman from the world. The more you fit into this world, the less you belong in heaven. I'm not preaching salvation but sanctification. You might be saved—but are you holy?

Sanctification isn't losing things but being set free from them. "For this is the will of God, your sanctification: that you should abstain from sexual immorality" (1 Thessalonians 4:3 NKJV).

For years now, I wake every morning and ask the Lord for a word. I pray that He'll tell me what I need to learn that morning. I can say with all honesty that, in general, the word He gives me is a rebuke of the way I'm thinking or living my life. If you're getting pats on the back for the words you hear, consider that you might be listening to yourself or to the devil. You can be sure that every day of your life, El Hakkadosh (the Holy God) will bring up something in you that needs to be changed. So long as you think this isn't true, you're wrong.

God sanctifies the saint. "To those who are called, sanctified by God the Father, and preserved in Jesus Christ" (Jude 1:1 NKJV).

You cannot walk in the power of the Holy Spirit unless you're being sanctified by the Holy Spirit. One precedes the other.

We have the wrong idea that being chastised by the Lord is bad. In reality, it's a sure sign that He loves you. We have the unholy and worldly idea that Yahweh Qadosh (the Holy One) wants our life to be easy. He wants you to be holy, and the easy life doesn't get you there. When once we understand God's goal for our life, we'll understand why He is being so hard on us. He is beating the hell out of us so we can be filled with heaven.

What a work in us He does! Sometimes, we think He's either absent or reckless in the process, unable to see today what can be correctly seen only from tomorrow. But as we gain each new level of sanctification, we can remember back to the prior. Though we may not see His plan, we can trust and know that He can.

Oswald Chambers said, "If you say you are sanctified, show it." Stop talking over the theology of sanctification and start working it out in the life you live. Chambers also said, "God not only expects me to do His will, but He is in me to do it."

The greater your calling, the greater your sanctification must be.

Child of God, I know it's a hard process to be sanctified. The process will most certainly bring tears. But there's a great purpose that El Yeshuatenu (the God of our salvation) has for you, while He makes you holy in one area of your life at a time. His work in you is worth the tears, because His work is always productive. His changing you will bring a blessing to you and to those around you, while He continues forming into you all that you were meant to be.

Prayer

Holy Spirit, I welcome you fully into my life, to sanctify me in all areas. Change me, I pray, so I become who the Father intends for me to become. Help me wash away all those things in me that don't belong, so that I'm useful to the Lord Jesus in all I do.

Challenge

List out things that you do each day—work, play, ministry, relationships, chores, entertainment, whatever it is you do. List out the activities and responsibilities one by one. Next, beneath everything you listed, write a prayer asking the Holy Spirit to sanctify you completely in all these things. Ask the Lord to show you how He wants to change you in each thing you've listed, then write His answer next to each one. Sanctification is a journey that will begin only when you take the first step.

Going further

If you want to put the rubber to the road in your sanctification, you must determine in your will each and every day to press into it. It will not be by your striving, but by your surrender—and you must surrender every day. The Lord will sanctify you, but you must put yourself before Him so that He will. Believe that He can change you, then let Him do the work. Choose each day to let the Lord continue what He started. *Ask the Lord what you need to change, then ask Him to help you.* "Create in me a clean heart, O God, and renew a right spirit within me. Cast me not away from your presence, and take not your Holy Spirit from me" (Psalm 51:10-11 ESV).

16

Consecrated

If you want to walk in a higher faith,
you have to let go of the lower things.

"'For I am the LORD your God. You shall therefore consecrate
yourselves, and you shall be holy; for I am holy.'"
–Leviticus 11:44 NKJV

The higher faith goes places where
the lower things cannot go.
To go higher, you must let go
of the lower things.

To be set apart, you have to let go. "'Consecrate [be set apart] yourselves therefore, and be holy, for I am the LORD your God. And you shall keep My statutes, and perform them: I am the LORD who sanctifies [cleans] you'" (Leviticus 20:7-8 NKJV).

Sanctification—as we explored in the last chapter—is the work being done in you by Yahweh Mekoddishkem (the LORD who sanctifies you). He's at work to cleanse you from all that doesn't belong in you. It's as if He throws you into His divine washing machine and turns it on, letting it run for the rest of your life. Consecration is different. Consecrating is both a separation and a joining—separating you from what's wrong, and joining you to what's right. It's the Lord telling you that as you're being washed, you need to stay out of the mud and draw near to Him to stay clean.

Consecration is the higher calling. You have a high calling, so you need a higher walk. Only if you walk higher will you reach the higher places. "Who may ascend into the hill of the LORD? Or who may stand in His holy place? He who has clean hands and a pure heart" (Psalm 24:3-4 NKJV).

The more reconciled to God, the more consecrated from the world. "Do not be conformed to this age, but be transformed by the renewing of your mind, so that you may discern what is the good, pleasing, and perfect will of God" (Romans 12:2 HCSB).

The problem with the Christianity peddled in our day is that holiness is not lifted up as the God-honoring way of life for a believer to walk in. We hear more messages on grace than we do on obedience. If we do hear a message on obedience, it's often filled with exceptions and excuses for continuing to live under the rule of our flesh. The reason so few teach on holiness is that few are willing to go there themselves. We teach as high as we are, because we never want to feel lower in ourselves. Go higher, then teach from there.

There are no compromises in a consecrated life. "'You shall consecrate them so they will be most holy, and whatever touches them will be holy'" (Exodus 30:29 NIV).

You're not set apart from it if you're part of it. If you act the same as everyone in the world, what makes you different? Don't try to fit in where you don't belong. "Then the LORD said to Moses, 'Go to the people and consecrate them today and tomorrow'" (Exodus 19:10 NKJV).

Stop limiting your faith to the meager levels of faith so often preached in our day. Look to the Word of God for the calling of El Hakkadosh (the Holy God) to the level of holiness you should walk in. The Lord means what He says and never changes His mind. From His Word, we've heard what He wants us to do—to be holy. If you want a higher faith, you have to live a holier life. If you want to live a holier life, you must have a life consecrated to the Lord.

The apostle Paul wrote, "Present your bodies a living sacrifice, holy, acceptable to God, which is your reasonable service" (Romans 12:1 NKJV). *Be the offering. Be the sacrifice. Change begins where excuses end.*

The Lord Jesus taught, "Whoever of you does not forsake all that he has cannot be My disciple" (Luke 14:33 NKJV). *This is not a question of salvation but of consecration. When Jesus is the only thing you cannot live without, that's where the life of a disciple begins.*

We need to ask Yeshua HaMashiach (Jesus the Messiah) what we need to be consecrated from, then be willing to do what He tells us. For several years, the Lord Jesus had me consecrated from all television, radio, and movies—not just worldly programs, but everything, even Christian movies. I remember people asking me how I could survive without watching the news. Oh, friend, you have no idea the freedom there is from the things we think we cannot live without. You're being influenced by everything you allow in your life, so use that as the gauge of what you should allow.

For some things, you need to draw a line, step over it, and vow never to return. "You certainly heard about him, and as his followers you were taught the truth that is in Jesus. So get rid of your old self, which made you live as you used to—the old self that was being destroyed by its deceitful desires. Your hearts and minds must be made completely new" (Ephesians 4:21-23 GNT).

Consecration from something means you're consecrated to another. When there's a consecration, we must know what we're to be consecrated *from*, while at the same time, knowing what we're to be consecrated *to*. You must get this right; otherwise, you might find yourself giving up one bad thing only to take hold of something just as bad or worse. Be deliberate in what you do, or you'll suffer the consequences.

Every new day is a chance to be a new you. Moses said, "Consecrate yourselves today to the Lord, that He may bestow on you a blessing this day" (Exodus 32:29 NKJV).

Sometimes our consecration isn't from something bad but from something good, so we can be consecrated to something better. I remember getting involved in serving the Father in so many capacities that I wasn't spending enough time with Him. In our serving, we often become a works-based machine serving in such a way that we don't really have to surrender. We're operating in our own strength and not resting in His power. One of the principles of serving El Elyon (God Most High) more completely is to surrender to Him more. He's measuring your surrender to Him more than your service to Him.

The Lord doesn't say to be consecrated to a church or a cause, but to Himself. The tighter you hold on to the things of men, the less you can be consecrated unto the Lord. "But know that the Lord has set apart for Himself him who is godly; the Lord will hear when I call to Him" (Psalm 4:3 NKJV). *When you consecrate yourself to God, He consecrates you to Himself.*

Consecrating yourself takes discipline and resolve. To gain these two things, you must rely on the power of Ruach Ha'Kodesh (the Holy Spirit). Stop complaining about failing in your efforts to grow higher in your faith while you're relying only upon your own strength. Of course you can't do it on your own! Your Father knows this, and that's why He sent you the Holy Spirit to help you. If you're failing, it's not because you're weak in yourself but because you think yourself too strong, and you're refusing to let the Holy Spirit help you. Pride stands tall in the life of a believer who isn't growing spiritually. Drop to your knees and admit you can't do it. Then ask the Lord to help you.

Consecrating your life is done one step at a time, and with each higher step you take, you'll be stronger to go even higher. Don't despair about how hard the journey is, but take comfort in knowing the Lord Jesus will help you. Don't think it will get easier. Ascending natural mountains gets harder the higher you go, and so it is in your faith. The higher you go, the more difficult the journey will be. Yet the sojourner who continues will experience a growing confidence in facing all that lies ahead, because of what they've seen the Lord do all along the way. The more you trust El Olam (the eternal God), the more your trust in Him will grow.

I'm always more impressed by a man or woman who lives their faith than by one who only argues about it.

The test of a saint is never in what they know, but in what they live. "'Who then is willing to consecrate himself this day to the LORD?'" (1 Chronicles 29:5 NKJV). *The way to debate truth and never lose is to simply live it out.*

Some things you may be consecrated from are for a season, though that season may last for many years. The Lord had me consecrated from meat for seven years. Other times, the Lord has had me fast from all sweets for six months. Sometimes, it doesn't matter what the Lord is separating you from, because the real exercise will be simply in your commitment to do as the Lord leads you. How far are you willing to go with Yahweh Raah (the LORD is my shepherd)? Let Him test you, for in the testing, He'll prove to you how far you're really willing to go.

Stop holding on to mediocrity, and grab hold of the consecrated life.

Prayer

Lord Jesus, show me everything You want me to be consecrated from. Give me the wisdom and the strength to consecrate myself from whatever does not belong in heaven. Help me, Lord, to be consecrated to You.

Challenge

Write down a list of everything you need to be consecrated from in your life. Ask the Lord to help you make this list. This list isn't only bad things, but also includes any good things that interfere with what the Lord has purposed for your life. Then make another list of what you need to be consecrated *to*, and again, ask the Lord to help you with this list. Keep these two lists before you. Change comes after commitments are made. Make a commitment.

Going further

There are some people in your life right now that you need to consecrate yourself *from*. Their influence is not good for you, and the outcome of spending more time with them will only get worse as time goes by. Be wise in your decision, and do only what God Himself approves. If you have commitments to this person, keep those commitments intact, but limit yourself from any negative influence they're having on you. *The greatest reflection of who you are is who you're with.* "'Can two walk together, unless they are agreed?'" (Amos 3:3 NKJV).

17

Successful Suffering

Jesus loves you so much that He'll withhold no suffering from you that would draw you nearer to Himself.

For our light affliction, which is but for a moment, is working for us a far more exceeding and eternal weight of glory.
—2 Corinthians 4:17 NKJV

The classroom of suffering is where we learn the most about growing into a higher faith.

Successful suffering is when the Christian accepts the suffering as part of the journey we all must go through. This doesn't mean we want to suffer, nor that we choose to remain in it, but that we realize that everything is part of God's plan. The Lord uses suffering to change us into all that He would have us become. When we learn to see our suffering through the lens of eternity and the purposes of Yahweh Raah (the LORD is my shepherd), we'll gain a new perspective by which we can better understand all that we're going through.

Learn to let suffering complete its work in you before God might remove it. "After you have suffered for a little while, the God of all grace [who imparts His blessing and favor], who called you to His own eternal glory in Christ, will Himself complete, confirm, strengthen, and establish you [making you what you ought to be]" (1 Peter 5:10 AMP).

A sculptor uses the heaviest hammer and the hardest chisel to break away the largest sections of rock that won't be part of the final statue. The bigger the piece that must be removed, the harder the sculptor must strike with the hammer. The Lord is doing the same thing with you. We protest on every swing of His hammer. We're protesting the circumstances He's using as His hammer and chisel in order to shape us. But we can be sure of this: Only the Lord can see the final shape He has purposed for us to become.

There are two forces that create the nature of Christ in you—an outward breaking away and an inward giving away. The outward is the hammer and chisel of external circumstances. The inward is the willing submission of your life to Jesus. The less submission, the harder the hammer must strike you. "Thus says the LORD, who stretches out the heavens, lays the foundation of the earth, and forms the spirit of man within him" (Zechariah 12:1 NKJV).

Successful suffering is when you can pray for help and give it to Yahweh Rapha (the LORD who heals) to be answered however He wants. You don't wonder whether He hears you, because you're fully confident that He does. You don't question whether He'll help you, but only trust Him that someday He will. All you do is take your problems to Him while knowing how much He loves you. Suffering can mature us in our faith as nothing else can, if we'll allow it to.

Jesus had faith that the Father could save Him from suffering. He also had faith that the Father would help Him through it. Just before He was crucified, Jesus prayed, "O My Father, if it is possible, let this cup pass from Me; nevertheless, not as I will, but as You will" (Matthew 26:39 NKJV).

Successful suffering is where we ask the Lord to show us how He's trying to shape us through the suffering. We know and trust that Yahweh Mekoddishkem (the LORD who sanctifies you) will never waste what suffering can accomplish in our lives. We realize that there's a great cost in our suffering, so we don't want to squander that cost by complaining. When we complain, we're telling God that He isn't faithful. Praise God because He is always faithful!

We think that every good thing is from God, and all suffering is from the devil. Yet the Lord uses suffering for our gain, and the devil uses the good pleasures of life for our demise. "For the LORD will not cast off forever. Though He causes grief, yet He will show compassion according to the multitude of His mercies" (Lamentations 3:31-32 NKJV).

Successful suffering seeks out how we might serve Him in our suffering, or after we've recovered from it. Consider that there are people we could not otherwise reach apart from our suffering. When we suffer, we can reach others who are suffering in similar ways, and we can reach them in a way nobody else could. Suffering is a harsh teacher that gives a hard lesson; through it we can learn how to have compassion toward others.

Some of the depths of suffering I've endured in my life left me with compassion for others. I learned that for others—as well as for myself—pain may be deep and hidden and weighing so heavily upon one's soul. I used to think that if someone suffered even half as much as I have, then they'd endured so much, and my heart would go out to them. Compassion is the fruit that can grow from suffering.

Let the suffering in your life mean something. Let it teach you this: The "God of all comfort...comforts us in all our tribulation, that we may be able to comfort those who are in any trouble, with the comfort with which we ourselves are comforted by God" (2 Corinthians 1:3-4 NKJV).

Successful suffering in a believer means they trust in the Lord during all that they go through. They know the Lord loves them completely and will never forsake them, even for a single moment. They believe in all that El Gibhor (the mighty God) can do, no matter what difficulty He chooses to bring into our life. When we realize how much God truly loves us, we can stop wondering why He allows us to suffer. We can trust Him with our life even in our hardest trials.

Don't be bitter about the trial that God is using to shape you. "'Look, I have refined you, but not [as severely] as silver; [rather] I have tested you in the furnace of affliction'" (Isaiah 48:10 CJB).

I remember going to church as a young boy. Because of my sensory condition, my suffering was always worse there, from being in a crowded building. I thought that God wasn't real—or that if He was, He wasn't a loving God, or else why did He let me suffer so much? Many years later, as I matured in my faith, I came to realize that the depth of God's love is unending. He allows us to suffer not because He doesn't love us, but because He *does*. Are you ready for this truth?

Suffering drives a person either to God or away from Him. "Therefore let those who suffer according to the will of God commit their souls to Him in doing good, as to a faithful Creator" (1 Peter 4:19 NKJV).

Successful suffering is not self-centered but Christ-centered. When we have self-pity, we look inward and find nothing we can hope for. But when we're Christ-centered, we look upward toward Him, and it's there we find hope. We must learn to take our eyes off ourselves, because inward focus takes our minds off God. Only when we're focused on God can we have peace, for there is peace in no other.

The measure of your peace is the measure your mind is focused on God. "You will keep in perfect peace all who trust in you, all whose thoughts are fixed on you!" (Isaiah 26:3 NLT).

Successful suffering is patient and confident that the Lord knows what He's doing. It doesn't question His timing nor complain about His inaction. Rather, it rests in Him and trusts in all that He does. The Lord has a purpose and a plan in all suffering, and sometimes, all we can do is trust Him. The greater the suffering, the more difficult it is to do this.

Patience is never born out of pleasure, but out of an ordeal from which we're going through. Learn to leave your requests at the feet of Jesus and not think you must always be repeating them. While we can be diligent in our prayers to end our suffering, we don't ever have to pressure Yeshua (Jesus) into action. Tell Him how you feel, ask Him for what you want, be confident that He has heard you—and know that He loves you. Then be patient while waiting for His answer. Trust Him with the answer.

Suffering does not reflect how God feels toward you; it reveals how you feel toward Him. "Though he slay me, yet will I trust in him" (Job 13:15 KJV).

Successful suffering accepts that the Father's plans don't always align with our own. We may think we could be more useful to the kingdom if we were healed, but sometimes, the Father can do more through a broken man or woman than somebody who seems to be whole by the world's standards. The Lord can use us in our brokenness more than when we're whole, because it's there that we must lean entirely on Him. Learn to embrace your weakness.

Never squander suffering, knowing all that God can do through it. Joseph told his brothers, "As for you, you meant evil against me; but God meant it for good, in order to bring it about as it is this day, to save many people alive" (Genesis 50:20 NKJV).

Elohim (God the strong and mighty one) has a ministry for you. It may be in a church, or it may be to an individual elsewhere. In that ministry, you'll find your purpose. It may be to preach, or it may be to pray; either way, it's service for the kingdom. The more God plans to use you, the harder the lessons must be on you. If you want to be effective for God to others, God must first do an effective work in you. There's no more effective way to change a man or woman than to put them through the fire of adversity, by which they can then be changed.

Before a man can change people, the Lord must change the man. The Lord said regarding His servant Paul, "For I will show him how many things he must suffer for My name's sake" (Acts 9:16 NKJV). *How few people we'd have in ministry if they knew in advance all that they would have to go through.*

Consider all that might be gained by your suffering when you minister into the life of another. Sometimes, we'll pay the price so that others will reap the benefits. When you're rightly serving God, you'll find that even when others gain the benefits and you don't, you'll rejoice all the same. A profit for the kingdom may come at your expense, but the cost is always worth it. In God's economy, a profit for one is a profit for all.

Pray that your suffering accomplishes His will for your life. "For God called you to do good, even if it means suffering, just as Christ suffered for you. He is your example, and you must follow in his steps" (1 Peter 2:21 NLT).

However you're suffering, I pray that it draws you nearer to the Lord. I pray that Yahweh Machsi (the LORD my refuge) will comfort you and also teach you all that He is doing. Pray for healing as you're led, but accept His answer if you're not yet healed. He is planning your eternity, so trust Him with today and every day.

Prayer

Lord Jesus, help me in my suffering to honor You and trust You with all that You're allowing me to go through. Help me be changed in every way that You want me to be changed, so that my suffering will not have been in vain.

Challenge

Write down the suffering you've been through in the past. Next to each item, write down how God has used it to change you for the better. Write down also any suffering you're experiencing right now. As best as you're able, write down how you believe God will use it to help you grow in your faith and be more useful to the kingdom. Ask God to help you understand how He has used your suffering in the past and how He is using it right now to shape you into something new.

Going further

In whatever you're going through, consider how you can help teach those around you to suffer successfully. Think about how your life could be a blessing to others by showing them how to have the peace of God upon you even in the midst of trouble around you. Write down some names of people that you know are suffering, and make a commitment to reach out to them and minister to them. As you minister to others, your suffering will gain meaning and have a purpose in your life. *Don't squander the cost of your suffering by being bitter.* "Not only that, but we rejoice in our sufferings, knowing that suffering produces endurance, and endurance produces character, and character produces hope, and hope does not put us to shame, because God's love has been poured into our hearts through the Holy Spirit who has been given to us" (Romans 5:3-5 ESV).

18

The Crucified Life

You can't have the resurrection life without first having a crucified life to be resurrected from.

That I may know Him and the power of His resurrection and the fellowship of His sufferings, being conformed to His death.
– Philippians 3:10 NASB

You'll ascend to a higher faith only after you've crucified your old life. You need resurrection power to take you higher.

*J*esus never peddled an easy Christian life, but a life crucified unto Himself.

There's a level in our faith that we cannot get to in any other way than to be crucified from our prior life. It sounds simple enough, and many Christians will profess to have done it, but only the rare man or woman has truly taken this step. The truth is that everything within us argues against this idea of dying to ourselves. We may understand the doctrine, but inwardly, we're opposed to it with every fiber of our being. Some might tell you how easily they've done it, but if so, it's doubtful they ever did.

There's no opponent more powerful, more cunning, more deceiving, more stubborn, more delusional, more ruthless, and more entrenched than yourself. That's why Jesus said you have to die to yourself, because He knows you'll never surrender. Our Lord Jesus taught, "Most assuredly, I say to you, unless a grain of wheat falls into the ground and dies, it remains alone; but if it dies, it produces much grain. He who loves his life will lose it, and he who hates his life in this world will keep it for eternal life" (John 12:24-25 NKJV).

A great many people have been willing to come to the cross of Christ and fall at His feet. In their brokenness and their fallenness, they call Jesus their Adonai (the Lord). These are the blessed ones who've received everlasting life and will spend all eternity in heaven.

It's a rare soul who goes further with Yahweh Sabaoth (the LORD of angelic armies)—who's willing to throw caution to the wind and give everything they have to the Lord. For such a man or woman as this, once they get to the cross, and perhaps stay there for quite some time, they'll climb up onto it and finally let their old man or woman be crucified with Christ.

Salvation comes once you kneel beneath the cross of Christ. Power comes once you climb up on that cross and crucify your natural man. Your spiritual life sprouts only from natural death. The only powerless Christians are those who refuse to crucify their own flesh. Jesus taught, "If anyone wants to be a follower of mine, let him deny himself and take up his cross and follow me" (Matthew 16:24 TLB).

When Jesus was crucified, it wasn't for anything He did wrong. It was because of the fallenness of you and me that Jesus hung on that cross, paying the price for our sins that we could never pay. When we climb on that cross and die to ourselves, we're not paying for our sins; only Christ can do that. No, all we're doing is agreeing with Jesus that our old nature must be done away with, so we can walk in the newness of life that only the Holy Spirit can put within us. This newness of life is the life of Christ that the Holy Spirit puts in us, which will cause us to live radically different. Once we're crucified with Christ Jesus, we'll then be raised with Him, and the same power that resurrected Him will be working in us. Once we completely die to Him, He will live completely in us.

The crucified life is freedom from the tyranny of you. It's freedom from your old nature, with the liberation of the power of Christ reigning within you. "'Whoever does not carry his own cross [expressing a willingness to endure whatever may come] and follow after Me [believing in Me, conforming to My example in living and, if need be, suffering or perhaps dying because of faith in Me] cannot be My disciple'" (Luke 14:27 AMP).

Our problem is that as soon as we hear about needing to be crucified with Christ, we start to negotiate a more "reasonable" deal from the perspective of our worldly minds. What will we really have to give up? What will we be able to hold on to? How far will this crucifixion thing really go? So long as you have such questions swirling in your head, you're not yet ready to be crucified. To be effective, your crucifixion must be voluntary—just as Christ's was. If you willingly die to your old self for Christ, you'll most assuredly have the Lord Jesus Christ ruling and reigning within you.

The shocking moment in the life of a saint is when they discover the truth that the sacrifice the Lord requires is their very life. To belong to Christ, you cannot belong to yourself. "Those who are Christ's have crucified the flesh with its passions and desires" (Galatians 5:24 NKJV).

We think that with our clever minds we can educate ourselves into a higher faith without ever having to throw ourselves helplessly before Yeshua HaMashiach (Jesus the Messiah). We want to be the mini-saviors of ourselves, doing those tasks as we're able that will lift us higher. But that strategy will never work. In God's kingdom, the wisdom of man is foolish, and man's schemes are never effective. The higher faith has nothing to do with you getting higher on your own, but only lowering yourself before Him. If you choose not to bow your knee to the Lord, you can be sure that someday, He will do it for you.

If you want to live higher, you must bow lower. "That at the name of Jesus every knee shall bow [in submission], of those who are in heaven and on earth and under the earth" (Philippians 2:10 AMP).

After you've crucified your life, a most wonderful truth is found: that the life you had before was not worth keeping. What we learn is that our prior life was so impossibly high-maintenance that it could never be sustained. Your pride worked you like a puppet, twitching your emotions up and down with every circumstance going on around you. The opinions of others mattered so much to you that you'd pay any price to change them, yet be left with nothing to show for it. It was as if you were on a giant hamster wheel, running as fast as you could but never able to get anywhere. The moments of peace were separated by long droughts of anxiety. The old life was exhausting, tiring your soul with each day you had to live in it.

Dead men don't sin. Determine that your "old man was crucified with Him.... For he who has died has been freed from sin" (Romans 6:6-7 NKJV).

The point of living a crucified life is that you're no longer alive to things that held you in bondage before. When you reach the end of your natural life, you'll no longer thirst or hunger as you did before. To die to the old self is to die to everything that was wrong within you. Most would argue that surely there were a few good things in their old life, but they're all wrong. Even the few good things you did were tainted by the old nature you were still alive to. You may have been busy serving others—but was it mostly self-serving?

You don't gain power in yourself, but through Christ in you. The crucified life gives way to the resurrection life in which the power of Christ will reign in you. "I want to know Christ and experience the mighty power that raised him from the dead" (Philippians 3:10 NLT).

When you finally crucify your flesh, your spirit man or woman will be ignited and filled by the power of the Spirit of God. Ruach Ha'Kodesh (the Holy Spirit) will place the essence of Christ's life deep within you. The power that raised Jesus will be the power that will raise you into a new life.

If you want to experience the fullness of God's power within you, you must be emptied of the old life you had before. The degree of your being led by the Holy Spirit is the degree to which you've crucified the old life that once led you. Oswald Chambers said, "You cannot imitate the nature of Jesus—it is either in you or it is not."

You cannot be full of yourself and also filled with the Holy Spirit. To be filled, you must first be emptied. To live the truth, you must first let go of the lies. The secret to being more is to become less, so that the more of Christ will reign in you. Lord Jesus, Your desire is not that we would be more, but that You would be the "more" in us. "Then you can be filled with everything God has for you" (Ephesians 3:19 ERV).

Yahweh (I Am, the Self-Existent One) will test your supposed crucified life. He does this to grow you, not humiliate you. One of the ways He allows this most often is through how other people mistreat you. We think we've already died to ourselves until someone comes along to mistreat us, slander us, and humiliate us in front of others. Just watch how quickly that old life of yours rears its head and comes out swinging. Don't worry about the other guy; just let your failures be a lesson. Learn to be corrected by your failures with humility in what you've done.

Sometimes, failing the test is the lesson God was trying to teach you. "'Jeremiah, say to the people, "This is what the LORD says: 'When people fall down, don't they get up again? When they discover they're on the wrong road, don't they turn back? Then why do these people stay on their self-destructive path? Why do the people of Jerusalem refuse to turn back? They cling tightly to their lies and will not turn around'"' (Jeremiah 8:4-5 NLT).

Don't despair when you fail the test, but be encouraged that El Deah (the God of knowledge) knew you were ready to be tested. The testing comes not so that we fail the test, but so that we learn how much further we have to go. You won't reach the end of the lessons, because the path is always one of perfecting, yet never getting to the end. It's more important to be on the right path than to be further along than you are now. But once you're headed in the right direction, be diligent to go even further. Only a few will dare to go all the way, but once they do, they discover that Yahweh Yireh (the LORD will provide) will give them everything they need. Your new spiritual life awaits you when your old natural life comes to an end.

You cannot be a Christian without the cross.

Prayer

Lord Jesus, thank You for the cross. Thank You for saving me for all eternity. Help me crucify my old life so I can have Your life reigning within me. Help me lose the idea that I need to keep any portion of the life I had before.

Challenge

Die to yourself. Get it into your mind that you'll make this a passion from which you can be driven to finally do it. Write out those areas of your life where your flesh is still ruling you, where your emotions are playing you, or where your desires are tugging you around like a helpless little soul. Then determine in your will to die to those very things that are holding you in bondage right now. Write out a declaration that you'll die to those things that don't belong in you.

Going further

Dying to oneself is never a one-and-done experience. *The reason we have to die to our flesh every day is because it wakes up every morning.* Don't get discouraged when you fail, but be encouraged that the Lord is there to help you. Start each morning in prayer, and ask the Lord to help you die to yourself and be made alive in Him, so that you walk in newness of life. Dare to live a life untethered by the corrupt nature of your flesh. *Sometimes, you need to burn the bridge so that you never go down that road again.* "Throw off your old sinful nature and your former way of life, which is corrupted by lust and deception. Instead, let the Spirit renew your thoughts and attitudes. Put on your new nature, created to be like God—truly righteous and holy" (Ephesians 4:22-24 NLT).

19

Alone
with God

Even pagans will answer a call to greatness,
but a man or woman of God will answer
a call to obscurity.

An angel of the Lord spoke to Philip, saying, "Arise and go"....
So he arose and went. – Acts 8:26-27 NKJV

The path to the higher faith will be a path of loneliness and obscurity. To go on with God, you have to be alone with God.

The Lord Jesus Christ desires that we be sanctified and consecrated, set apart to live a holy life before Him. Being holy is a prerequisite to growing higher in our faith. The more holy we become, the higher we can go in our faith. This doesn't happen by our effort but by the power of the Holy Spirit living within us. Yet Jesus must give us some lessons by which we'll then begin to grow higher. We'll find that everything we go through is meant to make us more holy. The Lord Jesus wants others to be able to learn about being holy just by watching how we live.

You must walk the high road to teach the high road, or else you have no frame of reference. "Show other Christians how to live by your life. They should be able to follow you in the way you talk and in what you do. Show them how to live in faith and in love and in holy living" (1 Timothy 4:12 NLV).

Yahweh Raah (the Lord is my shepherd) uses many lessons to teach you to be set apart. One of the most powerful lessons you can learn is in the classroom of obscurity, where you'll be isolated in your strangeness, unable to fit into the world around you. This world will often include your church, your job, and sometimes, even your family. Perhaps you already don't fit in and aren't popular—be glad for that, because the Lord can bless you in such a place. Maybe you're popular, and so the Lord will take that away from you. Let the Lord do as He will and know that His plan is always better. You have no true need for popularity, and it's actually hurting you because it builds up your pride.

Never seek to be popular with man; seek instead to be right with God. In obscurity, we discover who we really are. "Am I now trying to win the favor and approval of men, or of God? Or am I seeking to please someone? If I were still trying to be popular with men, I would not be a bond-servant of Christ" (Galatians 1:10 AMP).

There are many cliques in the world where people clamor to be popular, both in the secular realm and in the church. In our self-centered flesh, most of us long to be the center of attention. This doesn't go away just because we've stepped into our faith journey. We can be sure that all the baggage we were carrying into our faith was not removed at the beginning. Each bag we're holding on to must be removed one at a time. We're still clutching many bags that we're not even aware of, until Yahweh Tsidkenu (the LORD our righteousness) shows us.

The more self-centered you are, the less influence your life will have on those around you. "Don't be jealous or proud, but be humble and consider others more important than yourselves. Care about them as much as you care about yourselves" (Philippians 2:3-4 CEV).

In the world and in our churches, people long to be seen by others. And in the church, we often applaud them. In our unsanctified flesh, we still see through a worldly lens, and we wonder why we're not much different from the world. Yahweh Mekoddishkem (the LORD who sanctifies you) needs to sanctify us and put a new lens over our eyes so we see popularity for what it most often is: the pride of man lifted up before the world. We may sometimes wish we could fit into this popular crowd, but we should be thankful when we don't. It's only by ourselves that we'll spend more time alone with the Lord.

What if your lack of popularity proves you're in the center of God's will? "For we speak as messengers approved by God to be entrusted with the Good News. Our purpose is to please God, not people. He alone examines the motives of our hearts" (1 Thessalonians 2:4 NLT).

Another lesson Yeshua HaMashiach (Jesus the Messiah) will use to set you apart is to send you into the classroom of the wilderness. He will create a circumstance that separates you from others and leaves you with no other choice but to be alone with Him. If you're already a loner, this won't be hard. But for those who surround themselves with other people and with programs they pursue and places they visit, the wilderness is a barren place that leaves them in a state of despair. Never waste the despair that's from the Lord, because it's always meant to grow you. And when you're all alone, never complain that your only friend happens to be the Lord Jesus Himself.

Sometimes, God leaves us in a circumstance until we've learned the lesson. "Don't forget how the LORD your God has led you through the desert for the past 40 years. He wanted to find out if you were truly willing to obey him and depend on him" (Deuteronomy 8:2 CEV).

There have been times when I was jealous in a worldly way of those in the faith who were more popular than me. We must learn to see these fleshly feelings for what they are—a spirit of envy welling up within us. If we fail to see this, the deception is certainly strongest. Holy Spirit revelation is the only way to see ourselves as we truly are. Jealousy is covetousness, which is the selfish desire to have what others have. We must allow El Roi (the God who sees me) to show us our wrong feelings, to show us the reason we have them to begin with, and then to deliver us from such an evil trap that will only hinder us.

The worst thing you can do to yourself is to think only of yourself. "Where there is jealousy and selfishness, there is also disorder and every kind of evil" (James 3:16 GNT).

I'm thankful to live in obscurity, because it's a safer place from which I can live out my faith. I consider that I've been blessed to be the least popular person in the ministries I've been part of. At every church I've attended, I'm always on the fringes and known by very few. I get no credit for this humility, because it's the Lord who made me a loner. I'm thankful that God made me as I am. I'm thankful that He made this part of my faith journey easier by freeing me from the burden of popularity. There are some who have the great challenge of managing their pride in the face of their popularity. May the Lord give us only the popularity that won't puff up our pride.

Where pride rules, troubles begin. "Pride precedes a disaster, and an arrogant attitude precedes a fall" (Proverbs 16:18 NOG).

Being set apart is often equated to being separated from all that's evil. But that separation is only the beginning. We must learn that El Kanna (the jealous God) wants us to be set apart from anything that hinders our relationship with Him, even if they're good things. I know people who do many great things in the church, but they seem as far from God as anyone could be. These same people will serve God with their hands but reject Him in their hearts. I remember, as a young Christian, how shocked I was at the cruelty I found in some Christians in the ministries I served in. Some in the faith have become a hindrance to faith in others. But the question we must all be ready to answer—and the question we rarely want to hear—is, *What about us?* Perhaps the good things we do are a hindrance between us and God. Worse yet, are we being a hindrance between other people and God?

Don't let religion hinder your faith. You don't need rituals between yourself and the Lord, but a relationship. The Lord says, "For I desire mercy and not sacrifice, and the knowledge of God more than burnt offerings" (Hosea 6:6 NKJV).

When Abba ("dear Father" in Aramaic) wants to do a deeper work in you, He will get you all alone. It's hard to hide in a crowd when you're all by yourself. In your place of loneliness, the Spirit of God will address you. Don't despise any loneliness you must endure, because there the Lord has all your attention. Whatever the reason for your loneliness, know that the Lord has allowed it. God works only in your best interest, and it's up to you to trust Him, even if you can't see it. When the silence is deafening, and the clock seems to stand still, the Lord will teach you.

God calls you to be higher, then helps you get there. "Now may the God of peace make you holy in every way, and may your whole spirit and soul and body be kept blameless until our Lord Jesus Christ comes again. God will make this happen, for he who calls you is faithful" (1 Thessalonians 5:23-24 NLT).

When the Lord Jesus gets you by yourself, He will grow you more than He can at any other time. Let the time you spend alone with Him be special, anointed, and holy. Learn to pray without ceasing, not looking for the "amen" to end your prayer sooner. Put away the distractions of your phone and social media. Put away the distractions of your books and your things. Get alone with Him somewhere with nothing that can distract you. Clear your mind of your worries. Lose the anxieties that knock at the gate of your heart. Sit down and settle yourself before Him, where you're all alone with Him.

When your life is a prayer, the Lord will always be near you. "Make your life a prayer" (1 Thessalonians 5:17 TPT).

God says He will lift us higher when we're humble. But this lifting is not like our flesh thinks—to make us higher than those around us. No, it's far more holy and divine than that. God is lifting us to Himself, up to where He is, so we'll be blessed to be alone with Him. And when we're alone with Him, we'll bow low in reverence and adoration. When God lifts someone up, they'll always go much lower.

Too often, we see Scripture through our natural eyes, and we make natural interpretations. We look at everything in light of ourselves and how our lives could be made better and made higher before others. The Father has His better plan for us, and it's better than you could ever imagine.

Prayer

Father God, I want to be alone with You so I can learn to trust You more and more in every situation. Teach me to see the great blessing of being alone with You and serving You in obscurity, so that my service is an acceptable offering to You.

Challenge

In however you're serving God and aren't being noticed, write it down just for you and God to see. Ask the Lord to show you how He is working into you a higher faith through the unnoticed things you're doing for others. Ask the Lord to help you wash away any prideful self-serving you may still have in your life, and ask Him to set you apart for service that pleases Him. Determine in your mind to do or pray things in secret that only God will know.

Going further

If you're not serving the Lord in some regular way, make it your priority to discover what you can start doing for Him. If you're physically limited, make prayer your service and find some way you can learn the needs of others. Volunteer at your church, with a ministry, or in your family, so you can be used by God in even the smallest of ways. *You can't serve the Lord so long as you have your own agenda.* Jesus taught, "If anyone serves Me, he must [continue to faithfully] follow Me [without hesitation, holding steadfastly to Me, conforming to My example in living and, if need be, suffering or perhaps dying because of faith in Me]; and wherever I am [in heaven's glory], there will My servant be also. If anyone serves Me, the Father will honor him" (John 12:26 AMP).

20

Humbled
by God

God will humble you only if He has to.

"For everyone who exalts himself will be humbled
[before others], and he who habitually humbles himself
(keeps a realistic self-view) will be exalted." —Luke 14:11 AMP

You cannot go higher in your faith until you're humble
before men and El Elyon (God Most High).
Pride cannot stand in the higher faith.

There are many in the church who want to go higher in their faith, but only a few are willing to do what it takes to get there. In God's kingdom, the lower you go, the higher God will lift you. Conversely, the higher you try to go on your own, the lower God will set you down. The reason God won't let you go higher by your own prideful methods is that in His mercy, He doesn't want you to fall so far that you never get back up. God humbles you only to teach you that He alone can make you into something better.

God won't take you higher until you go lower. The Lord Jesus taught, "If you put yourself above others, you will be put down. But if you humble yourself, you will be honored" (Matthew 23:12 CEV).

We imagine ourselves far more humble than we really are. We think there's a perfect delineation between the proud and the humble. But that line of thinking is wrong. We're all proud, and to some degree, God must humble every one of us. The degree to which He must humble us isn't determined only by the level of pride we have, but also by the ferociousness with which we resist being humbled.

The bigger you think you are, the greater your distance is from God. "Though the LORD is great, he cares for the humble, but he keeps his distance from the proud" (Psalm 138:6 NLT).

The reason so few are willing to be humble before Yahweh Qadosh (the Holy One) is that they're not willing to be humble before men. People think they can remain in their pride with others while having a spirit of humility before God, but they're wrong. Just as light and darkness cannot be joined together, so it is that humility and pride cannot occupy the same space. A humble person will be humble before God and humble before others because they're humble at their center of their being. But the proud can only fake humility. They even think themselves quite humble. But God is never fooled, nor is He impressed by such hypocrisy.

The higher faith is a lower posture before God in heaven and before people on earth. "All of you, clothe yourselves with humility toward one another, because, 'God opposes the proud but shows favor to the humble.' Humble yourselves, therefore, under God's mighty hand, that he may lift you up in due time" (1 Peter 5:5-6 NIV).

Our problem is that we think we look weak and incompetent when we're humble before others. Our natural flesh wants to strike back and defend ourselves rather than giving the appearance that we're cowering down. Society speaks well of humility in theory but never promotes such a thing in practice. You'll find that being humble with others—either in the world or in the church—will hurt you more than anything else could. It goes against every fiber in our natural being to seemingly let other people walk right over us. We cannot believe that our El Rachum (the God of compassion and mercy) would actually expect us to do such a thing. But He does.

The lower the servant, the greater the saint. "And He [the Lord Jesus] sat down, called the twelve, and said to them, 'If anyone desires to be first, he shall be last of all and servant of all'" (Mark 9:35 NKJV).

When we get our pride hurt, it cuts deeper than physical wounds. Being humiliated in front of others can be so traumatic, it makes us physically ill. I remember a time when I was in the office of an especially arrogant man. He was perpetually rude and incredibly insulting. We were on a conference call with several others, and he began talking down to me and trying to make me look like I was incompetent in front of everyone. I became so angry I couldn't stay in the meeting. I got up and left without saying a word, and on the way out, I slammed his office door. This slamming caused a vacuum effect that lifted the ceiling tiles across a large room of workers. Everyone was shocked, because they'd never seen me this angry. It wasn't my finest moment. I failed that test, but I also learned a lesson. The Lord taught me that pride was still present within me. We need to look for the lessons God wants to teach us. Let Him teach you, and recognize that He will choose the way to test you.

If you're truly humble, nobody can hurt your pride. "A man's pride and sense of self-importance will bring him down, but he who has a humble spirit will obtain honor" (Proverbs 29:23 AMP).

El Roi (the God who sees me) knows our hearts. He sees the pride that's still standing tall within us. He will use other people in our lives and the circumstances we're in to bring about a humility that can come in no other way. If you want to be humble, you must be humbled. God uses worldly people to shape godly saints, and we complain about it while it's happening. Becoming humble is a journey that runs counter to our flesh but leads straight to the throne room in heaven. It's not a height to be climbed but a depth one must fall into. *Pride strives, while humility yields—and the difference will always matter.*

God can rarely change a person who doesn't think they need changing. "God is high and lifted up. He lives forever. His name is holy. He says, 'I live in a high and holy place, but I also live with people who are humble and sorry for their sins. I will give new life to those who are humble in spirit. I will give new life to those who are sorry for their sins'" (Isaiah 57:15 ERV).

Yahweh Shammah (the Lord is there) has allowed you to be humbled in the past, and He will most certainly cause you to be humbled again in the future. He will bring difficult people into your life to test you. They'll talk down to you in front of others. They'll talk about you behind your back. They'll justify their actions out of the pridefulness and self-righteousness they're walking in. God will use such people to deal with your pridefulness. The Lord will reveal your pride through the pride in others. We may think ourselves wise in how we see the pride in others, yet we see it so clearly only because we have it so completely at the core of who we are. We think the "log in the eye" story is about others, then continue to live with the log in our own eye.

If people would seek a higher faith as much as they do a higher position, they'd be giants in the kingdom. From the song of Mary: "He has done a mighty deed with His arm; He has scattered the proud because of the thoughts of their hearts; He has toppled the mighty from their thrones and exalted the lowly" (Luke 1:51-52 HCSB).

Being humble is hard, because people are always trying to humiliate us even more. We speak of honoring the humble, then we walk all over them as soon as we can. But God is ever watching, and He is always in control. It's the lowly ones who God helps; the prideful ones are on their own. Whatever you lift up as a sign of your humility, it's actually the banner of your pride. Pride seeks the attention of men, while humility is satisfied to be seen only by God. Pride speaks loudest, and pride stands tall, but the humble have the favor of the Lord.

The more humbly you walk with the Lord, the less you need to impress those around you. "The LORD God has told us what is right and what he demands: 'See that justice is done, let mercy be your first concern, and humbly obey your God'" (Micah 6:8 CEV).

To be humble, we must first see our own pride. We need the help of Ruach Ha'Kodesh (the Holy Spirit) to see ourselves as we truly are. From there, the pillars of pride can be taken down, one by one. The less pride that remains, the more humility can fill you.

Pride is one of the last things taken down in the life of a believer. Pride never goes easy, because it masquerades as something good. We stand pridefully on our intellect, we stand pridefully on our strength, and some of us stand pridefully in our own ministry. The tragedy we find is that when our pride is stripped away, there's so little left of what we were before. The beauty of this is that it's from here that God can make you holy, humble, and useful for the kingdom.

Humility is the path that leads to God. "He leads the humble in what is right, and the humble He teaches His way" (Psalm 25:9 AMPC).

There are some who walk in humility, and in so doing, they walk with God. Everything about them speaks of their humility without a word ever being spoken. The world will count them as weak, but the Lord is the strength within them. They've learned that the greatest strength is found in restraint and not allowing themselves to be moved by the manipulation of others. They've tasted the sweetness of not being tossed about by the opinions of other people. They've discovered the wonderful truth that in their humility, they sit in God's presence and hear all that He has to say. They're led by the Spirit because they follow Him in humility wherever He might take them.

Humility sets you free from the opinions of others. "Do not set your mind on high things, but associate with the humble. Do not be wise in your own opinion" (Romans 12:16 NKJV).

You can walk in humility. The time and the discipline that it takes to get there is up to you. God will crush you only as long as it takes for the wine to come pouring out. The more pliable you are in God's hands, the easier it will go for you. Stop looking at people as your enemies; see them as instruments of God whereby He is making you into something new.

Let God choose the circumstances, then let Him help you learn your lessons. Let the process of reaching your humility be the classroom of God's design where you can grow higher in your faith each day.

Prayer

Holy Spirit, reveal to me every part of me that is still prideful.
Convict me into a humility that's welcomed by God and
fits perfectly in the courts of heaven. Help me walk in
authentic humility before others so I can serve Yeshua
(Jesus) in a way that He's pleased with.

Challenge

Write down a list of the different things going on in your life that you find humiliating. It could be how someone is treating you or certain circumstances you're in. List as many things as you can. Then next to each item, write down how you think the Lord is using that person or circumstance to shape you into a humble servant for His kingdom. You'd be shocked if you knew all the things the Lord is doing to change you every day.

Going further

Walking in humility is one of the most difficult things we'll ever learn to do. Rarely do we do it willingly. But walking in humility is what you have to do if you want to go further with God. He will drag you kicking and screaming only so far—then He'll set you down and leave it up to you to decide just how far you want to go with Him. Determine in your heart on this day that you'll surrender everything to Him. *Stop stacking up new doctrines and clever programs, and just surrender all that He would change you. If ever you think worldly methods work, just look at the world.* "Surrender to God All-Powerful! You will find peace and prosperity. Listen to his teachings and take them to heart" (Job 22:21-22 CEV).

Building Up the Spiritual

If we want to grow in our faith,
we need to be planted in the Word.

"But the ones that fell on the good ground are those who, having heard the word with a noble and good heart, keep it and bear fruit with patience." – Luke 8:15 NKJV

The third pillar is that blessed part of our faith journey where God has stripped away the natural so we can start to grow in our spiritual lives with a greater intensity. First, we need the good ground, which is the foundation we stand on. Next, we need the natural ground to be broken up so seeds can be planted and roots can burrow downward. Then we get to the stage where the sprouts begin to push through the ground and bask in the light of His glory. Never rush your way to spiritual growth; wait for the Lord to prepare you.

We need to be more focused on growing with the right spirit than we are on gaining spiritual gifts without knowing where they came from. We must stay in the Word and keep our minds focused on Jesus so that we'll know the Holy Spirit and have His leading in everything we do. A test that we're being led by the right spirit is that we'll never be led down a path counter to the Word. If you don't know the Word, you won't know if you're on the right path. Get into the Word more than you are right now.

Christian, stay grounded in your faith. Make your life good ground from which the Lord can continue working the Word into your life. Stay humble before the Lord as your spiritual life begins to blossom, never letting a spiritual gift make you think you're higher. For your faith to go higher, you must go lower.

The danger in this stage is that as we grow spiritually, we might start looking down on others. Whenever we think we're really something, then we're not. The Lord will correct you when you get proud, and your degree of arrogance will determine how hard that correction needs to be. Learn your lessons quickly, and your faith journey will be easier.

If you'll stay humble on your faith journey and remain pliable in the hands of God, He'll begin to form you into something wonderful you haven't known before. Your spiritual life will be like nothing you've ever experienced, and will amaze you with how much the Lord can show you and do through you. Put down your pride, pick up your Bible, and buckle in for the ride of an eternal lifetime. *You were meant for something more.*

21

Increasing
Your Faith

*Waiting patiently is the work required
to increase one's faith.*

So Abraham received what God promised because
he waited patiently for it. – Hebrews 6:15 NOG

If you want to go higher in your faith, you'll do so one step
at a time. The amount of time you remain at each step
depends on how patient you are while remaining there.

You were meant to walk in a higher faith. Your faith is supposed to increase more and more as you travel along your faith journey. When you've placed yourself in the hands of El Yeshuati (the God of my salvation) and have let go of all your wasteful striving, it's there that He can start to build your faith. After the clay has been beaten down, the Lord picks it up to form it into something new. The Lord can do a work in you just as soon as you'll let Him. The process isn't easy to go through, but the outcome will always be worth it.

Sometimes, the only thing we can do is put ourselves in God's hands. "If I ascend to heaven, You are there; if I make my bed in Sheol, behold, You are there. Even there Your hand will lead me, and Your right hand will take hold of me" (Psalm 139:8,10 NASB).

We don't increase our faith by the programs of man but by the hands of the Father. The Father is calling us to draw near to Himself, and He'll change us once we do. When once the Lord has you in His grip, the work begins. The first stage is the hardest, in which the Lord reveals how weak our faith really is. It's never a pleasant thing to be shown ourselves as we really are. That great faith we thought we had—we never really had it. From this place of despair, Yahweh Ezer (the LORD our helper) can help us grow higher in our faith.

Self-delusion is that plot of land that stands between how we see ourselves and how we really are. "Search me, O God, and know my heart; test me and know my anxious thoughts. Point out anything in me that offends you, and lead me along the path of everlasting life" (Psalm 139:23-24 NLT).

For Yeshua HaMashiach (Jesus the Messiah) to grow your faith, He must begin from wherever you are right now. What it takes to grow your faith doesn't depend on your strength but on your weakness. Strong Christians are rigid and resistant to change. They dig their heels in deep and refuse to believe they could be wrong. Even when the Lord is able to push them along, they make it so much harder as they hold on with all their strength to their manmade religious viewpoints.

Be stubborn enough to never give up and pliable enough to let God help you. "Patient endurance is what you need now, so that you will continue to do God's will. Then you will receive all that he has promised" (Hebrews 10:36 NLT).

The Lord can change weak Christians further and faster, because they know how much they need Him. Pray to be weak before the Lord, then watch all that He can do in you. You'll be amazed at how far the Lord can take you. He doesn't need one teaspoon of your charm or one ounce of your abilities to make you an effective saint for the kingdom. All the Lord needs is your surrender before Him and your willingness to let Him do with you as He pleases.

The secret to overcoming is your willingness to let the Lord help you. "'If you are willing and obedient, you shall eat the good of the land'" (Isaiah 1:19 NKJV).

Our natural instinct when faced with any requirement for growth is to strive harder. This natural instinct prevents most Christians from growing higher in their faith. Christians who insist on growing their faith through their efforts won't have a growing faith. Your natural instincts don't work in the spiritual realm. But Christians who surrender to the Lord Jesus Christ will reach spiritual heights they never imagined. Jesus will pull you up when you reach for Him, because in that posture He can take hold of your hands.

The reason so few grow into a mighty faith is that they try doing it with their own power. "And the apostles said to the Lord, 'Increase our faith'" (Luke 17:5 NKJV).

We think in our carnal minds that the Lord is looking for those who can do everything for themselves. But the ones who insist on doing everything themselves are the ones who have the most pride. Your pride is the greatest hindrance to growing in faith. Yet we see many in the church who hold up their achievements and their talents as trophies that brought them to where they are today. We honor the proud leaders more than the humble servants, then wonder why our churches are floundering.

Your pride makes you think your faith is higher than it is. "'Look at the proud one, his soul is not right within him, but the righteous will live by his faith [in the true God]'" (Habakkuk 2:4 AMP).

Humility defeats pride in the kingdom of God. In His kingdom, the spiritual reigns over the natural, and the things of heaven reign over the things of the world. El Elyon (God Most High) will take you higher in your faith only as you kneel lower before Him. That's why He must often hurt you before He can help you. We would never wake up in the morning and ask the Lord to hurt us. And after being hurt, we rarely look to the Father to see how He might use it. Instead, we blame either the devil or the Father. Then we feel quite sorry for ourselves as the victim. If only you knew all the good that Father God was bringing about from all the bad!

The Lord allows the hard times because that's when we seek Him the most. "I will cry out to God Most High, to God who performs all things for me" (Psalm 57:2 NKJV).

Faith increases in levels. To get to the higher faith, it's as if there's a slow dial, not a switch. The Lord Jesus Christ will take you to each higher level when you've proven yourself ready. The proof always comes in trials, because faith cannot be tested in your pleasures. The testing is never to disqualify you but to prepare you to take you even higher. Never despise the testing that's helping you grow in your faith. Obstacles are not there to block you from growing but to build you up to go even higher.

The measure of faith is never answered by a yes or a no, but by "How much." Faith isn't a switch but a dial. You cannot turn it up by your power, only by His. "'Lord, I believe; help my unbelief!'" (Mark 9:24 NKJV).

As your faith goes higher, your life will become more peaceful. This peace isn't because your life is easier, because it will likely become harder. Each higher level of faith requires a higher level of testing. But as your faith grows, the tests won't seem as hard as they used to. The more we trust the Lord, the less we'll worry about all the troubles we're going through. The more we trust the Lord, the more we can rest in our circumstances. We'll appear strange to others around us, as if we're not even fully aware of what we're going through. We are aware, but we just aren't worried. Our peace is because we trust that Yeshua HaMashiach (Jesus the Messiah) has us.

Living worry-free doesn't mean your life is without problems; it means that you've given them to God. "Don't worry about anything, but pray about everything. With thankful hearts offer up your prayers and requests to God. Then, because you belong to Christ Jesus, God will bless you with peace that no one can completely understand. And this peace will control the way you think and feel" (Philippians 4:6-7 CEV).

We can never reach the end of how high our faith can go, but we'll have an eternity to keep trying. Your faith journey won't end on earth. Let the Holy Spirit take you places in your faith you never imagined you could get to. Trust that the Spirit of God can give you more faith and prepare you to walk in it. Believe that Jesus can help you, then watch Him as He does. Let the Father fill your life with a faith that can move mountains.

You can live higher than you are only if you let God help you. "'I am the LORD who makes you holy'" (Leviticus 22:32 NLT).

I'm embarrassed to admit just how many years it took the Lord Jesus to break me down before I let Him build me up. For such a long time, my faith was growing only in knowledge, and I had nothing of the power of the Holy Spirit. Even as I was serving the Lord with all my might, I was only proving to Him that I wasn't yet ready to go higher in my faith. The Lord has to bring us to the end of ourselves before we ever find the beginning of His life in us. This isn't a question of salvation but of sanctification, so we can be used by God so much more.

Growing in faith is not like climbing a mountain; it's like falling backward into a deep canyon. One is by your effort; the other has to rely entirely on Him. Everything you try to do yourself proves who you rely on. Stop white-knuckling your way to a higher faith, and simply fall into it. "God has apportioned to each a degree of faith [and a purpose designed for service]" (Romans 12:3 AMP). *Faith is not your ability to have Christ, but trusting entirely that Christ has you.*

The Lord arranged circumstances for me that crushed me, like a winepress crushes grapes, until there was nothing left that I could offer. After I was saved, I had been so excited to be used by God, and it never occurred to me that He didn't want me to serve Him with all my strength. We're called to love Him with all our strength, but to serve Him with all humility in complete surrender to His strength. I was nothing more than another zealous soul who thought I was fighting for God, but I was actually fighting against the principles of the kingdom. I was self-centered in my faith, and El Olam (the eternal God) would have none of that. The Lord had to crush me from this zealous attitude, beating the pride from hell right out of me.

Zealousness is like a rocket booster—it's great so long as you're pointed in the right direction. "Even so you, since you are zealous for spiritual gifts, let it be for the edification of the church that you seek to excel" (1 Corinthians 14:12 NKJV).

It's a most painful feeling to realize just how wrong we were with the direction we were heading, especially with all the zeal we had in doing so. If we're to increase our faith, we must have the right foundation of faith which the Lord Jesus Christ can build upon. We must have our own "road to Damascus" experience in which the Lord Jesus confronts us and calls out our zealously prideful nature. We need that spiritual reset button pushed by the Lord Jesus, so we can reboot into something new.

Good motives are like good soil—get the foundation right, and good things can grow from it. "People may be pure in their own eyes, but the LORD examines their motives" (Proverbs 16:2 NLT).

Be willing to let the Lord give you a course correction in your faith journey. Stop thinking that somehow you're more clever than others, and ask El Roi (the God who sees me) to show you where you're wrong. You're human, and it's okay to be wrong. I'm not perfect, and neither are you. Let the Lord kick the zealous, religious, prideful spirit right out of your life. Let Him knock you to the ground, and then impart a new heavenly vision into your life. From this, your faith can grow higher than you ever imagined.

A successful faith journey makes course corrections along the way. "You will hear a voice behind you saying, 'This is the way. Follow it, whether it turns to the right or to the left'" (Isaiah 30:21 GW).

Prayer

Holy Father, thank you for showing me where I've been off in my thinking and where I had been serving You in my might, not Yours. Help me walk with You in humility and surrender to Your strength, so my faith is built upon nothing less than Your power.

Challenge

Write down a list of different ways you've served God—perhaps things you've done for your church or some organization, or the care you've given to your children or parents or others around you. These are all commendable. Then write down whether you did these things in your own strength or through reliance on the power of God. Be honest, since God already knows anyway. You can't con a God who knows everything.

Going further

Write down a list of ways that you feel led to serve God now or in the future. Pray to the Lord Jesus to help you know what He really wants you to do. Be willing to accept an answer other than what you may be hoping for. Next to each item on this list, write down how much you'll need to rely on the Lord. One way we know we're being led by the Holy Spirit is that He will give us a mission that can be accomplished only by His strength. *If you walk beneath your calling, you won't accomplish all He has for you.* "That is why we always pray for you. We ask our God to make you worthy of the life he has called you to live. May he fulfill by his power all your desire for goodness and complete your work of faith" (2 Thessalonians 1:11 GNT).

22

The Foolish and the Weak

God chooses the foolish and the weak because they rely on His wisdom and strength.

But God chose what is foolish in the world to shame the wise; God chose what is weak in the world to shame the strong.
— 1 Corinthians 1:27 ESV

If you want to go higher in your faith, you need the power of El Shaddai (God Almighty) to help you get there. So long as you're relying on your own wisdom and strength, you won't get far.

G od isn't looking for the proud and the strong, but for the foolish and the weak. He isn't looking at how independent you can be, but at how much you know you need Him. He isn't looking for the self-made person, but for the person willing to be made new by Him. The most wonderful truth in the world is that God chooses the foolish and the weak; that's the low standard we're held to in order to be used by Him.

When you're weak before God, He will be your strength before men. "He gives power to the weak, and to those who have no might He increases strength" (Isaiah 40:29 NKJV).

We often think we're useless to the Father because we know all too well our own faults and limitations. Thinking He needs our help more than we need His is a great error born in our pride. The first step is to realize how needy we are. Then we must trust that He will help us.

The most powerful prayer comes from a weakness in self and faith in God, who can do anything. "And whatever you ask for in prayer, having faith and [really] believing, you will receive" (Matthew 21:22 AMPC).

Yahweh Yireh (the LORD will provide) doesn't need your wisdom to make you wise, nor does He need your strength to make you strong. We must realize that to be effective for the kingdom, we don't need the self-promoting attributes lifted up by the world. What the world covets, our Lord doesn't need, nor will He use. The Lord uses the least because they rely on Him the most.

God's purposes for you do not depend on your abilities. "But God has selected [for His purpose] the foolish things of the world to shame the wise [revealing their ignorance]" (1 Corinthians 1:27a AMP).

If you want to go higher in the kingdom, you must go lower in the world. We sometimes think that it's the most famous believers who accomplish the most, but that line of thinking follows the values of the world. No matter how small you think His task for you is, just do what He calls you to do, and you'll be a blessing to the kingdom.

When once you realize El Hanan (the gracious God) can work through your foolishness and your weakness, you'll stop needing to pretend you're something greater. In your humble perspective of yourself, God will start to use you the most. Once He does, your life will be a blessing to those around you.

Pray for the strength to be weak before God. "God has selected [for His purpose] the weak things of the world to shame the things which are strong [revealing their frailty]" (1 Corinthians 1:27b AMP).

Too many times, we miss all that Yeshua HaMashiach (Jesus the Messiah) would do through us because our eyes are fixed on what's happening to us. In whatever situation you're in, trust that the Lord can use you. Ask Him to show you what that person before you needs, then let Him help you minister to them. When you minister to others, you'll find that you'll be ministered to as well.

In the kingdom, when we yield ground, we gain ground. "When I am weak, then I am strong—the less I have, the more I depend on him [Christ Jesus]" (2 Corinthians 12:10 TLB).

Your kingdom role is not given by the approval of man but by the assignment of God. Jesus isn't looking at how high your title is, but at how low you're willing to bow beneath Him. Your stature in heaven is measured not by all the Scripture you might know, but by the Scripture you live by. The giants in the kingdom aren't the ones who know the most, but who live the most in what the Holy Spirit has taught them.

The Lord's power is greater in your weakness. The Lord said, "My grace is all you need. My power works best in weakness" (2 Corinthians 12:9 NLT).

It's one thing to know the truth, and quite another to walk in it. I've come to understand well that the Lord Jesus could use me even though I was weak and foolish. I'm the way that I am by the Lord's design. Because I was born with the strangeness of a broken sensory system, my life has been a series of difficult and awkward moments at every turn. Socially, I'm a flop at best and a loner most of the time. Since I live in this strange world of mine that so few understand, I'm left to walk in isolation, unable to explain why I'm the way that I am.

The Lord prevails through your weakness, and the world cannot understand. The Lord says, "The Holy Spirit helps us in our weakness" (Romans 8:26 NLT).

My weakness is my inability to tolerate the pain from sensory inputs that surround me. The worst part is that this hurts me not only during the problem but also beforehand, when I'm anxious about the sensory pain I may have to face. What we fear happening is often as bad or worse than the reality. We need to trust the Lord with our future so we won't have to worry about it.

To grow in your faith, the question isn't, "Can you be strong enough?" but "Can you be weak enough?" "My flesh and my heart may fail, but God is the strength of my heart and my portion forever" (Psalm 73:26 ESV).

My foolishness is found in being around people when most of my life I've been a loner. I never learned how to operate normally around people. I've always been far more comfortable being around animals that cannot speak back than around people to whom I may have to speak. I love the people around me, but I just never felt comfortable being around most of them. Even among my family, I'm often off by myself.

The question is never if God can use you, but will you let Him? "For you see your calling, brethren, that not many wise according to the flesh, not many mighty, not many noble, are called" (1 Corinthians 1:26 NKJV).

What I learned after many years is that when El Yeshuati (the God of my salvation) allowed me to have this condition, it placed me where I drew near to God to find His strength and wisdom, because of how much I needed it. The principle of the weak and the foolish is that the weaker and more foolish you are, the more God can give you from His own strength and wisdom. It's not to my credit that He gives me anything, but I'm blessed by it. And friend, you can be too. In whatever ways God has made you foolish or weak, thank Him for that.

As a diamond is formed in adversity, so it is that the Lord allows His servants to be formed. Never think the tough times have no meaning, because they're the times that have the most meaning in who we become. "Yea, though I walk through the valley of the shadow of death, I will fear no evil: for thou art with me; thy rod and thy staff they comfort me" (Psalm 23:4 KJV). *He never promises an easy life, but a life in which He'll never leave you.*

We all have things about us that make us feel weak and foolish. We all have flaws in our bodies, errors in our minds, goofy personality traits that are in us from birth, and the odd ways we act, which are driven by experiences we've gone through. Whatever the reasons are that have made you weak or foolish, know that this is where God can help you. Not only can Yahweh Ezer (the LORD our helper) help you, but because of your weakness and foolishness, God will choose you to be His own special vessel to the world just as soon as you put down the facade of what you're pretending to be.

God isn't looking for your strength to stand before Him, but for your weakness to fall before Him. "The high and lofty one who lives in eternity, the Holy One, says this: 'I live in the high and holy place with those whose spirits are contrite and humble. I restore the crushed spirit of the humble and revive the courage of those with repentant hearts'" (Isaiah 57:15 NLT).

The Father turns the world upside down with the principles of His kingdom. When we start to operate on kingdom principles, we start seeing just how different the kingdom really is. You'll start to see that people you thought were so high in the church are still low in the kingdom, because they're still operating by the principles of the world. They appear to be strong and full of wisdom, but our Father is laughing at their natural abilities being performed like a circus act before others. They don't have a lick of the power of the Holy Spirit within them.

Whenever we're not strong in a spiritual gift, it's because we're not weak before God. "As you yield freely and fully to the dynamic life and power of the Holy Spirit, you will abandon the cravings of your self-life" (Galatians 5:16 TPT).

As you start to get filled with the strength of Christ and the wisdom from heaven, you'll learn just how great the exchange truly is. When you're relying upon Yahweh Tsuri (the LORD is my rock), you have a trustworthy Lord who can do infinitely more through you than you could ever have hoped to accomplish on your own. You'll come to thank Him for all the things about yourself where He can be your all in all. One of the greatest days in the life of a believer is when they learn to be comfortable in their own skin, as they're filled by the Holy Spirit.

Our problem in ministry is that we have too many strong ministers. Paul said, "The weakness of God is stronger than men" (1 Corinthians 1:25 NKJV).

When the Lord called me to go into prisons and minister there, I thought He couldn't have chosen a worse candidate than me. I was right. By every measurement of man, I should never have been picked to do anything of the sort. Because of my sensory condition and the issues it causes, I should've been disqualified before I'd even signed up. But the kingdom of God operates on a different set of principles. The principle of God choosing the foolish and the weak is found time and again in Holy Scripture. If God chooses you, know that this was never by your qualifications, but by His grace. Nobody truly chosen by God can stand proudly, because they know He chooses the foolish and the weak. Do you qualify?

Prayer

Lord Jesus, help me see that You can do more in my foolishness
and weakness than with anything I can bring to the table.
Help me not to worry about what other people think of me,
but to only be encouraged that You can help me.

Challenge

Write down two lists, one with all the foolish ways about you, and the
other with all your weaknesses. If you struggle to do this on your own,
consider asking a trusted friend or mentor to help you. It's important
to be honest with ourselves about this. Once you have these two lists
completed, give them to God. These are the qualifications He's looking
for so that you'll rely upon Him. These are the things God can use in
your service for His kingdom.

Going further

Each day, pray for the Lord Jesus to be your strength and your wisdom.
Before you approach anything that requires physical or emotional
strength, pray to the Lord that His strength will fill you. Confess your
weakness before Him and plead with Him to give you His strength
to accomplish whatever purposes He has placed before you. Before
you do anything, pray that He'll give you His wisdom to understand
and discern what you should do. Confess your foolish thinking before
Him and ask Him to help you be wise. Make this your daily pledge,
and watch how your life will change. *You'll accomplish more by resting
in the Lord than by striving on your own.* "'Stop striving and know that I
am God; I will be exalted among the nations, I will be exalted on the
earth.' The LORD of armies is with us; the God of Jacob is our strong-
hold" (Psalm 46:10-11 NASB).

23

The Spiritual Life

*You won't trip over natural things
when you're walking in the Spirit.*

Walk by the Spirit and you will not carry
out the desire of the flesh. –Galatians 5:16 HCSB

If you want to go higher in your faith, you must
go higher in your spiritual life; that's where you'll
get closer to El Elyon (God Most High).

Many Christians talk about growing spiritually, but they don't understand what it means to be spiritual. We all know what it means to live in the natural, because we all live in the natural each day. But for many Christians, the spiritual seems so foreign and mysterious because it's a place they've never been to. Their most common mistake is to think *soulful* is the same as *spiritual*; they mistake something emotional as something spiritual.

Another common mistake is to think the spiritual life means living a notch or two above the natural. Christians know about their natural level of unholiness before their salvation, and so they imagine the spiritual as being an improved version of themselves. As they overcome a sin or two and begin to do a few good things, they start to think of themselves as more spiritual. Their progress may be commendable, but their efforts and their measurements remain firmly planted in the natural realm. Even the pagans abstain from doing some evil and will do a few good things in this world. The spiritual life is something so much higher.

Spiritual power is not built up but poured in. Moses said, "Oh, that all the Lord's people were prophets and that the Lord would put His Spirit upon them!" (Numbers 11:29 NKJV).

The problem with thinking that the spiritual is slightly better than the natural is that the spiritual goal will be set too far below what Yahweh Hoseenu (the Lord our maker) would have you reach for. The measurement is still of this world. And if we're honest, we set the goal to a level we can get to on our own. When you're relying on yourself, the limit is you, and that will be the level you try to attain. You can be sure this is nowhere close to where God wants to take you.

Stop using earthly measures when you're trying to reach heavenly goals. "The person without the Spirit does not accept the things that come from the Spirit of God but considers them foolishness, and cannot understand them because they are discerned only through the Spirit" (1 Corinthians 2:14 NIV).

Another error Christians make is thinking the spiritual is so mysterious and beyond understanding that they give up and don't try to get there. They justify their thinking by saying the spiritual life is a level we can get to only in heaven, while the natural is all we can experience while here on earth. They're wrong. We're meant to live a spiritual life here on earth.

God can show you in a moment what you couldn't learn in a lifetime. "This is what Yahweh says: Call to me, and I will answer you. I will tell you great and mysterious things that you do not know" (Jeremiah 33:2-3 NOG).

The problem with putting off the spiritual life until we get to heaven is that we squander everything God wants to do in us and through us while we're here on earth right now. We were meant for more, and if we don't take hold of it, we're a hindrance to all that God could do through us. We're meant to have heaven come down into our lives right now so we can be a vessel that God works through to reach those around us.

Until we believe that the spiritual life is meant for us, we'll never be able to walk in it. It's not something to be attained by our striving or the programs that institutions can offer. Rather, it's a life that surrenders to God so He can fill it with the Holy Spirit. God provided everything you needed in order to flourish in your natural life. He has already done the same thing for your spiritual life. Will you receive it?

The purposes of God are never dependent upon the provisions of man. "Abraham named the place Yahweh-Yireh (which means 'the Lord will provide'). To this day, people still use that name as a proverb: 'On the mountain of the Lord it will be provided'" (Genesis 22:14 NLT).

The spiritual life isn't just a little higher than the natural life; rather, it turns the natural life upside down. It's so radically different from worldly measurements that the scales of man can't be used to see what level your spiritual life has risen to. You can work hard and get stronger in your natural strength, and it's by your determination that you do it. But it always takes the Spirit of God to strengthen and equip the spirit of a man or a woman so they can grow and flourish in their spiritual life.

Seek to live a spiritual life that turns your worldly life on its head. In the world, the more you take, the more you have. In the spiritual, the more you give, the more you have. In the world, the ends justify the means. In the spiritual, the means justify the ends. In the world, the stronger you are, the more you can do. In the spiritual, the weaker you are, the more El Gibhor (the mighty God) can do through you.

Divine power flows in natural weakness. "He gives strength to the weary and increases the power of the weak" (Isaiah 40:29 NIV).

The test of how much higher your spiritual life needs to go will be how much your natural life still controls you. You're either pleasing to the Lord or just pleasing your flesh. The spiritual life is not a switch but a dial, an ever-increasing way of living your life, controlled either by you or by the Holy Spirit.

The spiritual life is where the flesh is no longer reigning, and the inner spirit is strengthened by the power of the Holy Spirit. This doesn't mean your flesh won't sometimes win a battle, but it has surely lost the war. Yeshua HaMashiach (Jesus the Messiah) came and saved you from your sin. The Holy Spirit came to give you power over sin.

Just because you're in the flesh doesn't mean you cannot walk in the Spirit. "That the righteous requirement of the law might be fulfilled in us who do not walk according to the flesh but according to the Spirit" (Romans 8:4 NKJV).

The spiritual life is a life where the unseen is seen and the hidden is revealed. One of the greatest revelations will be when the Lord opens your eyes to deeper truths held within the pages of Holy Scripture. You might see angels and perhaps a glimpse of heaven, but Holy Scripture is where you'll see the greatest sight one can ever see—the heart of the Father.

The spiritual life is where you can hear the Holy Spirit because you're listening with your spiritual ears. The Holy Spirit will open your ears and gently whisper to you. He'll teach you all things and guide you in everything you're doing, if you're willing to listen and then obey.

Some of you need deliverance from your stack of books. It's good to study the things of man, but without the Holy Spirit, you'll never understand the things of God. The Lord Jesus taught, "The Helper, the Holy Spirit, whom the Father will send in My name, He will teach you all things" (John 14:26 NKJV).

The spiritual life is the life where you can see in the spirit because the Holy Spirit has opened your spiritual eyes. You'll see the spirit behind the things people say and do. You'll see where there is light or darkness that surrounds people. You'll see the anointing on other people, as well as the spiritual facade that so many people wear.

The spiritual life is the life of the Spirit of Christ reigning within you by the power of the Holy Spirit, who is upon you. When Jesus lives inside you, His light will shine out from you. You'll have a greater sense of grace and mercy for those around you. His peace will be upon you. His life will emanate from you.

Christ through you is the evidence of Christ in you. "Test yourselves to see if you are in the faith; examine yourselves! Or do you not recognize this about yourselves, that Jesus Christ is in you—unless indeed you fail the test?" (2 Corinthians 13:5 NASB).

The spiritual life is the life from above brought down to earth, so that you're a vessel for God and a blessing to His kingdom. It's a life of revelation in all that God wants to do through you. The more He pours in, the more you'll pour out because you simply have no place in which to keep it all.

The spiritual life is a life in which Yahweh Tsidkenu (the Lord our righteousness) can entrust you with spiritual gifts that aren't for you, but to be used through you to the benefit of His other children.

You won't seek these gifts nor take any credit or applause for them. Rather, you'll humbly receive these gifts to help others whom God puts before you.

Not every gift is a guarantee; they're given only as the Lord deems necessary. "Are we all apostles? Are we all prophets? Are we all teachers? Do we all have the power to do miracles? Do we all have the gift of healing? Do we all have the ability to speak in unknown languages? Do we all have the ability to interpret unknown languages? Of course not!" (1 Corinthians 12:29-30 NLT).

The spiritual life will fill you with God's everlasting love and make you a vessel through which His love will pour out onto others. As the Holy Spirit pours the Father's love into your heart, His love will flow out from you through your words and actions to those around you. Your life will become a reflection of the Father's love.

Spiritual growth is revealed in practical outcomes. "Let everyone see that you are gentle and kind. The Lord is coming soon" (Philippians 4:5 ERV).

The spiritual life is a selfless life with a servant's heart and a soul that's filled with compassion for others. You'll be more concerned for the eternal well-being of others than for the temporal things of this day. You'll learn what it means that there can be a great profit in heaven for the things we count as a loss here on earth.

The spiritual life is as complete in the valleys below as it is in any mountaintop experiences above. Though we love and get refreshed on the mountaintop with our El Shaddai (God Almighty), we're equally blessed and honored to do His work in the valleys below. We get our anointing on high, then carry it down to the valleys below.

God is so upside down to our worldly thinking, so stop trying to understand your circumstances right side up. "'For as the heavens are higher than the earth, so are My ways higher than your ways, and My thoughts than your thoughts'" (Isaiah 55:9 NKJV).

The spiritual life is a life that prays in the Spirit, in holy communion with the Holy Spirit as we go about our day. We'll learn that we can speak to the Holy Spirit always, never thinking that prayer time has any limits. Where we used to stop our prayers on time, we now gladly take them further as we go on with the Lord in our faith journey.

The spiritual life sees the leading of the Lord with all that's going on around them. In good times and bad, with ministry and work, with relationships and divine appointments, we'll ask the Lord to show us what to say and do. It's a precious spiritual connection that never ends, and it always guides us in everything we do.

When you surrender all, you gain so much more. "For whoever wants to save his [higher, spiritual, eternal] life, will lose it [the lower, natural, temporal life which is lived only on earth]; and whoever gives up his life [which is lived only on earth] for My sake and the Gospel's will save it [his higher, spiritual life in the eternal kingdom of God]" (Mark 8:35 AMPC).

The spiritual life believes that El Chay (the living God) can do anything, even when He doesn't seem to act as we would want. It's where we pray, knowing that God can do all things, and we never question Him about what He doesn't do. We see miracles in the answers to many prayers, and have hope for any requests still outstanding. When you truly believe God can do all things, your prayer life will go infinitely higher.

Prayer

Holy Spirit, help me build up my spiritual life so that I'm filled with the life of Jesus within and reaching to heaven above. Help me learn what it means to have a spiritual life. Then help me get there.

Challenge

Go online to your favorite Bible website, such as Biblegateway.com, and search for the words "spiritual" and "Holy Spirit." Read through all the verses you find. Pray to the Lord beforehand to open your spiritual eyes to spiritual truths. Don't stand on the traditions of man, but seek the wisdom from above in order to learn what it means to be a spiritual man or woman. If you're already living a spiritual life, seek the truth that will take you higher. There's so much higher that you can go.

Going further

Think about some spiritual giants in times gone by and consider that God wants to use you in the same way. Stop thinking that you were never meant for something more, because you are. Be daring enough to ask the Lord how He wants to take you higher in your spiritual life, and be determined to wait until He answers you. You'll be surprised what God has in store for the soul who is willing to go further with Him. *The same Holy Spirit who was dwelling in Peter dwells in you.* "They even carried their sick out into the streets and put them on cots and sleeping pads, so that when Peter came by at least his shadow might fall on one of them [with healing power]" (Acts 5:15 AMP).

24

Authentic Spirituality

*You must know the authentic in order
to discern the counterfeit.*

Dear friends, do not believe everyone who claims to speak by the
Spirit. You must test them to see if the spirit they have comes from
God. For there are many false prophets in the world. – 1 John 4:1 NLT

If you want to grow higher in your faith, you must
be able to discern what is *not* the higher faith.

So many confuse a soulful life with a spiritual life because the outpouring of the soul can match what we think the spiritual life should look like. We'll see someone in some state that pours from their soul to their body, and we think it's something spiritual to be admired. There's nothing wrong with having your soul touched and to be moving in a soulful way, but it doesn't mean the experience is spiritual.

Being soulful is an outward expression for men to see. Being spiritual is an inward expression seen only by God. The result of soulfulness is the praise of men. The result of being spiritual is that all praise is to the Lord Jesus. "I heard a loud voice of a great multitude in heaven, saying, 'Alleluia! Salvation and glory and honor and power belong to the Lord our God!'" (Revelation 19:1 NKJV).

So many seek after spiritual gifts with a fleshly appetite to prop themselves up before others. They'll seemingly have good intentions, and they're convinced they'll be honored by both men and God. Yet their motives and their goals prove them wrong; because of their pride, they're a hindrance to all that God might do through them. In their fervor to be more spiritual, they'll often pretend to be more spiritual, seeking the praise of men instead of approval from God. Yahweh Qadosh (the Holy One) doesn't approve of anything that's false.

We aren't supposed to chase spiritual gifts, but to walk in them. "So it is with you, since you are so very eager to have spiritual gifts and manifestations of the Spirit, strive to excel in ways that will build up the church [spiritually]" (1 Corinthians 14:12 AMP).

The devil counterfeits the authentic in order to deceive the elect. However, the elect will often become so afraid of the counterfeit that they reject the authentic. They miss out on wonderful truths that help them avoid every lie. The devil wins when people fall for the counterfeit lie. The devil also wins when they reject authentic truth. What we need is spiritual discernment of the authentic so we can separate out and reject only the counterfeit.

We're so afraid to be united to what's wrong that we're separated from what is right. "Now I plead with you, brethren, by the name of our Lord Jesus Christ...that there be no divisions among you, but that you be perfectly joined together in the same mind and in the same judgment" (1 Corinthians 1:10 NKJV).

If we avoid authentic spirituality to avoid the counterfeit, we limit all that the Lord can do through us. We set our boundaries at the natural and forfeit the spiritual in our lives. The Father never intended for the church to operate apart from the Holy Spirit. We were meant to live a Spirit-filled life. There are many in the church in our day who speak out against the spiritual, all the while thinking themselves righteous—as if they're protecting the church. But they're hurting the church and grieving the Holy Spirit with their powerless faith that's grounded only in the natural intellectualism of our day.

Stop organizing the Holy Spirit out of your services. If you never leave room for Him, don't be surprised when He doesn't show up. "But know this, that in the last days perilous times will come: [beware of people] having a form of godliness but denying its power. And from such people turn away!" (2 Timothy 3:1,5 NKJV). Don't miss the point in these verses that Paul was warning about people in the church.

Authentic spirituality will be aligned with the Word of God and will never be limited by the traditions of man. It will not rely upon the knowledge of man or the power within oneself, but on the divine inspiration and outpouring of power from heaven.

Don't preach to be popular, lest the power of God be diluted by the opinions of man. Yeshua (Jesus) schooled the religious authorities of His day, "All too well you reject the commandment of God, that you may keep your tradition...making the word of God of no effect through your tradition which you have handed down" (Mark 7:9,13 NKJV).

Authentic spirituality will never promote the person, but exalts only the Lord whom we serve. It is more concerned with honoring God than being honored by men. It is more interested in living doctrines than in arguing over them with others, especially with those who debate only to puff up their pride by parading their worldly knowledge and perspective of Scripture.

When you promote yourself, you demote yourself in all that God might do through you. "'For whoever promotes himself will be humbled, and whoever humbles himself will be promoted'" (Matthew 23:12 CJB).

Authentic spirituality doesn't seek gifts so they can be on display before men, but seeks to serve the Lord however He uses us, with or without gifts. To the degree you want to be seen by men, the Holy Spirit isn't effectively working in you. It takes our surrender to the Lord for Him to be victorious through us.

The greater your surrender to Christ, the greater His victory will be in you. "I no longer live, but Christ lives in me. The life I now live I live by believing in God's Son, who loved me and took the punishment for my sins" (Galatians 2:20 GW).

Authentic spirituality waits for the Holy Spirit and listens for all He will say. It doesn't rely on the power of man but seeks the provisions that come from heaven. It doesn't look at natural limits but trusts in spiritual abundance, which has no end, because heaven's warehouses are stocked up into eternity.

Scarcity is a natural problem, whereas abundance is a spiritual reality. "And God is able to make all grace abound toward you, that you, always having all sufficiency in all things, may have an abundance for every good work" (2 Corinthians 9:8 NKJV).

Authentic spirituality knows that the real power is in prayer, because it's in prayer that we reach into the resources of heaven. The highest peak in the life of a person with authentic spirituality is kneeling down low in private and speaking humbly with their Abba ("dear Father" in Aramaic).

When you have nothing but a prayer, you have everything you need. "Yahweh is near to everyone who prays to him, to every faithful person who prays to him. He fills the needs of those who fear him. He hears their cries for help and saves them" (Psalm 145:18-19 NOG).

You can have an authentic spiritual life only if you ask Him for this. When you ask Him for something He also wants, and your motives are right, He will most certainly give it to you. He can take you higher, once you're willing to go lower before Him.

If the prayer is right, the answer is coming. "You ask [God for something] and do not receive it, because you ask with wrong motives [out of selfishness or with an unrighteous agenda], so that [when you get what you want] you may spend it on your [hedonistic] desires" (James 4:3 AMP).

The opposite of being authentic is being a counterfeit. Counterfeit is just another word for a lie. Not being authentic is being in a lie. An embellishment is nothing more than a lie mixed together with a little bit of truth. It's your pride that causes you to embellish a story. It's easy to keep your story straight when you don't add to it. Anything fake will crumble, and anything false is not of El Olam (the eternal God). You have to be authentic in the little things before you can have a higher faith.

I can always tell someone who has a self-made spirituality with a self-made calling. They hold their head very high. If your spirituality is formed by God, and you've been called to service by God, then very little pride will remain—it has been crushed in His hands as He formed you into something new. "But the jar he was making did not turn out as he had hoped, so he crushed it into a lump of clay again and started over" (Jeremiah 18:4 NLT). *Be wary of vessels that appear desirable to man; they're rarely a product made new by God.*

It is better to be authentic with a little than to be fake, no matter how much you might have. Beware of the competition that causes you to want to fake something beyond what you are. Being genuine in a little faith matters more than having a higher faith. You won't get the higher faith unless your faith is genuine. Authentic faith is always built upon authentic faith; that's the only foundation that can hold it.

So long as your faith is built upon your feelings, you're standing on shaky ground. "'The heart is deceitful above all things, and desperately wicked; who can know it?'" (Jeremiah 17:9 NKJV).

I've come to see that the authentic spiritual life isn't what you do in front of other people, but how you are with El Roi (the God who sees me) when you're all alone with Him. If you ever want to truly walk in the Spirit, you'll first have to learn to crawl in the Spirit. This sounds easy, but it's the hardest thing a natural person can do. We cannot study our way to a spiritual life, only surrender to the Holy Spirit; He alone is able to help us grow spiritually.

You need never plead for the Holy Spirit to fill you, only ask. "I pray that He may grant you, according to the riches of His glory, to be strengthened with power in the inner man through His Spirit...so you may be filled with all the fullness of God" (Ephesians 3:16,19 HCSB).

To be spiritually authentic, we must first admit how unspiritual we really are. Our flesh rules us more than we care to admit, and more deeply than we can imagine. We sometimes think of ourselves as spiritual, until someone pokes us in the natural, and we see how fast that old natural man rises up. Let your spiritual failures be the lessons that help you grow higher. Reject the idea that growing spiritually is easy for others and hard only for you. You've no idea what others went through to walk in the spiritual life they have now.

The Lord can often do more through us in our failures than in our successes. It's when we're broken that the Lord can form us into something new. After David's adulterous affair with Bathsheba, and his killing of her husband, his crimes were exposed. Then for seven days, David "fasted and went in and lay all night on the ground" (2 Samuel 12:16 NKJV).

Yahweh Shammah (the LORD is there) will bless your spiritual life not when it seems so much higher, but when it is pure and authentic. Lose the idea that you need to impress anyone with how spiritual you are. It's your pride that wants to impress others. Only in your humility can God help you grow spiritually. Let others think of you as they will, but let God know you'd rather be looked down upon than be thought one inch higher than you really are.

So long as you try to impress men, you cannot please the Lord. "Don't be selfish; don't try to impress others. Be humble, thinking of others as better than yourselves. Don't look out only for your own interests, but take an interest in others, too" (Philippians 2:3-4 NLT).

I've found that for me to be authentic in my faith, I've had to endure being mistreated. The worst part is when people who mistreat you then justify it according to their own personal opinion of what is right. What I've learned is that to be authentic, I have to be in the Spirit and respond in love when others come after me with critical words. We're taught to be loving, yet we struggle with that the most. The minute someone strikes out at us, we don't really want to "turn the cheek" but to return the slap, and we think ourselves justified. But when we seek only to be justified by El Hakkadosh (the Holy God), we're able to be authentic before others. Being authentic is measured by God's approval, not by any person here on earth.

You can have an authentic spiritual life. This life is not hindered by whatever errors you have in your past; it depends only on your surrendered will to the Lord, who can help you going forward. There's nothing you need to bring to the table, because the Lord has everything you need. As you grow in this blessed authentic spiritual life, you'll be a blessing to those around you. Your life will be an extension of heaven, and you'll be used by God to reach into the lives of those closest to you. When the spiritual is real, the natural will shudder.

Prayer

Lord Jesus, help me live a humble life, simple in what I do, yet filled with all the spiritual truths that pour out from heaven. Help me be authentic in everything I say and do, knowing it's from You that all things are given, and to You, all glory is due.

Challenge

In both your natural and your spiritual life, make it your determined prayer that you'll be authentic in everything you do. In your journal, be daring enough to admit each day where you've fallen short and where you'll pray that the Lord will change you. If you aren't real with yourself, you won't be real with God, and you have no hope of being real with others.

Going further

The higher faith will happen only when the spiritual life is authentic. As you begin to mature spiritually, you'll find this life is far more simple than you imagined. Think about others you know who are spiritually mature. Write down the attributes of those people that indicate their spiritual maturity. Then write next to this list of attributes how you measure up and where you need to work. Pray to the Lord to help you in each area. Don't stop praying over this list until you've crossed off each item. It might take years to do this, so get started. *Your thought life is the one place where you decide whether to be the master or the slave.* "Keep your thoughts continually fixed on all that is authentic and real, honorable and admirable, beautiful and respectful, pure and holy, merciful and kind. And fasten your thoughts on every glorious work of God, praising him always" (Philippians 4:8 TPT).

25

<hr style="border:none;" />

The Spirit-Filled Life

You can accomplish more in one day filled with the Holy Spirit than in a lifetime full of yourself.

Barnabas was a good man, full of the Holy Spirit and strong in faith.
And many people were brought to the Lord. – Acts 11:24 NLT

If you want to grow higher in your faith, you must live a life
that's filled with the Holy Spirit in everything you're doing.

Too often, Christians equate the Spirit-filled life with having spiritual gifts, walking in miracles, or operating in the prophetic. Those are good things, but they're not the main characteristics of what being Spirit-filled truly means. Being Spirit-filled is having the fullness of the Holy Spirit reigning within us. The evidence of the Holy Spirit in us is the Holy Spirit working through us.

Yeshua HaMashiach (Jesus the Messiah) said we would know the true prophets by their fruits. What better fruit could we look for in a believer than the fruit of the Holy Spirit? By this fruit the believer can grow and become ready to walk in the Spirit, experiencing the gifts and the miracles we were meant to walk in. This fullness of the Spirit is not to elevate us above others, but for us to simply be utensils in His hands.

Once you're filled with the Holy Spirit, your life will never be the same. Our Father God promised, "I will put my Spirit inside you. And I will help you live by my rules. You will be careful to obey my laws" (Ezekiel 36:27 ICB).

The Spirit-filled life is one in which Ruach Ha'Kodesh (the Holy Spirit) is reigning in you, and your flesh has surrendered. The Spirit reigns more as you yield more. It's not like a switch but a dial, an ever-growing submission to the power of God and the leading of the Holy Spirit. It's a journey that goes the distance from who you were to who the Father intends you to become. The Spirit-filled life is the new life you were meant to have. When once you ask God to help you in this Spirit-filled life, He will help, for this is most certainly at the center of His will for you.

When we're filled with the Holy Spirit, we're filled with the purposes of God. "It is God who produces in you the desires and actions that please him" (Philippians 2:13 NOG).

The Spirit-filled life isn't measured by His miracles through you or the spiritual gifts placed on you, but by the Holy Spirit that's within you. God may decide to pour a few miracles through you from time to time, but His Spirit reigning in you will change the way you behave each day. The Lord may give you spiritual gifts to help you in your calling, but the humility you have along the way is what will prove that the Holy Spirit is within you. The grandest thing that Yahweh Mekoddishkem (the LORD who sanctifies you) does within us is to change us into something new.

"God washed us by the power of the Holy Spirit. He gave us new birth and a fresh beginning" (Titus 3:5 CEV).

People chase spiritual gifts as if they're prizes, and they long for spiritual visions as if they were a badge of honor. But the real prize that comes from heaven is a changed life. The Spirit-filled life will be a life filled with the fruit of the Holy Spirit. You'll have greater influence for the kingdom with your attitude than with any spiritual gift God gives you. The problem with spiritual gifts is that they can puff up your pride. The beauty of spiritual fruit is they replace your pride with the attributes of heaven.

The filling of the Holy Spirit is measured by the fruit that flows out. "But the fruit of the Spirit is love, joy, peace, patience, kindness, goodness, faithfulness, humility, self-control" (Galatians 5:22-23 CJB). *The fruit is in your attitude.*

The rest of this chapter is broken up into sections focusing one by one on the spiritual fruit listed in Galatians 5:22-23. If you want to grow higher in your faith, you must first have the Holy Spirit grow higher in your life. There's no shortcut or alternative for the higher faith, only a journey with God to be filled with the Holy Spirit, and to live a life that proves it.

When you're filled by the Holy Spirit, you're no longer just a man or a woman. "But you will receive power and ability when the Holy Spirit comes upon you" (Acts 1:8 AMP).

Love: The Spirit-filled life is filled with love. The Holy Spirit pours into our hearts the love of the Father, and this love then pours out onto those around us. The love from God is not like the love found in the world. It's a love that's sacrificial, not self-serving. It's a love that has no end and no set of conditions by which it can be attained. This love is pure, holy, and joined with the things found in heaven. This love is poured into us, then flows from us as we serve as God's vessels to a needy world.

The measure of God's love in us can be seen in how much we love those who are against us. "God's love has been abundantly poured out within our hearts through the Holy Spirit who was given to us" (Romans 5:5 AMP).

Joy: The Spirit-filled life is filled with an unexplainable joy that persists even in the bad times. This joy overcomes gloom and protects against depression. It invigorates the soul to wake up each day and embrace the blessed life God has given us. This joy is filled with hope and isn't deflated by the problems in this world. It acknowledges obstacles, but remains confident in the power of El Shaddai (God Almighty).

Count your blessings and give your problems to the Lord. "Always be joyful. Always keep on praying. No matter what happens, always be thankful, for this is God's will for you who belong to Christ Jesus" (1 Thessalonians 5:16-18 TLB).

Peace: The Spirit-filled life has an abundance of peace. There'll be peace like a river that's always flowing and never striving, only winding its way through life without worry. This peace will be more than just within; it will pour outward, seeking peace with all those around you. The peace from heaven never depends on our circumstances on earth. No matter what you're going through, the peace of Yahweh Shalom (the Lord is peace) can remain upon you. Let peace rule in your heart, and your peace will give hope to those around you.

The peace of Christ in you is the message of hope through you. Jesus taught, "I have told you all this so that you will have peace of heart and mind. Here on earth you will have many trials and sorrows; but cheer up, for I have overcome the world" (John 16:33 TLB).

Patience: The Spirit-filled life is filled with patience. It's a life of trusting in God for every situation before us. It's a patience that perseveres through the trials that inevitably come. It's a patience that holds us up so we can endure. Patience waits with trust and faith that Christ is always with us. As you trust the Lord more, you'll be more patient in whatever you're going through. Patience is the gauge of our faith and the test of how much we believe in all that God is doing. Patience believes Yahweh Ezer (the LORD our helper) is at work even when we can't see it.

If you wait for God's timing, you'll be on time. "Be still in the presence of the LORD, and wait patiently for him to act. Don't worry about evil people who prosper or fret about their wicked schemes" (Psalm 37:7 NLT).

Kindness: The Spirit-filled life has evidence of an outpouring of kindness. It speaks words of kindness that are born out of genuine thoughts of kindness. It extends kindness to those who deserve it as well as to those who don't. It's a kindness that's noticed and admired for how it makes people feel. Barely anyone will remember the words you might tell them, but they'll surely remember the way you made them feel. Be kind to everyone, knowing we're all in this together.

Don't be consumed by how others treat you, but be convicted in how you treat them. "Never be bitter, angry, or mad. Never shout angrily or say things to hurt others. Never do anything evil. Be kind and loving to each other. Forgive each other the same as God forgave you through Christ" (Ephesians 4:31-32 ERV).

Goodness: The Spirit-filled life is a life of goodness. It's a life that thinks about good things and longs to do good things for others. It's a life filled with the goodness of God that overflows onto those around us. The goodness isn't like what the world will peddle as good, which is usually self-serving. Rather, it's a goodness that will stand the test of time and the judgment of Christ as the Lord looks upon what we're doing.

How we are practically reflects who we are spiritually. "Therefore, as we have opportunity, let us do good to all, especially to those who are of the household of faith" (Galatians 6:10 NKJV).

Faithfulness: The Spirit-filled life is filled with faithfulness. It is faithful to Jesus and to friends and loved ones. It is faithful to every promise spoken. It's a faithfulness in commitments even when things become very hard. It's a faithfulness that causes others to trust us, knowing we'll do what we say. It's a life that displays what being true means, so that we're an example to others. Being faithful is being who Jesus Christ wants you to be.

Don't compromise an inch, and God will give you a mile. "Yahweh will make you the head, not the tail. You will always be at the top, never at the bottom, if you faithfully obey the commands of Yahweh your Elohim that I am giving you today" (Deuteronomy 28:13 NOG).

Gentleness: The Spirit-filled life is filled with a gentleness born out of humility. It's a life that, in humility, speaks gentle words that soothe the soul and lift up those around them. This life has a gentleness that's evident in the way you walk and how you look at others with your eyes. The gentler you become, the more comfort you'll bring to those around you who are hurting. Your life will become a safe place for people to go and a welcome place for people to stay close to you. Your gentleness toward others will be a testimony of the life of Christ reigning in you.

Gentle words flow from gentle souls. "Be beautiful in your heart by being gentle and quiet. This kind of beauty will last, and God considers it very special" (1 Peter 3:4 CEV).

Self-control: The Spirit-filled life has self-control and is able to overcome things that try to overpower you. On your own, you could never achieve what only the Holy Spirit can help you achieve. Self-control is possible only when you have the Holy Spirit within you, giving you the strength and guidance to live rightly. This doesn't mean you'll never fail, because you will. Sometimes, you'll try to do things on your own. After you fail, submit yourself once again to the Holy Spirit. By His strength, you can prevail.

You won't have a Spirit-filled life by consuming the things of this world. "Don't be drunk with wine, because that will ruin your life. Instead, be filled with the Holy Spirit" (Ephesians 5:18 NLT).

Don't despair with where you are, but have confidence in where the Lord can take you. When Yahweh Sabaoth (the LORD of angelic armies) gets you in His grip, there's no wiggling out of where He's taking you. Though you may not be able to imagine yourself filled with the Spirit of God and full of the fruit from the Holy Spirit, be sure that God can both imagine it and make it happen. He knows what He can do once you give Him the right of way in which to do it. Determine in your heart today that you'll let Him help you—and He will.

We must realize that what is written in the Word is for us. We can all be filled with the Holy Spirit. Some think it's not possible, but a few simply ask God to give it to them. Be daring enough to ask God.

Prayer

Father God, You promised to put Your Spirit inside me and to change me forever. I pray that you'll help me yield my life to the Holy Spirit, so the fruit of the Holy Spirit will grow abundantly in me. Help me have an attitude that's possible only by the power of the Holy Spirit within me.

Challenge

Write down the list of spiritual fruit from Galatians 5:22-23. Next to each one, write down in what ways you can see the evidence of the Holy Spirit working within you. Then write down next to each one the evidence of where you have not yet yielded yourself to the Holy

Spirit. Finally, write below this list a prayer asking the Holy Spirit to change you, and give Him permission to do so.

Going further

Write down these verses from Galatians 5:22-23 and devote a time each day of the week to read these verses and pray over each fruit of the Spirit. Pray that you yield to the power of the Holy Spirit both to plant that fruit and to make it grow abundantly within you. Believe that God can do it, and surrender yourself to Him so He can get started. *Don't focus on the problem outside you but on the deficiency it reveals within you. Every problem in your life reveals which fruit of the Spirit has not yet ripened in your life.* "The fruit of the Spirit [the result of His presence within us] is love [unselfish concern for others], joy, [inner] peace, patience [not the ability to wait, but how we act while waiting], kindness, goodness, faithfulness, gentleness, self-control. Against such things there is no law" (Galatians 5:22-23 AMP).

26

Spiritual Discernment

Don't pray only for a sign from God;
pray also for the discernment to know
what the sign means.

O Lord, listen to my cry; give me the discerning mind you promised.
—Psalm 119:169 NLT

If you want to grow higher in your faith, you'll need
spiritual discernment to help you find your way.

We must read the Word and grow in our knowledge of God's truth. If we don't know the truth in the Word, we're susceptible to being deceived by the world's lies. Keep learning, because the times are upon us when lies are becoming more deceptive, and the truth is no longer desired in the world. In these days, we're seeing how the lie is presented as the truth, while the truth is dragged through the mud and then called a lie. Spiritual discernment has never been as important to the believer as it is now.

We must discern when a lie has a sprinkling of truth, lest we be deceived by the lie that's hidden within. "'Everyone will deceive his neighbor, and will not speak the truth; they have taught their tongue to speak lies; they weary themselves to commit iniquity'" (Jeremiah 9:5 NKJV).

Knowledge by itself won't be enough to protect us from deception. Your ability to discern the truth by what you know will fall short of the deceptions that will come at you. We must grow in our spiritual life so we can discern by His Spirit in us what we could never discern in our own power. We must lose the idea that we're smart enough and clever enough to keep ourselves safe from the deceptions in our day. Having the Holy Spirit indwelling us to show us the truth is so important.

Before you can know the truth, you must be able to discern the truth. "For everyone who partakes only of milk is unskilled in the word of righteousness, for he is a babe. But solid food belongs to those who are of full age, that is, those who by reason of use have their senses exercised to discern both good and evil" (Hebrews 5:13-14 NKJV).

Spiritual discernment will show you what books cannot teach you. When the Holy Spirit reveals a thing, then gives you discernment to know what it means, you can operate in the natural using the discernment given to you in the spiritual. We need to lean more on El Deah (the God of knowledge) and trust less in ourselves. Even when we think we know a fact, we need to pray to the Lord to reveal all that's really there. So often, we see only the external and make conclusions about all that's inside. This is as true in our perceptions of people as it is with our view of the circumstances going on around us. Don't be satisfied that what you see is the way things are, but pray the Lord will give you more discernment.

The greatest weapon the devil has in spiritual warfare is the deception that this fight is in the natural realm. Stop focusing on that one person who is attacking you; focus instead on the spirit behind them. "For we do not wrestle against flesh and blood, but against principalities, against powers, against the rulers of the darkness of this age, against spiritual hosts of wickedness in the heavenly places" (Ephesians 6:12 NKJV).

When Yeshua HaMashiach (Jesus the Messiah) asked people if they had eyes to see or ears to hear, He was not speaking to their natural senses but their spiritual senses. If you want to grow in the Spirit, you must yield to the Spirit to greater degrees. To the degree you rely upon yourself, the Holy Spirit cannot help you. We need the Lord to open our spiritual eyes so we can see what our natural eyes miss—not only to look at angels or demons, but to see spiritual forces at play around us. We must learn to see the evil so we can be more aware of what's against us. Also, we need to see the good so that we can be secure in the power of God who is with us.

You won't hear until you're willing to listen. "'Anyone with ears to hear must listen to the Spirit and understand what he is saying to the churches'" (Revelation 3:6 NLT).

Spiritual discernment is not only for the prophets and the priests but for any man or woman who dares to go further in their walk with Yahweh Sabaoth (the LORD of angelic armies). The Lord pours out His wisdom to those who ask and to those who are humble enough to receive it. The proud don't ask. The humble don't delay in pleading for the Lord to help them.

We all know the verse that says, "Do not lean on your own under-standing" (Proverbs 3:5 ESV), but we still lean far too often on our own understanding. We do this because we were taught to do so from an early age. We must undo the natural lessons we've been taught, so we can redo ourselves in the spiritual. Stop jumping to your feet, and just drop to your knees. The Lord helps those who ask, period.

The key to making good decisions is asking the Lord to help you. "If you need wisdom, ask our generous God, and he will give it to you. He will not rebuke you for asking" (James 1:5 NLT).

There's a spiritual realm right before us, if we would only see it. There are angels around us, yet we believe only what we can see, and this limitation keeps our eyes firmly closed to what's going on right before us. Believe beyond what you can see, and you'll find that the Lord is with you. If you close your mind to the spiritual, you'll be trapped in the limits of the natural. This doesn't mean you have to see everything that's in the spiritual; be glad that you don't, because there's much evil you wouldn't want to see. But be willing to let the Lord show you what He will, and believe that He can do it.

The things of this world are anchors to the spiritual realm. "If the Holy Spirit is living in us, let us be led by Him in all things" (Galatians 5:25 NLV).

No matter what your question is, without spiritual discernment, you're on your own. You may get advice from people, but you must learn to be discerning, and God will remain silent until you're ready to ask Him. Spiritual discernment will come by your faith and your humility, not by any title given by man. What matters is not what people call you, but what God entrusts to you as your spiritual life begins to blossom. God may give you a little, or He may give you a lot, and we must be thankful to receive anything at all. Let Yahweh Ezer (the LORD our helper) open your eyes, and you'll start to see all that He is doing.

No matter how bad things look, don't give up, because you have no idea what God is doing behind the scenes to help you. "Then Elisha prayed, 'O LORD, open his eyes and let him see!' The LORD opened the young man's eyes, and when he looked up, he saw that the hillside around Elisha was filled with horses and chariots of fire" (2 Kings 6:17 NLT).

Spiritual discernment isn't just for the big decisions in your life, but also for the daily walk in which you're living. The more you're led by the Holy Spirit, the less you'll go your own way. When you go the way God has for you, you'll experience peace. His will is better than yours. When the Spirit is leading you, and you're following Him, your path will show it. Even the mundane things in life will take on a greater meaning. Nothing is wasted in His kingdom, and everything has a purpose in the plans of El Elyon (God Most High).

Trust God with your decisions, then wait for Him to answer. "The LORD directs the steps of the godly. He delights in every detail of their lives. Though they stumble, they will never fall, for the LORD holds them by the hand" (Psalm 37:23-24 NLT).

There are people around you who desperately need you to spiritually discern what's going on in their lives and how you might pray for them. When we see the spirit behind someone, good or bad, we gain the discernment by which we can better understand what's really going on. Pray that your eyes will be opened.

The Holy Spirit cannot do a work through you until He has first done a work in you. "We are setting these truths forth in words not taught by human wisdom but taught by the [Holy] Spirit, combining and interpreting spiritual truths with spiritual language [to those who possess the Holy Spirit]" (1 Corinthians 2:13 AMPC).

Spiritual discernment is a difficult burden at times, as you become aware of the deception and the manipulation people are using against you. You'll see right through people in your work life, personal life, or ministry, and you'll recognize the hidden things they're doing against you. This is when you must embrace the teachings of Christ to love your enemies, of which some are your enemies without even knowing it. Rarely will God lead you to reveal a thing that He has shown you in someone who is coming against you. Yet He has shown you these things for a reason. Let the Lord lead you on what to do in these situations.

Sometimes, we're not meant to overcome our enemy but to win them over. The Lord Jesus taught us, "You have heard that it was said, 'You shall love your neighbor and hate your enemy.' But I say to you, love your enemies and pray for those who persecute you, so that you may prove yourselves to be sons of your Father who is in heaven" (Matthew 5:43-45 NASB).

Spiritual discernment is a powerful thing when you're ministering to others. El Rachum (the God of compassion and mercy) will show you their hidden hurts or maybe even their secret sins. Rarely will you share this with them, but it will help you as you minister to them. I've been blessed many times by the Lord to get a word for someone as I'm ministering to them. You must first carefully discern whether the word for them is from the Lord; you must also discern whether the Lord intends for you to give it to them. Sometimes, you won't even know the full meaning of the word, but the Lord will let you find out from them, so you'll be confident as you're praying over others in the future.

The Holy Spirit may lead you to speak, but it's the flesh that refuses to shut up. "Let two or three prophets speak, and let the others judge. But if anything is revealed to another who sits by, let the first keep silent. For you can all prophesy one by one, that all may learn and all may be encouraged. And the spirits of the prophets are subject to the prophets" (1 Corinthians 14:29-32 NKJV).

Spiritual discernment is the compass and the map for your spiritual life, so that your course can be guided by Yahweh Raah (the LORD is my shepherd), and your destination will be the purposes He has for you. There are no classes or programs for learning to discern better; such learning comes only through an ongoing walk with the Lord. My prayer for you is to be filled with the Holy Spirit and be spiritually discerning in your life. May the Lord open your eyes and open your ears, giving you the spiritual enlightenment by which you can be discerning in the world around you. The time is now. We need to discern the times we're in.

There's a great burden that goes along with spiritual discernment. You'll discern others as they try to peddle their lies and manipulate you. Discerning the truth is not an easy thing to do when people are coming against you. Often, you cannot confront them with what you've discerned, because by man's understanding, there's no way you could know. Thank the Lord for the discernment, then ask Him to lead you in how to respond to it.

Prayer

Lord Jesus, give me the spiritual discernment I desperately need to find my way and go higher in my faith. Help me make wise choices as I learn to rely upon the leading of the Holy Spirit in everything I say and do.

Challenge

The Holy Spirit is your teacher, but we all need spiritual mentors to help us stay the course. Seek out that person in your life you can call on, and watch how the Lord uses them to help you along the way. Never be too proud to seek help, and never be so arrogant that you don't think you need help. Be willing to learn, and you will. Pray for the discernment to find the right person for this season in your life. Even if you're a mentor, get mentored yourself.

Going further

Be determined in your faith journey to grow ever higher. The minute you think you're there, you'll go no further. Know that the Lord can take you ever higher if you let Him. Pray to the Lord to show you areas of your life that you need to grow in. If you're listening, He will surely tell you. Once you have your list, keep it before you and humbly pray for the Lord to help you in each of the things on your list. *The best way to change a situation is to ask God to change you.* "Create in me a clean heart, O God. Renew a loyal spirit within me. Do not banish me from your presence, and don't take your Holy Spirit from me" (Psalm 51:10-11 NLT).

27

Spiritual Sight

You need spiritual eyes to see spiritual truths.

Jesus taught, "The eye is the lamp of the body; so if your eye is clear [spiritually perceptive], your whole body will be full of light [benefiting from God's precepts]. But if your eye is bad [spiritually blind], your whole body will be full of darkness [devoid of God's precepts]." —Matthew 6:22-23 AMP

Spiritual sight improves only with spiritual maturity. It's not enough for us to be given sight; we must also use it.

Newborn babies won't always open their eyes right away, and when they do, they can focus only on what's very close to them. Initially, they're interested only in the flashy and moving things before them. Their vision will improve as they grow and mature in their new natural environment. As they mature in years, their eyes will come to appreciate the beauty of a sunset far away and the stillness of the moon in the night sky.

When a person is born again in the Spirit, they don't open their spiritual eyes right away. They're not yet aware of this sense. Many believers aren't even taught what it means to have spiritual sight, so they fail to press into all that it can offer. You can be born again spiritually but still have your spiritual eyes closed. You must have your spiritual eyes opened before you can see in the spiritual.

It's not that God hides truth from us, but that our eyes are not open so we might see it. "Deal bountifully with Your servant, that I may live and keep Your word [treasuring it and being guided by it day by day]. Open my eyes [to spiritual truth] so that I may behold wonderful things from Your law" (Psalm 119:17-18 AMP).

For believers, the greatest hindrance to opening their spiritual eyes is the failure to mature in their spiritual life. They're born again in spirit, but remain spiritual babies. They rely only on their natural senses and don't seek to grow spiritually. They don't read the Word of God, or if they do, they study and strive with only their natural intellect. What they learn may be impressive to man, but it won't get them any closer to El Elyon (God Most High). Their natural efforts only hinder their spiritual progression.

It wouldn't be so hard for you to move in the spiritual if you weren't trying so hard in your natural. "A person who isn't spiritual doesn't accept the teachings of God's Spirit. He thinks they're nonsense. He can't understand them because a person must be spiritual to evaluate them" (1 Corinthians 2:14 GW).

When we focus on the natural realm, we become obsessed with circumstances that surround us. We're moved by the seen and remain oblivious to the unseen. We're consumed by the world and don't take hold of the things from heaven. You cannot discern spiritual truths using your natural intellect. This doesn't mean you should not increase intellectually, but you also need to increase spiritually. Increasing intellectually is through your own effort, whereas increasing spiritually comes only from your willingness to let the Lord help you.

We understand how to mature in the natural realm because we can see it with our own two natural eyes. In the natural, we can use the scales of man to prove our progress. Yet even at the peak of natural maturity, one can remain a spiritual baby, helpless in the spiritual realm. Spiritual growth takes time, but time alone won't bring it about. In the natural, you mature by your own efforts. In the spiritual, you mature when you let El Shaddai (God Almighty) help you. In the natural, you go as far as you're able. In the spiritual, you go as far as you let Him take you.

Spiritual growth never occurs through the power of man. "Receive your power from the Lord and from his mighty strength" (Ephesians 6:10 NOG).

You can grow into spiritual maturity, and you can have your spiritual eyes opened. It doesn't come by your efforts or the programs of man, but as a gift to the one who is willing to receive it. Pray to your heavenly Father that He will open your spiritual eyes today.

You'll know your spiritual eyes are open when you start to peer behind the curtains of what was veiled by your natural eyesight. The Lord may start to give you dreams or visions, or He may let you see the spirit that's behind people you come across. Your natural sight can sometimes be deceived, but spiritual sight cuts right past the natural facade and shows us what's behind the person we're looking at.

Never let the limit of your sight be the limit of your faith. "And Elisha prayed, and said, 'Lord, I pray, open his eyes that he may see.' Then the LORD opened the eyes of the young man, and he saw. And behold, the mountain was full of horses and chariots of fire all around Elisha" (2 Kings 6:17 NKJV).

Even when our spiritual eyes are opened, we're often moved by all that we see in the natural. Only through persistent prayer can we come to trust in the unseen power of the Holy Spirit within us and not be moved by the circumstances around us. Part of growing in our spiritual eyesight is learning to see past the natural that's staring us right in the face. Sometimes, to see more clearly in the spiritual, you need to simply close your natural eyes and pray for Yeshua HaMashiach (Jesus the Messiah) to show you the spiritual reality.

When you're looking up, you won't feel down. "To You I have raised my eyes, You who are enthroned in the heavens!" (Psalm 123:1 NASB).

Spiritual sight has more to do with trusting in the unseen presence of God than it does with seeing angels and demons around you. There may be times when the Lord will allow you to see in the spiritual realm, but most often, He gives you the faith to know He's there even when you don't see anything. When we can believe without seeing, our faith will grow even higher.

It's more important to have the presence of God than to feel it. "'God did this so that they would seek him and perhaps reach out for him and find him, though he is not far from any one of us'" (Acts 17:27 NIV).

Late one night, I came home after I'd been ministering in one of the darkest of prison yards. After a while, I lay down to sleep. But I couldn't fall asleep because I felt something demonic standing next to my bed. I opened my eyes, and the Lord let me see in the spiritual. I saw the most horrific demon looking over me. It had followed me home from the prison. I knew Ruach Ha'Kodesh (the Holy Spirit) was with me, so I told the demon to leave—and he was gone.

In whatever you're going through, He has you. "The LORD himself goes before you and will be with you; he will never leave you nor forsake you. Do not be afraid; do not be discouraged" (Deuteronomy 31:8 NIV).

We don't always see demonic spirits, but we can be sure they're around us. We need to learn to tell the demons to leave our homes and our churches by the authority given to us by the Lord Jesus Christ. Demons may not move on our account, but by the authority of His name, they cannot stay. I've heard people say they want to see in the spiritual realm, but they fail to realize this means they'll see much that is frightening. The Lord won't open your eyes until you're ready. Until He does, trust Him that He has you.

No matter how bad things look around you, just remember that He is with you. "Even when I walk through the darkest valley, I will not be afraid, for you are close beside me" (Psalm 23:4 NLT).

One of the most powerful forces given to us by Yahweh Yireh (the LORD will provide) is our imagination. Some in the modern church have turned this idea of imagination into a thing of childish daydreaming or demonic strongholds. They've thrown the baby out with the bathwater, and they think themselves wiser for it. But imagination is built on the mind God created in us, and if we have a spiritual mind that longs for God, our imagination will be a blessing. We must discern whether what we imagine is from God, and we must let God use our imagination to reach us. Learn to imagine yourself in the presence of God, then wait for all He will show you.

God's imagination is never limited by yours. "Glory belongs to God, whose power is at work in us. By this power he can do infinitely more than we can ask or imagine" (Ephesians 3:20 NOG).

When we have spiritual sight, we'll see the natural realm from an entirely different perspective. On this earth, we have demons. But also on this earth, we have angels. In this life, we have trouble. But also in this life, we have Jesus. Don't allow what you see in the natural to outweigh what's in the spiritual. Pray that El Rachum (God of compassion and mercy) will open your eyes to see deeper into the lives of those around you. Be willing to be taught a lesson for thinking one way about others, then having the Lord Jesus show you just how wrong you were. When we start to see the truth, we can then discern the lie.

Don't look at the storm; look at Jesus. "Peter went over the side of the boat and walked on the water toward Jesus. But when he saw the strong wind and the waves, he was terrified and began to sink. 'Save me, Lord!' he shouted. Jesus immediately reached out and grabbed him. 'You have so little faith,' Jesus said. 'Why did you doubt me?'" (Matthew 14:29-31 NLT).

Pray today that Yahweh Qadosh (the Holy One) will open your spiritual eyes. Believe today that He can do it. Allow yourself to acknowledge that God is always with you. Speak His power over every circumstance that comes up against you. Get ready to see everything around you in a whole new way. Get into a quiet place and close your natural eyes. Focus on any situation in your life, then ask the Lord to show you something you could never have seen with your natural eyes. Can you believe that the Lord sees better than you? He most certainly can.

You cannot see an open heaven with a closed mind. As Stephen said, "Look! I see the heavens opened and the Son of Man standing at the right hand of God!" (Acts 7:56 NKJV).

Prayer

Father God, open my eyes so I can see into the spiritual realm and be aware of what You want me to see. Put the spirit of wisdom and revelation upon me so I understand more of what You're allowing me to see.

Challenge

Every day, spend time with God before you read His Word. Ask Him to open your eyes to see in His Word the truth that will speak to the way you're living. Ask His Holy Spirit to reveal more and more of what's in the Word to change you. Spiritual vision begins in the classroom, which is in the presence of the Lord. Write down truths discovered as the Holy Spirit reveals them, and praise God that He trusts you with them.

Going further

Pray that the Lord will start revealing to you the truth behind the people you come across. Ask Him to first prepare your heart so that any knowledge of people you gain will be kept in confidence and meant only to help them. Don't look at the outward through their emotions, but look for the inward that only the Holy Spirit can show you. Don't use your natural eyes to try and see spiritual truths, but only seek the Lord's vision. *Revelation is not seeing something new, but having something revealed that was there all along. It's not that God has hidden the truth, but that we're naturally blind to see it and deaf to hear it, with a heart that cannot understand.* "'Yet the Lord has not given you a heart to perceive and eyes to see and ears to hear, to this very day'" (Deuteronomy 29:4 NKJV). *Spiritual senses are never attained, only received. It's never a matter of trying harder, but of yielding more.*

28

Spiritual Wisdom

*If you want to increase in spiritual wisdom,
you need to decrease in natural foolishness.*

We ask God to give you complete knowledge of his will and to give you spiritual wisdom and understanding. Then the way you live will always honor and please the Lord, and your lives will produce every kind of good fruit. – Colossians 1:9-10 NLT

If you want to grow higher in your faith, you must increase in spiritual wisdom. Spiritual wisdom isn't attained through men but given by God.

Knowledge is information, some true, some not. Knowledge may know a truth without walking in it. Spiritual wisdom is knowing the truth and then walking in it. Knowledge is gained through books and classrooms. Spiritual wisdom is received when you're submitted to the Lord. Knowledge often puffs up, whereas spiritual wisdom comes from a posture of lowliness. Knowledge can be a weapon, whereas true spiritual wisdom is helpful to all who are willing to listen.

Nobody is judged by their knowledge, but by how they treat others. "But the wisdom that is from above is first pure, then peaceable, gentle, willing to yield, full of mercy and good fruits, without partiality and without hypocrisy" (James 3:17 NKJV).

We need to understand wisdom at a higher level if we're to ever have a higher faith. Worldly wisdom may have some limited value, but it is always far lower than the wisdom that comes from heaven. Spiritual wisdom isn't just a little higher than the wisdom of this world; it turns the wisdom of this world on its head. Growing higher in your faith comes through spiritual growth, and that growth won't happen apart from having spiritual wisdom in the way you live.

The deep things of God are never found in the shallowness of man. You cannot take hold of heavenly truths so long as you desire only the knowledge of man. The Lord Jesus taught, "If I have told you earthly things and you do not believe, how will you believe if I tell you heavenly things?" (John 3:12 NKJV).

Worldly wisdom operates by the principles of the world. Worldly wisdom will say, "Money can buy you happiness." People will do anything to get more money, believing the lie that happiness will be found where money is. They go through their entire lives thinking that if only they had more money, they'd be happier. They try to save as much as they can for as long as they can, thinking that if they have enough, they can finally feel secure. But money can never satisfy the needs of an eternal soul, and it's a fool's game whenever we think that money will do what it never can.

That which has the greatest value will cost you nothing monetarily. "'Why do you spend money for what is not bread, and your wages for what does not satisfy? Listen carefully to Me, and eat what is good, and let your soul delight itself in abundance'" (Isaiah 55:2 NKJV).

Spiritual wisdom operates by the principles of heaven. Spiritual wisdom will say, "When you put all your trust and focus on Yahweh Magen (the LORD is my shield), He will give you everything you really need." Spiritual wisdom says that being happy is when we have Yeshua HaMashiach (Jesus the Messiah). Spiritual wisdom says that the more you give, the more you have. Spiritual wisdom says that you need not horde anything, since you can take nothing with you when you leave this earth. Spiritual wisdom says that we can trust the Lord with all we need, and our true security will come from Him. When you truly trust the Lord, you'll find that you have everything your eternal soul ever needed.

It's not that you're seeking the wrong things, but that you're seeking them in the wrong order. "'Seek the Kingdom of God above all else, and live righteously, and he will give you everything you need'" (Matthew 6:33 NLT).

If we want to grow in our faith, we must grow spiritually. We must gain a heart of spiritual wisdom that can be given only by Elohim (God the strong and mighty one); there's no natural way to gain it. Natural effort will yield only natural gains, which fall pitifully short of the heights of heaven. This doesn't mean you should skip your natural studies and programs, but they're only a beginning step to get you started on the next level. Don't neglect your natural studying, but don't let the natural studies keep you from reaching into the heavens for spiritual truths.

The logic of heaven isn't bound by the books of man. "These things we also speak, not in words which man's wisdom teaches but which the Holy Spirit teaches, comparing spiritual things with spiritual" (1 Corinthians 2:13 NKJV).

Keep yourself firmly rooted in the foundation of the Word, while at the same time, reaching for the things of heaven. If you only burrow down, you'll miss the higher. If you only reach for the higher, you'll lose your footing. "But the natural man does not receive the things of the Spirit of God, for they are foolishness to him; nor can he know them, because they are spiritually discerned" (1 Corinthians 2:14 NKJV).

When we ask God for wisdom, it's given to us by Ruach Ha'Kodesh (the Holy Spirit). Wisdom is a gift to receive and not a goal reachable by the programs of man. The problem most Christians have is that they've grown only by their own strength, and they've stopped at the limit of themselves. Their natural pride or their lack of spiritual knowledge will prevent them from going any higher. Many simply haven't been taught that you can grow in spiritual wisdom, and so they've never pressed into it. The proud will redefine spiritual wisdom down to their own level of worldly wisdom, so they can think of themselves as spiritually elevated above others. The humble simply ask God to give them heavenly wisdom.

Just because you're smart doesn't mean you're right. "Stop deceiving yourselves. If you think you are wise by this world's standards, you need to become a fool to be truly wise. For the wisdom of this world is foolishness to God. As the Scriptures say, 'He traps the wise in the snare of their own cleverness'" (1 Corinthians 3:18-19 NLT).

Be willing to let El Hanan (the gracious God) open your eyes so you can see spiritual truths and receive spiritual wisdom as never before. Do this today. It's never too late until it is. Spiritual wisdom discerns truths that are beyond what is seen, and allows us to see what's behind the curtain. You cannot peer into the spiritual realm with natural eyes, and you cannot spiritually discern using only your natural intellect. You need a humble heart as you humbly ask the Holy Spirit to help you. Make it your prayer to ask for spiritual wisdom.

Natural wisdom says to know more, then study more. Spiritual wisdom says that to know more, you need to spend more time with the Holy Spirit. "'If you, then, being evil [that is, sinful by nature], know how to give good gifts to your children, how much more will your heavenly Father give the Holy Spirit to those who ask and continue to ask Him!'" (Luke 11:13 AMP).

Spiritual wisdom gives us the power to change. Knowledge can know the truth, and can know what's right and what's wrong, but wisdom is something far deeper. Wisdom gives us not only the ability to know the truth but also to be changed by it and to act upon it. If you're living wisely, it means that you're making wise choices. A wise man or woman considers each choice in the light of God's Word and the leading of the Holy Spirit.

It's either your way or God's way—and your choice matters forever. "'Today I am giving you a choice of two ways. And I ask heaven and earth to be witnesses of your choice. You can choose life or death. The first choice will bring a blessing. The other choice will bring a curse. So choose life! Then you and your children will live'" (Deuteronomy 30:19 ERV).

You can know that the Holy Spirit is within you. But to walk in the wisdom of the Holy Spirit means that you can then operate in the power of the Holy Spirit. Knowledge will take you only so far; you need heavenly wisdom to go higher. It's not enough to know about the Holy Spirit; you must be filled with the Holy Spirit. Spiritual wisdom flows outward only when you're filled inwardly with the Spirit of Yahweh Ezer (the LORD our helper).

The proof of the Holy Spirit in you is the Holy Spirit through you. The waters are not still, but flowing. The Lord Jesus said, "He who believes in Me, as the Scripture has said, out of his heart will flow rivers of living water" (John 7:38 NKJV).

Wisdom is an action. You can know everything and act foolishly. But wisdom causes us to act wisely. We're not called to be wise in our own eyes but to reflect on ourselves with a measure of humility, knowing what fools we are apart from God. The mark of a wise man or woman is someone who doesn't try to show off how wise they are. They'll walk in humility, knowing that any wisdom that may be in them is from the Lord and all credit is to Him alone. No one can look at spiritual wisdom and slap a label on it that says "mine."

Don't live in regret for time wasted; be wise with the time you have left. "Therefore see that you walk carefully [living life with honor, purpose, and courage; shunning those who tolerate and enable evil], not as the unwise, but as wise [sensible, intelligent, discerning people], making the very most of your time [on earth, recognizing and taking advantage of each opportunity and using it with wisdom and diligence], because the days are [filled with] evil" (Ephesians 5:15-16 AMP).

If you see yourself as wise, that's your pride, and there's no wisdom there. If you act with spiritual wisdom, that's from your humility, because you're acting counter to what your natural flesh wants you to do. Spiritual wisdom is always counter to fleshly desires. Whatever is driven by your flesh will result in foolishness. Worldly wisdom is foolish as well, because it may sound good to man but runs counter to the wisdom from heaven.

The higher your faith, the lower your opinion will be about yourself. "Do not be wise in your own eyes; fear the Lord and depart from evil" (Proverbs 3:7 NKJV).

In the natural, you want to strike back when someone speaks against you, slanders you, makes fun of you, or speaks down to you. Or you close the door, and you wallow in your bitterness. These are natural reactions to natural events that happen in our lives. No one is exempt from being treated unfairly. People will treat you wrongly, and your reaction says everything about how spiritually wise you really are.

Nobody can put you down if you already are. You fear being humbled only if you're not already humble. "A man's pride will bring him low, but the humble in spirit will retain honor" (Proverbs 29:23 NKJV).

If you have spiritual wisdom and someone speaks ungodly words toward you, they won't touch you, because you're walking in the

Spirit. Acting wisely means you're not moved by the foolishness of man. A wise believer is not owned by the ungodly opinions of others, but the judgment of El Elyon (God Most High). Spiritual wisdom cuts loose the puppet strings of man and sets the believer free in Christ. Spiritual wisdom stands strong and firm in the face of human foolishness.

It's hard to offend a person not ruled by their pride. "When pride comes, then comes shame, but wisdom is with those who have no pride" (Proverbs 11:2 NLV).

God says that to overlook an offense is better than responding to it. The world says to get even. The world will say that the greatest revenge is your success. God says all vengeance belongs to Him. Spiritual wisdom will give you power over your ungodly natural reactions to others. One of the greatest benefits of spiritual wisdom is being set free from the opinions of others and being able to feel a peace that's beyond human understanding.

The more you can overlook an offense, the less it will bother you. "A person's wisdom yields patience; it is to one's glory to overlook an offense" (Proverbs 19:11 NIV).

Prayer

Holy Spirit, pour into me spiritual wisdom from heaven so that I live wisely by Your power working within me. Help me walk in heavenly wisdom that pours out goodness and kindness to those around me.

Challenge

Write down the areas in your life in which you're not yet walking with spiritual wisdom. This may include every area of your life, so start perhaps with the top three areas that matter most to you. Take this list to the Lord in prayer and ask Him to help you grow in spiritual wisdom. Ask Him to make it plain to you how He wants you to grow. In your humility, God can do the greatest work in your life. Add more areas of your life to this list for prayer as God reveals them to you.

Going further

Make a list of those people whose opinions are still holding you tethered in your life. Next to each person's name, write a prayer asking God to set you free from their opinions so you can focus on being right with the Lord. *There's power in the freedom of not being tethered by the opinions of man.* "It is dangerous to be concerned with what others think of you, but if you trust the LORD, you are safe" (Proverbs 29:25 GNT).

29

Hearing Holy Spirit

The reason so few hear from the Holy Spirit is that so few believe He will talk to them.

Jesus taught, "But when He, the Spirit of truth, comes, He will guide you into all the truth; for He will not speak on His own, but whatever He hears, He will speak; and He will disclose to you what is to come." —John 16:13 NASB

If we want to grow higher in our faith, we must be led by the Holy Spirit. To be led by Him, we must have spiritual ears to hear Him.

If you want to grow higher in your faith, you'll need the help of the Holy Spirit. The natural man or woman can climb only as high as they can go on their own. The Holy Spirit can take you places you could never get to on your own. This is one of the most exciting and adventurous seasons in the life of a believer who's willing to go further with God. The promise of the Holy Spirit is for you and for me, if we're willing to receive Him.

Many people know the Holy Spirit by name but have never spoken with Him. "The grace (favor and spiritual blessing) of the Lord Jesus Christ and the love of God and the presence and fellowship (the communion and sharing together, and participation) in the Holy Spirit be with you all. Amen (so be it)" (2 Corinthians 13:14 AMPC).

You can earn degrees in theology and be a leader in the church for decades, and yet not have a lick of Holy Spirit power in your life. God doesn't care two cents about your credentials; instead, He's looking for the man or woman who dares to go further with Him. You can go further than yourself only when you're humble enough to ask your Father to help you. When you can put down your pride, your Father can pick you up and do something with you.

God helps those who know they can't help themselves. "For thus says the High, Exalted One who lives forever, whose name is Holy: 'I live in the high and holy place but also with the broken and humble, in order to revive the spirit of the humble and revive the hearts of the broken ones.'" (Isaiah 57:15 CJB).

Do you believe that Ruach Ha'Kodesh (the Holy Spirit) can speak to you? If you've heard His voice, that's wonderful; keep listening for more. If you haven't heard His voice, ask for it in prayer, then start listening. If you'll believe and stop leaning on your own understanding, you'll get a wonderful revelation from Him. Our problem is that we spend more time telling the Lord Jesus what we want from Him than we do listening to what He wants from us. We fear He may just ask for more than we're willing to give Him.

As Christ sacrificed His life for us, so we should sacrifice our lives to Him. "Offer yourselves as a sacrifice, living and set apart for God. This will please him" (Romans 12:1 CJB).

We were meant to hear the voice of the Holy Spirit. In the plans and purposes of El Yeshuatenu (the God of our salvation), the Holy Spirit is with us and guiding us in all we should do. By the words of Christ Jesus, we're to be comforted and taught by the Holy Spirit. We're not alone. We're supposed to hear His voice, then be obedient to all He's calling us to do. *You were meant for something more.*

There are some things that only the Holy Spirit can teach you. Jesus promised, "The Helper is the Holy Spirit. The Father will send Him in My place. He will teach you everything and help you remember everything I have told you" (John 14:26 NLV).

Several years ago, I met with a man for breakfast to discuss ways in which I could search for a job. He belonged to a conservative church that I went to at the time. He was a leader in the church and respected by many. Because I'm a loner, I've always been an outsider at the churches I go to. So when I get a rare chance to meet with a brother in Christ, it's a special privilege.

A life well lived encourages others to do the same. "Be an example to all believers in what you say, in the way you live, in your love, your faith, and your purity" (1 Timothy 4:12 NLT).

I didn't know the history of this man. I assumed he was not Spirit-filled, since most at this church were not. He started telling me he had grown up in a Spirit-filled church. My spirit man leaped with joy that perhaps I had found another Spirit-filled believer at this church I belonged to! But then this man told me this about the people he knew from his old church: "It's so cute that they think they can hear God."

It saddens me to see Christians mocking Christians. Sometimes, it seems the pagans treat their own better. Divisions are often of the devil.

The more you criticize others, the more it says about you. "Why do you criticize or despise other Christians? Everyone will stand in front of God to be judged" (Romans 14:10 NOG).

I find it interesting that some of the smartest intellectuals will use the false crutch of fallacious arguments to make an unsound point on something they have no spiritual understanding about. So many in our churches lean on charged-up emotional messages in order to protect their own weak faith that relies more on their oratory skills than on the power of El Shaddai (God Almighty). Intellectualism sometimes makes a mockery of the spiritual because it isn't spiritual. One can have knowledge of God but not have one iota of His supernatural power in their lives. Prideful intellectualism always tries to discredit humble spirituality.

If you want to teach about being Spirit-led, you must be Spirit-led in your teaching. "We don't speak about these things using teachings that are based on intellectual arguments like people do. Instead, we use the Spirit's teachings. We explain spiritual things to those who have the Spirit" (1 Corinthians 2:13 NOG).

A few years ago, I sat down for lunch with my earthly father along with my prison ministry partner of many years, Joe Diaz. My father had just turned ninety the year before. (He's ninety-three as I write this book.) For much of his life, he walked in the calling of hospitality, serving many people, including the elderly, single mothers, prostitutes, and widows, over decades of humble, unseen service.

Over several years, my parents allowed twenty-eight different unwed pregnant mothers to come and live in their home, where these young moms could deliver their babies. Many of them were prostitutes, and they all needed a safe place to stay. It's one thing to pray against abortion, and quite another to have twenty-eight pregnant women come live with you to save their babies. My father now is unable to do all the physical labor he did before, so he has graduated to being an intercessor.

We won't be rewarded by what we know but by what we have done.

What you do matters eternally. Jesus tells us, "And behold, I am coming quickly, and My reward is with Me, to give to every one according to his work" (Revelation 22:12 NKJV).

That day at lunch, my father was telling Joe and me of a time the Holy Spirit spoke to him. He had heard the Holy Spirit as if He were talking out loud. The Holy Spirit told him to paint the house of a couple who went to his church, though he barely knew them. Yahweh Raah (the LORD is my shepherd) calls us out of our comfort zone so we can rely on Him. He may give us words to speak or practical things we should do, and it's up to us to obey Him. My father had grown up in a conservative church, and here he was now listening to the Holy Spirit guide him.

God isn't interested in your background but in your willingness to hear Him. *You won't reach new heights sitting in your comfort zone.* "'Have I not commanded you? Be strong and of good courage; do not be afraid, nor be dismayed, for the LORD your God is with you wherever you go'" (Joshua 1:9 NKJV).

My father said he resisted this word from the Holy Spirit for a few weeks. He was unsure if it was from the Lord, since it was something outside what he had experienced before. But the Holy Spirit persisted, and my father finally yielded to God. He approached this couple and told them what God had told him to do. That's the other part of our spiritual journey—after the Lord has spoken to us, we should let others know that the Lord is still speaking to this day. My father didn't tell them this to impress them with the fact that he was hearing God; he wanted only to be obedient to what God was telling him to do.

You never have to pray for the Lord to speak to you, but only that you'll have ears to hear Him. Jesus taught, "For nothing is concealed except to be revealed, and nothing hidden except to come to light. If anyone has ears to hear, he should listen!" (Mark 4:22-23 HCSB).

My father believes that this couple agreed to it because he had told them he was directed to do it by the Lord— by Yahweh Shammah (the

Lord is there). This couple had no money for the paint, so my father paid for it all, which was about five hundred dollars worth. He didn't think two seconds about the price of the paint or about how long it would take him to do all this work.

You know you're truly serving God with all your heart, all your mind, and all your strength when you don't question Him or complain to Him about what He is asking you to do.

My father borrowed my spray-painting gear for this job (I have lots of gear for getting big jobs done, and I love to do things myself at my house). But I'm humbled to see how much my father is willing to do for others. I remember when he was seventy-five, and I had busted up my leg in a motorcycle accident. I was just starting to refloor my house before the accident, but was out of commission for months from my injuries. He drove a hundred miles round-trip daily for weeks and refloored my entire house. He took care of my yard and other things too. Watching his labor at my house was absolutely the best godly sermon I've ever heard preached.

Your life is bigger than yourself, because it touches everyone around you. "'Let your light so shine before men, that they may see your good works and glorify your Father in heaven'" (Matthew 5:16 NKJV).

It took my father a few weeks to finish the painting project for this couple. The works we do matters. At the end of the project, he received a letter in the mail. He opened the letter and inside found a check he wasn't expecting. The check amount was about five hundred dollars, the same amount it had cost him to buy the paint for the house God told him to paint. Don't you dare tell me this wasn't of God. My father didn't need this money, and didn't expect it either. But it was a confirmation from Yahweh Yireh (the Lord will provide) that my father had done exactly what the Lord had wanted him to do.

What pours out of your heart fills the cup you'll drink from. "The work of righteousness will be peace, and the effect of righteousness, quietness and assurance forever" (Isaiah 32:17 NKJV).

Child of God, the Holy Spirit is speaking. If you believe, then you will hear Him. We were meant to live with the Holy Spirit in us forever. Some, however, have been taught that the Holy Spirit cannot speak; that teaching is wrong. God is not mute, but most men and women are spiritually deaf, lest they might hear Him. If you want to hear the still small voice of God, you must stop being so big in yourself and noisy in your ramblings. Get off by yourself, quiet your soul, and let the Holy Spirit speak to you on this day.

When you quiet the soul, the Holy Spirit will quicken you. Yeshua (Jesus) taught, "It is the [Holy] spirit that quickeneth; the flesh profiteth nothing: the words that I speak unto you, they are spirit, and they are life" (John 6:63 KJV).

Pray for those leaders and elders in the church who don't believe that God can speak to us. Pray for our pastors to all come to believe in the power of God and the truth of His Word, so they preach the truth that the Holy Spirit can speak to us all. The promises in the Word are true if we just believe them.

There are more promises in the Word than we have accepted. "For every word God speaks is sure and every promise pure. His truth is tested, found to be flawless, and ever faithful" (Psalm 12:6 TPT).

Prayer

Holy Spirit, speak to me with such clarity and conviction that I have no doubts that it's You directing me. Help me be ready not only to hear You but to be obedient to You in however You're leading me.

Challenge

Pray to the Holy Spirit and ask Him to tell you what needs to change in your life. Also, ask Him what menial service He wants you to do for someone else. The reason so many don't hear the Holy Spirit is that they only want the gifts or the revelations that will elevate them above others. Pray to be corrected where needed and pray on where you should serve, and the Holy Spirit will most certainly be willing to answer such a prayer. Be willing to humbly obey His every command.

Going further

When the Holy Spirit leads you to say something to someone or to do something for them, be willing to share with others how God was leading you. Don't do this to boast that you can hear from God, but in humility, tell others to encourage them that the Holy Spirit can lead them too. We need to encourage others to listen to the Holy Spirit so their lives will be a blessing to others. *The Lord will bless your life as much as your life is a blessing to others.* "'Give, and you will receive. Your gift will return to you in full—pressed down, shaken together to make room for more, running over, and poured into your lap. The amount you give will determine the amount you get back'" (Luke 6:38 NLT).

30

Spiritual Maturity

*Christians who learn to get things right are
Christians who learn to see where they're wrong.*

But solid food is for the [spiritually] mature, whose senses are
trained by practice to distinguish between what is morally
good and what is evil. – Hebrews 5:14 AMP

If you want to grow higher in your faith, you must become
more spiritually mature. This maturity doesn't happen
based on how long you've been a Christian, but on
your willingness to let the Lord change you.

In several areas in our lives, there's the potential for reaching a higher level of maturity. We can mature physically, emotionally, intellectually, and spiritually. These areas are all intertwined; to mature to our full potential, we must mature in them all.

Maturing in faith is not agonizing in all you've done wrong, but persevering in all you should do right. "So let's not get tired of doing what is good. At just the right time we will reap a harvest of blessing if we don't give up" (Galatians 6:9 NLT).

For the natural, the maturing process begins the moment we're born. For the spiritual, the process begins the moment we're born again in the Spirit. It's possible to mature in each area, but each area will determine the degree to which you can mature in the other ones.

The mature believer learns to become like a little child. Jesus taught, "Whoever will humble himself therefore and become like this little child [trusting, lowly, loving, forgiving] is greatest in the kingdom of heaven" (Matthew 18:4 AMPC).

Spiritual maturity is not measured by years but by where you are in your journey. There are many who advance in years but don't mature along the way. Others are mature beyond their years and are quickly reaching the heights of their potential. The maturing of a saint isn't a competition with others, but a measure within oneself. What matters is not where you are in comparison to someone else, but where you are in relation to the potential God has for you. Maturing spiritually is the race you're in by yourself, and your potential is the goal line.

The maturity of a believer isn't in how long you've been a Christian, but in how much of a Christian you really are. "You have been believers so long now that you ought to be teaching others. Instead, you need someone to teach you again the basic things about God's word. You are like babies who need milk and cannot eat solid food" (Hebrews 5:12 NLT).

Physical maturity is the process by which our body grows and changes over time. We'll all age as we grow older, but we can choose how well we take care of ourselves along the way. The mature believer will treat his or her body as if it were not their own. No matter where you are with your physical condition right now, you can choose to make the best decisions going forward. Maturing doesn't mean we won't fail, but only that we learn from our mistakes. To be our best, we must learn from our worst. Ask Yahweh Hoshiah (the LORD saves) to help you.

Stop treating your body as if it belongs to you. "Or do you not know that your body is the temple of the Holy Spirit who is in you, whom you have from God, and you are not your own? For you were bought at a price; therefore glorify God in your body and in your spirit, which are God's" (1 Corinthians 6:19-20 NKJV).

Another area in which we can mature is with our emotions. We can learn to control our emotions instead of letting our emotions control us. Reaching emotional maturity doesn't mean we don't express our emotions, but that we're able to restrain them. If you can't manage your emotions, you're a puppet to them. Emotional maturity doesn't just happen, but requires your willingness to change. Invite Yeshua HaMashiach (Jesus the Messiah) to help you control your emotions. When your emotions are controlled, your life will flourish.

You have to reflect inwardly to change how you act outwardly. "Be angry and do not sin; on your bed, reflect in your heart and be still" (Psalm 4:4 HCSB).

We have the potential to mature intellectually. This isn't merely adding facts and figures to what we already know. Nor is it the ability to manipulate others with our intellectual prowess. Rather, it's the process by which we learn to use sound reasoning in a variety of circumstances, so we can discern the truth from the lie. If we want to reason rightly, we'll need wisdom from El Deah (the God of knowledge) to help us. It's about becoming wiser, not smarter. Pray to the Father that He will help your mind to mature with heavenly wisdom.

The world's idea of a mature Christian is someone who has more knowledge of the truth. God's idea is one who lives more truth. Knowledge can know the truth, but wisdom lives it. "If any of you need wisdom, you should ask God, and it will be given to you. God is generous and won't correct you for asking" (James 1:5 CEV).

Spiritual maturity comes from the spiritual power that emanates from the presence of Ruach Ha'Kodesh (the Holy Spirit) within you. We cannot use the measurements of man to determine when we reach the spiritual heights measured only by the scales of heaven. What may look right to us may very well be an offense to God. Your spiritual maturity is not born out of striving, but out of surrendering to all that the Holy Spirit might do in you. Reaching new heights is done by becoming ever lower in yourself so that the Lord will take you higher. It's not about having more miracles in your life, but about having more grace toward those around you.

In the natural order, as we mature, we're able to do more on our own. In the divine order, as we mature, we rely upon the Lord to do more through us. "For it is God who is at work in you, both to desire and to work for His good pleasure" (Philippians 2:13 NASB).

We're so blessed if we know even one or two spiritually mature Christians in our life. They'll serve as a "true north" for us in our spiritual journey of where we should get to. The spiritually mature Christians I know have so much wisdom, but they don't parade it about for attention. They don't add to your comments and to your prayers, as if you missed something and they need to make up for it and correct you. They just listen and genuinely want to hear what you have to say. They don't teach down to you, but put their arm around you and sit with you. They're interested in the real you and what you're thinking.

One of the greatest signs of a mature faith is in the mercy shown to others. "He has shown you, O man, what is good; and what does the LORD require of you but to do justly, to love mercy, and to walk humbly with your God" (Micah 6:8 NKJV).

The spiritually mature don't point out your faults, but instead, encourage you on where you can get to. It's a great blessing to have someone who speaks into your life and is full of mercy. The words they use help you, building you up. They say good things about you, not with shallow flattery but with a genuine love.

The maturity of your Christian faith is revealed in how you criticize other Christians. "For the Kingdom of God is...living a life of goodness and peace and joy in the Holy Spirit. If you serve Christ with this attitude, you will please God, and others will approve of you, too. So then, let us aim for harmony in the church and try to build each other up" (Romans 14:17-19 NLT).

The mark of a spiritually mature believer is that there's a humility about them. Not that they're putting themselves down, but they're not propping themselves up. They aren't out to prove to others what they can do spiritually, but what they do spiritually will be edifying to all who are blessed to know them.

Beware of the person who always reminds you of who you were. Seek out the person who speaks to you about who you can become. Then become that person you seek to find. "Therefore comfort each other and edify one another" (1 Thessalonians 5:11 NKJV). *To edify is to build up; it is constructive, not destructive. You cannot lift each other up if you're tearing each other down.*

The spiritually mature don't use big words to impress you with their intellect, but use simple words to help you understand. They don't talk above you, but speak deep down into your heart. They don't try to impress you with where they are, but they encourage you to reach the potential you were meant to get to. There's a selflessness about them. They'll focus on you and not be easily distracted. They'll make you feel special and valuable.

Some of our greatest accomplishments are what we encourage others to do. "We must also consider how to encourage each other to show love and to do good things" (Hebrews 10:24 NOG).

For the spiritually mature at a gathering, you'll rarely find them at the highest seat or at the center of attention; they'll be in the lowest seat and on the fringes. They won't tell you about the degrees they may have, but you can sense their wisdom in every word they speak. They won't judge you; rather, they want to help you in whatever way you're struggling.

God has worked salvation into you, but it's up to you to work it out. "Work out your salvation [that is, cultivate it, bring it to full effect, actively pursue spiritual maturity] with awe-inspired fear and trembling" (Philippians 2:12 AMP).

They show kindness and respect. They have a peace about them, and they don't worry. They're confident. When they pray, their prayers are intimate because they know the Lord. Once you know someone who's spiritually mature, it reveals to you the areas of your own immaturity. This is not to shame you, but to encourage you to be all that Yahweh Mekoddishkem (the LORD who sanctifies you) wants you to be.

Being kind is more important than being seen as right. "If all these things [which includes kindness] are in you and growing, you will never fail to be useful to God. You will produce the kind of fruit that should come from your knowledge of our Lord Jesus Christ" (2 Peter 1:8 ERV).

You should want to become so spiritually mature in life that others will be drawn to you, learn from you, and long to be like you. They'll want to be around you and be influenced by you. They'll hope that some of you might rub off on them. You can be such a blessing to other people if you simply allow Yahweh Sabaoth (the LORD of angelic armies) to help you grow. While on this earth, you can have such a high faith that the change you have to make when you get to heaven will be small. Live a life on earth as you would in heaven.

Jesus doesn't expect you to be perfect, but He wants you to try. Jesus taught, "You, therefore, will be perfect [growing into spiritual maturity both in mind and character, actively integrating godly values into your daily life], as your heavenly Father is perfect" (Matthew 5:48 AMP).

My prayer is that you'll seek ever-growing maturity in your spiritual life. Don't think yourself unable based on your current way of living, or be worried about the opinions of man, but only be convinced by the truth that God can take you higher. Ask Yahweh Ezer (the LORD our helper) to do what only He can do. Then let Him do it.

Prayer

Father God, help me mature spiritually into that soul You want me to be. Help me grow higher spiritually while remaining lowly before others, not worrying about the opinions of man. Help me please You in all I do.

Challenge

Think of that one man or woman you know who is the most spiritually mature person you've ever met. Write down a list of those characteristics in them that are evidence of spiritual maturity. Place that list before you and write out where you are in your life with each of these characteristics. Then place your answers before the Lord and pray that He'll help you mature in each of these areas.

Going further

One of the greatest baseball players of all time was Babe Ruth, who once said, "It's hard to beat a person who never gives up." That's how you need to be with maturing spiritually. You're going to fail along the way, many times. You'll run into obstacles and not think you're able to overcome them, and you're right. You need the Lord to help you. Start praying more than you're striving, and with God's help, you'll get there in due time. *When God asks you to do something, He expects you to let Him help you.* The apostle Paul said, "God helped me, and he is still helping me today" (Acts 26:22 ERV).

Going Higher with God

You can always tell a saint who is close to God. The things of the world just don't matter to them much anymore. They're at peace, even when there's a good reason not to be. They're humble because they know just how great and holy God really is. They speak to God as a friend, because He is. They'd rather see God than be seen by other people.

Inside the Tent of Meeting, the Lord would speak to Moses face to face, as one speaks to a friend. – Exodus 33:11 NLT

The most blessed saints are those who make it to this fourth pillar, going higher with God. No one who makes it to this level has any pride left within them. They've come this far only through great humility. And though their journey was difficult and their path full of trials, they wouldn't change a thing, but only keep going higher with the Lord.

A child of God who makes it to pillar four has spent much time in the fields, laboring on the foundation of their faith, laying the groundwork that they might grow higher. From there, the Lord took them and broke them so He could make them into something new, a vessel He could use. After this, the Lord took them into the wilderness and helped them grow spiritually, so they would be humble and strong in their spirit.

Pillar four begins a most precious stage of our faith journey with God while we're still here on this earth. We grow ever closer to Him, learning more about the Lord personally and not just intellectually with facts and doctrines we used to hold on to so tightly. We stop striving so hard, and instead, start resting more as we know the Lord will help us. We become less critical of others, because we've become more aware of ourselves and all that the Lord is yet doing in us.

The soul who is walking in pillar four no longer competes in the races of men but walks in the fields with angels. They don't desire to impress others with where they are, but long to draw others to be nearer to God. They don't need anything from God because they have God Himself, and God has them. They start to see the futility of the faith they used to have, which relied on themselves. They're starting to learn what it means to be devoted to the Lord and separated from the world.

Nothing compares to being nearer to God. Nothing on earth is comparable to what is stored in heaven. When we fix our eyes properly on the Lord Jesus, we'll see that He is all we need. We'll see that Jesus has a plan and a purpose for us while we're here on earth. Our one task in this life is to walk in what the Lord has for us. Do that, and you'll have done well. You'll be a pleasing aroma to the Lord and a blessing to those around you.

31

Simple Faith

The simpler your faith,
the easier it is to walk in it.

"What does the LORD require of you?
To act justly and to love mercy and to walk
humbly with your God." – Micah 6:8 NIV

As you go higher in your faith, your faith will
become simpler. We learn along the way
that faith isn't really that complicated—
just love God and love others.

When the Lord Jesus starts to take you higher in your faith, He takes you down a path you never expected. We look for higher things from the perspective of the world, but the Lord Jesus has something much higher than that. As He draws you higher, you'll begin to understand the higher faith from the perspective of your Father in heaven. One of the greatest revelations of the higher faith is that it's a simple faith. Don't let your expectations be an anchor that prevents you from being drawn up into the simplicity of a higher faith that Jesus Christ has for you.

Simple does not mean shallow. The deeper truths are the simple truths. It's in something as simple as water that we encounter a depth so great that we can never reach the bottom. "The purposes of a person's heart are deep waters, but one who has insight draws them out" (Proverbs 20:5 NIV).

The higher faith is a simple faith that trusts in Yahweh Machsi (the Lord my refuge). The simplicity of trusting Him will be a paradigm shift in your life. Times of testing and periods of trials will prove your trust and leave you at peace in the midst of all you're going through. You'll find that this one simple act of trusting God supersedes your knowledge of a hundred doctrines that, just a short time ago, you used to analyze and debate as if your faith depended on them.

The thing you fear the most, you need to trust Him with the most. "But when I am afraid, I will put my trust in you. I praise God for what he has promised. I trust in God, so why should I be afraid? What can mere mortals do to me?" (Psalm 56:3-4 NLT).

What matters is not the higher truth you know, but the simple truth you walk in. Jesus promised, "If you abide in Me, and My words abide in you, you will ask what you desire, and it shall be done for you" (John 15:7 NKJV).

The higher faith is a simple faith that believes that Yahweh Shammah (the Lord is there) is with you. This will no longer be a cute phrase that you barely believed before, but an experience to which nothing else can be compared. When you're in the presence of God, everything else pales in comparison. When you can feel Him near to you and know that He is as close to you as the air you breathe, this will be the place of higher faith.

Do your best, don't stress, and know the Lord is with you. "Even though I walk through the [sunless] valley of the shadow of death, I fear no evil, for You are with me; Your rod [to protect] and Your staff [to guide], they comfort and console me" (Psalm 23:4 AMP).

Never think a simple truth is beneath you. You may understand complicated things, but do you walk in the simple truths?

The higher faith is a simple faith that knows Yeshua HaMashiach (Jesus the Messiah) will never leave you. You won't think that you're two sins away from being abandoned by Him. You'll rest in the fact of His faithfulness to you, even when you've not been faithful to Him. No one can separate you from Christ Jesus, because no one can overpower the King of kings. When once you've felt securely held by Him, nothing will be able to shake you ever again.

Never give up on God, because God will never give up on you. Jesus promised, "My Father, who has given them to Me, is greater than all; and no one is able to snatch them out of My Father's hand" (John 10:29 NKJV).

To grow in your faith is to lower yourself into a simpler faith. It comes not by knowing more, but by simply trusting more. It increases not by changing more, but by being more willing to be changed.

The higher faith is a simple faith that knows Jesus truly loves you. No longer will you live in the false idea that somehow your failures can separate you from the love of Christ. If He loved you when you were yet His enemy, how much more does He now love you as His friend? There's a powerful force of absolute safety when you're held in the grip of El Yeshuatenu (the God of our salvation) and covered by His unconditional love.

Let the foundation of your faith rest upon the truth that Jesus loves you. Jesus promised, "I have loved you just as the Father has loved Me; remain in My love [and do not doubt My love for you]" (John 15:9 AMP).

The greatest truths are so simple that many people never see them.

The higher faith is a simple faith that doesn't have to understand everything to know that Yahweh Sabaoth (the LORD of angelic armies) has them in everything. You'll stop trying to figure out things that are beyond you, and start entrusting things to a Lord who is sovereign over them all. You'll set things before the Lord and gladly leave them there, never to pick them up again. You'll have freedom from the bondage of the things you held so tightly before. When you don't have to figure everything out, you can just relax and let God handle things.

The simpler your faith, the more pure it is. "We conducted ourselves in the world in simplicity and godly sincerity, not with fleshly wisdom but by the grace of God" (2 Corinthians 1:12 NKJV).

The more you simplify your life, the less complicated things will be.

The higher faith is a simple faith that holds no grudges and harbors no resentment toward others. It forgives faster than one can be offended, and forgets about all those things that don't really matter. You'll lose the idea that grudges are justified as you come to learn just how deeply the Lord Jesus has forgiven you. You'll discover the freedom found by not being entangled in the pain of your past. You'll simply forgive others and move on.

Faith is simple—love God and love others.

We're better at preaching forgiveness than practicing forgiveness. "God has chosen you and made you his holy people. He loves you. So your new life should be like this: Show mercy to others. Be kind, humble, gentle, and patient. Don't be angry with each other, but forgive each other. If you feel someone has wronged you, forgive them. Forgive others because the Lord forgave you" (Colossians 3:12-13 ERV).

The higher faith is a simple faith that believes like a little child. You'll start to pray for bigger and better things, knowing just how true it is that nothing is impossible for God. You won't agonize over problems, because deep in your heart you'll trust that God can help you with them all. You'll simply go to Him as your Father and not question either His motives or His abilities, only believing that He can help you with all things. When we approach our Father like a child, we're rightly placing our life in His hands.

Believing is both the simplest and the hardest thing for us to do.

Don't be such a grown-up that you're no longer a child of God. Jesus said, "Learn this well: Unless you dramatically change your way of thinking and become teachable, and learn about heaven's kingdom realm with the wide-eyed wonder of a child, you will never be able to enter in" (Matthew 18:3 TPT).

A simple faith takes you further because it's not weighed down by the complexities of man.

The higher faith is a simple faith that asks Yahweh 'Ori (the LORD our light) for His directions, then follows Him no matter what He says. A higher faith trusts Him higher. We ask for His guidance because we trust that He will send us in the right direction. We'll go where He says because we trust in His leading. Sometimes, He'll ask us to do things and go places that make no sense to us, but we follow Him anyway. Kingdom principles run counter to the world. As we continue to follow Him, we'll find that His paths are always right.

It's better to pray about decisions than about consequences. "With every step you take, think about what he wants, and he will help you go the right way" (Proverbs 3:6 ERV).

Man makes faith complicated. The Lord just says, "Follow Me."

The higher faith is a simple faith that prays more and worries less. There's a place we can get to in our faith where anxiousness has no room to stay. It's where the peace of God is complete and the worries of this world aren't allowed. Others will see the impossible challenges that surround us, but we'll be focused on the Lord who goes before us. Where we once were buried in worry, we find ourselves floating in faith and trusting that the Lord will take care of us. Our prayers will be as confident as if the thing we're praying for is already done.

It's not enough to pray for direction; you must also go where He leads you. "I will instruct you and teach you in the way you should go; I will counsel you [who are willing to learn] with My eye upon you" (Psalm 32:8 AMP).

I remember, as a young Christian, how intimidated I was by what I thought were very high Christians. I felt so low next to them. But then I met a few very humble Christians. I came to see that they were very near to God. I learned that these humble ones were truly in a higher faith. They never stood over me with their religiousness but sat next to me with a simple and humble faith. I felt God's love through them. I've learned that the more Christians try to impress you with their spiritual height and teach down to you so they can try to prove it, the less they know God, and the less God can do through them.

The more simple your faith, the more pure your faith will be. "So continuing daily with one accord in the temple, and breaking bread from house to house, they ate their food with gladness and simplicity of heart" (Acts 2:46 NKJV).

If you're younger in your faith, don't be put off by arrogant Christians, nor allow yourself to be intimidated and pushed away from the church. God will deal with the proud; you just remain humble and place your confidence in the Lord. If you're more mature in your faith, determine never to make another believer feel that they're beneath you. Only then will you be effective for the kingdom. Beware of the religious spirit: "For they loved the praise of men more than the praise of God" (John 12:43 NKJV).

The proof that you've made your religion more important than God is in how complicated you've made it.

Keep your faith simple. Be humble before men and before El Shaddai (God Almighty). The higher faith is found by those willing to kneel lower. You'll do more for the kingdom in your simple humility than in any other way. You can reach a higher faith through a simple path of a surrendered heart that lives only to please the Lord.

Have a simple faith, and your life will be a blessing to those around you. "That your faith should not be in the wisdom of men but in the power of God" (1 Corinthians 2:5 NKJV).

Prayer

Lord Jesus, help me have a faith so simple and so focused on You that all the ways I've complicated it begin to fade away. Show me the simplicity of loving the Father and loving others, and help me walk in humility everywhere I go.

Challenge

Every one of us has made our faith far more complicated than it needs to be. We've argued doctrines to the point that we're no longer living them. Write out for yourself a list of confessions. In this list, tell the Lord where you've made your rituals or your arguments more important than simply loving Him and loving others. Ask Him to show you where you're wrong. Be willing to be wrong.

Going further

Some of us don't self-reflect very well, and we need the Lord to bring a correction. The correction will often be in the form of a difficult circumstance. Look at your life right now and consider what difficult circumstances you might be going through. Consider how the Lord might be using these trials to bring you back to a simple faith. Pray that the Lord will show you. *Sometimes, God won't change your circumstance until the circumstance changes you.* "And we know that God causes everything to work together for the good of those who love God and are called according to his purpose for them" (Romans 8:28 NLT).

32

Praying Higher

A believing prayer warrior is a dangerous thing in the midst of an evil world.

The LORD is close to everyone who prays to him, to all who truly pray to him. – Psalm 145:18 ICB

The path to a higher faith will be found in a prayer life that takes you there. The more time you spend in prayer, the higher you'll go.

As the Lord Jesus Christ draws you higher in your faith, you'll go higher in your prayer life. You can have a prayer life so high, it's as if you're breathing the air of heaven. A prayer life where you close your eyes and begin to pray, and it wouldn't surprise you in the least that if you peeked, you might see the Lord Jesus sitting on His throne with angels singing all around Him.

Have a prayer life such that your voice is recognized in the throne room of heaven. "One day Jesus told his disciples a story to show that they should always pray and never give up" (Luke 18:1 NLT).

We're meant to pray higher. Jesus looks at you while you're praying and can see in you how much faith you really have. The height of your prayer time is equal to the height of your faith, and there's no fooling an infinitely all-knowing God. The wonderful thing is that Jesus can help you pray higher. Make it your prayer to pray higher.

We pray as high as we believe. "'Whatever things you ask in prayer, believing, you will receive'" (Matthew 21:22 NKJV).

When you pray higher, you pray nearer to the level of all that El Gibhor (the mighty God) can do. There's nothing impossible for God, and so there should be nothing too hard for us to pray for. We think we have a great faith until we need one; then we find ourselves struggling to even bring our problem to the Lord and letting Him have it. In our greatest trials, we'll find out just how high our faith is and how high we can really pray.

If you want to know where you lack faith, it's what you think is impossible for God to do. Jesus prayed: "Abba! (that is, 'Dear Father!') All things are possible for you" (Mark 14:36 CJB).

We must learn to pray unreasonable prayers with the same conviction as we do when we pray for something reasonable. We need to take everything to the Lord and just place it before Him and believe that He can do it. Too many believers don't even believe enough to ask Him. And even if they do ask, they don't really believe He can or will do what they ask. Be the prayer warrior that people go to, knowing that you're bold enough to ask Yahweh Yireh (the LORD will provide) for anything they might need.

Be the one in your circle of influence who believes for the impossible. "'For with God nothing [is or ever] shall be impossible'" (Luke 1:37 AMP).

If you don't believe, your prayers will fall flat before you even say them. An unbelieving prayer is telling God you don't trust Him to do it or that you don't think He can. With a weak faith like that, your prayers will likely not move a grain of sand, let alone a mountain. Admit where you're wrong, then pray that He makes you right, so your prayers reach up into heaven.

Jesus is interested not in what you know, but in what you believe. He said, "'When the Son of Man comes, will He really find faith on the earth?'" (Luke 18:8 NKJV).

Throw caution to the wind and cast your doubts away, then fall to your knees and pray like a believer should pray. Pray for El Shaddai (God Almighty) to help you have a faith that can move mountains. Turn away from the world's sense of reasonableness and just sit before your Father, with whom all things are possible, and ask for whatever it is you need.

Knowledge says that mountains can be moved—faith moves them.

Your faith journey should be a progression of believing more and doubting less. "Jesus told his disciples: Have faith in God! If you have faith in God and don't doubt, you can tell this mountain to get up and jump into the sea, and it will. Everything you ask for in prayer will be yours, if you only have faith" (Mark 11:22-24 CEV).

Don't worry about what people think about you. Just keep your eyes on Jesus. Know that God will bless you when you pray to Him with whatever is on your heart. When you hand your burdens over to Yahweh Hoshiah (the LORD saves), you'll become so light that you'll almost float into heaven. Your prayer life can be so high that it places you right into the heavenly realm.

When you don't know what to do, just take it to the Lord. "The LORD says, 'I will guide you along the best pathway for your life. I will advise you and watch over you. Do not be like a senseless horse or mule that needs a bit and bridle to keep it under control'" (Psalm 32:8-9 NLT).

There are times when I close my eyes and step into a vision. Almost always, it's a place I've never seen, and sometimes, I cannot make sense of what's meant by the images I see. I need the Lord to help me understand such things. It's so precious when Ruach Ha'Kodesh (the Holy Spirit) pulls back the curtains and allows me to see something from the Father. You're one blink away from a vision that the Lord is just waiting to show you.

By the prayers of Christ, you can have heaven opened up before you. "While He prayed, the heaven was opened" (Luke 3:21 NKJV).

I was once at a prayer meeting, sitting on the floor alone, when I felt a strong presence of the Holy Spirit. I closed my eyes, and in a moment, I was standing in a place deep in the heart of heaven. I don't know how I knew I was in heaven; I just knew. As we grow in our faith, we'll discern the "amen" in our spirit when the things of God are revealed before us.

You won't have heavenly visions with your eyes fixed on earth. The apostle Paul said, "I have not been disobedient to what was revealed to me from heaven" (Acts 26:19 TPT).

In my vision, I was in a room so large you couldn't see the edge of where the walls were, nor how high the ceiling was. The expanse of the room was so great that you could hardly call it a room, yet it was. There was a stone floor, like what you might find in an old castle. The stones were not cut perfectly, but with natural shapes, the shapes made by God.

There was a stone wall more than waist-high, of which I couldn't see the end in either direction. Beyond the stone wall was a great expanse, so great I couldn't see where it ended. There seemed to be a deep canyon beyond the wall, but I was too far away to look down it.

God speaks in dreams and visions so that the natural man gets out of the way. "'For God speaks again and again, though people do not recognize it. He speaks in dreams, in visions of the night, when deep sleep falls on people as they lie in their beds'" (Job 33:14-15 NLT).

High above me was a bluish-purple haze. It was like looking into the night sky because I couldn't see as high as the ceiling was. The colors above me were deep and rich and majestic. The colors highlighted the majestic place that I was in. Still higher, I could see a long, thick curtain, like a thick, wavy veil, so thick that it didn't move. The veil was a deep purplish-red color and was at a right angle from the edge of the stone wall, extending out a long way across the stone floor in front of me. I could see the edge of the veil, and it was close to where I was standing. It was surreal, yet real—so real that I could touch it.

Never ignore what the Lord is trying to show you. "One night, the Lord spoke to Paul in a supernatural vision" (Acts 18:9 TPT).

I couldn't see the area on the other side of the veil because the fabric was so thick, so I walked forward to see what was on the other side. I came to the end of the veil, then stepped around it. And there I saw Him. I saw Yeshua HaMashiach (Jesus the Messiah) kneeling in prayer. I didn't see His face, but from the back and the side, I knew it was Him. I could feel His presence. I could feel the love in the room. It was when I saw Him that I realized I was in the prayer room of the Christ.

When you anchor your soul into Christ, who is in heaven, there's no storm on earth that can move you. "This hope we have as an anchor of the soul, both sure and steadfast, and which enters the Presence behind the veil, where the forerunner has entered for us, even Jesus" (Hebrews 6:19-20 NKJV).

That's all I remember from this vision, but it gave me such a deep sense of being covered in prayer by the Lord Jesus Himself. How much our lives would be different if we truly grasped that the Lord Jesus was interceding for us from heaven. Through prayer, the Lord Jesus reaches out to us, and through prayer, we can reach out to Him.

The Lord Jesus promised us, even to this day, "I do not pray for these alone [the disciples], but also for those who will believe in Me" (John 17:20 NKJV).

I am confident that Jesus prays the same for you and me what He says He did for Peter: "I have prayed for you, that your faith should not fail" (Luke 22:32 NKJV).

When you always have Jesus praying for you, what in the world are you so worried about? "Therefore he [Jesus] is able, once and forever, to save those who come to God through him. He lives forever to intercede with God on their behalf" (Hebrews 7:25 NLT).

Your prayer life *is* your life. Growing spiritually is growing in prayer. In prayer, we step into the spiritual realm. In prayer, we reach into heaven. Growing higher in faith is possible only as we learn to pray higher, trusting that Yahweh Hoseenu (the LORD our maker) is listening, and trusting that He can help us.

If you're going to pray for a little, you may as well pray for a lot. "Now to him who by his power working in us is able to do far beyond anything we can ask or imagine" (Ephesians 3:20 CJB).

You don't need a vision of heaven as much as you need the faith that Jesus Christ is praying for you. We often think the highest faith prays the highest, and we're right. Jesus has the highest faith, and He is high in heaven while praying for us. Our prayers may be weak, but His prayers for us are always strong. Pray that the Lord Jesus will help you pray higher.

The deepest prayer has no room for words. "Christ Jesus is the One who...is at the right hand of God interceding [with the Father] for us" (Romans 8:34 AMP).

When you pray, imagine the Lord Jesus kneeling next to you, and pray knowing that He hears you, and it'll be there that you're praying in His presence. Jesus always hears you, and He is always with you, and our prayers should be spoken believing that truth. Be the prayer warrior to the people around you that they need you to be.

Pray to God's limits, not yours. Jesus taught, "With God all things are possible" (Matthew 19:26 NKJV).

Prayer

Lord Jesus, I thank You that You're praying for me. Help me realize that I'm covered in Your prayers and that You long for me to grow in my faith. Help me pray higher as You take me higher, so that my prayers will be a blessing to those around me.

Challenge

If you don't already have a place where you can tuck away by yourself just to pray to the Lord, choose that place today. It could be in a car, in a certain chair, on a bench, under a favorite tree, or in a quiet room. Anoint this place with oil as a sign that you're setting it apart to spend time with the Lord. When you pray at this place, ask the Lord Jesus to be with you and help you grow higher in your prayer life. You'll never go wrong asking the Lord to help you in your prayer life.

Going further

Write out a prayer list of people in your life who need specific prayers for something. Don't try to help God by listing out how the prayer might be answered, but simply present to the Lord the problem that needs to be solved. Keep adding to this list as new prayer requests need to be prayed for. When a prayer is answered or no longer needed, cross it off. Trust that the Lord can answer every prayer on your list, and you're starting to walk on holy ground. Watch in amazement at the requests being crossed off. *Pray so high that only God can get the glory for the outcome.* "Now to Him who is able to [carry out His purpose and] do superabundantly more than all that we dare ask or think [infinitely beyond our greatest prayers, hopes, or dreams], according to His power that is at work within us, to Him be the glory in the church and in Christ Jesus throughout all generations forever and ever. Amen" (Ephesians 3:20-21 AMP).

33

Listening Higher

*When you don't know what to do, ask God,
then wait for Him to tell you.*

You are my God. Show me what you want me to do, and let your
gentle Spirit lead me in the right path. – Psalm 143:10 CEV

When we grow higher in our faith, we'll hear
His voice more clearly. In the kingdom,
listening is more beneficial than speaking.

There are many who claim that God no longer speaks in our day. They preach from a platform of spiritual emptiness, trying to explain faith at the meager levels in which they live. Yet God has not lost His voice, and He never will. Our job as Christians is to learn how to discern His voice.

You won't get a fresh word eating the canned goods of man. "Therefore, as the Holy Spirit says: 'Today, if you will hear His voice...'" (Hebrews 3:7 NKJV).

If you want to discern the voice of Yahweh Shammah (the LORD is there), you must compare it to the written Word of God. To discover the counterfeit, you must compare it to the original. The more you know the Word of God, the better you can discern the voice of God.

If you're not standing on the Word of God, you're sinking in the sands of your delusion. "Another reason we regularly thank God is that when you heard the Word of God from us, you received it not merely as a human word, but as it truly is, God's Word, which is at work in you believers" (1 Thessalonians 2:13 CJB).

There are three voices competing for your attention: the voice of God, the voice of Satan, and the voice of your own flesh. You're always listening to one of these voices, but are you always discerning? We mustn't think we're ever beyond error, because we're wrapped in error by the very flesh that surrounds us.

The bridge between good intentions and good outcomes is good discernment. Some of the worst outcomes grow out of the best of intentions that have not yet been tested by godly discernment. "Yes, if you cry out for discernment, and lift up your voice for understanding.... Then you will understand the fear of the LORD, and find the knowledge of God" (Proverbs 2:3,5 NKJV).

The voice of the devil will always question the truths of God. Satan works on our emotions and twists the truth until it becomes a lie. The devil will lie to you so well that you may think it's the truth. But truth has no basis in the devil, and we must stand on the truth as told in the Word of God. You need to remain firmly rooted in the Word of God.

When you make room for the devil, be sure he is going to take it. "Don't give the devil a way to defeat you" (Ephesians 4:27 ERV).

Your flesh has a voice that shouts loudly. The flesh takes natural urges and twists them into evil desires. The flesh will use hunger and thirst in a thousand ways to destroy you. The flesh will always lead you somewhere higher, but then abandon you and let you fall.

Anybody can listen to their flesh, but it's the blessed person who's led by the Spirit of God. "If you use your lives to do what your sinful selves want, you will die spiritually. But if you use the Spirit's help to stop doing the wrong things you do with your body, you will have true life. The true children of God are those who let God's Spirit lead them" (Romans 8:13-14 ERV).

It's the most blessed child of God that can discern the voice of Ruach Ha'Kodesh (the Holy Spirit). They don't seek attention from others with their voice, but want only to listen to His voice. They recognize Him because they're immersed in the Word of God and come to know the truths that He tells them.

Yahweh Mekoddishkem (the LORD who sanctifies you) will not always tell you what you want to hear. But if you dare to listen, He will surely say those things you need to hear. Always beware if the voice you hear is in agreement with the flesh which surrounds you. If you don't think your heart is deceitful, you're treading in dangerous waters.

If you want to hear from God, you need to spend time with Him. "In the morning, O LORD, You will hear my voice; in the morning I will prepare [a prayer and a sacrifice] for You and watch and wait [for You to speak to my heart]" (Psalm 5:3 AMP).

The Holy Spirit may speak aloud or, more likely, deep into your heart. He may convey a message to you by a vision, in a dream, or through a circumstance. He can speak through a person who is young in their faith or through someone very mature in their spiritual life. He can even speak through a donkey. God makes a statement through the stars in the sky. Be sure of this—He is speaking to you every day.

When you walk with God, you can talk with God. "'Listen to His voice, serve Him, and cling to Him'" (Deuteronomy 13:4 NASB).

Listening higher is meant to take you deeper into all the things Yeshua HaMashiach (Jesus the Messiah) will show you. As you grow in your spiritual senses and hear all the things that the Lord will tell you, this will have a profound impact on your life. With just a few words, what the Spirit of Christ says can change the direction of your life forever.

You can be inspired by the words of men, but a word from the Lord changes the course of your life. "'Go and tell Hezekiah, "Thus says the LORD, the God of David your father: 'I have heard your prayer, I have seen your tears; surely I will add to your days fifteen years'"'" (Isaiah 38:5 NKJV).

Listening higher will guide you in where you should go and what you should do in your life, whether in ministry, in secular work, in your personal affairs, and most importantly, with every relationship you have. As you mature more in listening to Yahweh Raah (the LORD is my shepherd), you'll ask Him to help you with more decisions. You'll learn the most wonderful truth beneath heaven—that the Holy Spirit is with you and can guide you every step of the way.

You can't walk in your calling if you don't listen to God. Jesus said, "My sheep hear My voice, and I know them, and they follow Me" (John 10:27 NKJV).

Listening higher will bring greater revelations of the truths held in the Word of God. You'll open the Bible each day with the excitement and expectation of all that the Holy Spirit will show you. As you read one verse, many other related verses will fire off in your head, and the teachings of Scripture will come together for you as never before. You'll start to hear the Word in your heart as you see the Word with your spiritual eyes.

Holy Scripture is like a precious diamond—a singular truth, but with many intricate facets. There are many ways in which the truth can be seen, but it's a singular truth that can never be changed. In every truth, there may be different views, but these are always complementing, never contradicting. Truth is like a mirror; it never changes but reflects back onto the man from where he is. "The grass withers, the flower fades, but the word of our God stands forever" (Isaiah 40:8 NKJV).

Listening higher will show you the deeper things in the souls of those you're ministering to, so that you might pray for them or reveal to them all the Lord is telling you. The Holy Spirit will tell you things that only the other person can know. The Lord will have you pray about this privately, then possibly also let the person know that the Lord has revealed it to you. Always be careful to let the Holy Spirit lead you on what to reveal to someone else with what He has revealed to you.

If you want to hear the Lord's voice, you need to quiet your own. "Be still, and know that I am God" (Psalm 46:10 NKJV).

Listening higher will bring revelations about yourself and what the Lord has done and is doing in your life. The Lord will tell you things to let you know why you've suffered or why things didn't work out the way you had hoped for. He will entrust you with the truth of how every difficult thing was allowed to make you who you are. However, He won't tell you everything, because you must learn to just trust Him.

Theology should be your foundation, not your walls. Never limit God by what you know, and He will show things you never knew. "'Call to Me, and I will answer you, and show you great and mighty things, which you do not know'" (Jeremiah 33:3 NKJV).

Listening higher will deepen the relationship between you and the Lord Jesus, because the conversation will no longer be one-sided. You'll start to pray more gently and with a growing expectation that He'll answer you. No longer will you go to Him with only a laundry list of requests that He might answer; instead, you'll include a growing list of thanksgiving for all that He has done.

Listening higher may bring prophetic words meant to warn of all that may be coming at you or to those around you. These words may be to help you or someone that you love. They may be for something immediate or for something a long way out. This will test you the most to see how much you trust Him when He is revealing a thing that has not yet happened.

Prophetic words are not bound by the timelines of man. "'For the vision is yet for an appointed time; but at the end it will speak, and it will not lie. Though it tarries, wait for it; because it will surely come, it will not tarry'" (Habakkuk 2:3 NKJV).

Listening higher will give you peace; you'll be comforted by His gentle voice into a place of rest. Where you once had frustration or anxiousness, you'll find a growing sense of the divine presence of Yahweh Shalom (the LORD is peace). As His peace fills the room, everything else must leave. As He speaks to you, He'll comfort you with words of love and gentleness.

Listening higher will bring you lower before the Lord, with all He is telling you. When God speaks, even the angels know to sit in silence. Sometimes, His voice can hurt as it addresses something in us that needs to change. We'll learn that at such times, we're so blessed that He is willing to help us grow higher.

It's hard to hear the Lord when you're talking so much. "Yahweh is in his holy temple. All the earth should be silent in his presence" (Habakkuk 2:20 NOG).

Listening higher will change your life. It will lift you from shallow worldly thoughts into the highest of heavenly thoughts, and you'll never forget their impact. Your worldly thoughts will dissipate into oblivion as you start to fill your mind with the things of El Hakkadosh (the Holy God). What used to matter so much before will lose all its appeal, and new and wonderful blessings from the Lord will fill you and satisfy you as you've never been satisfied before.

Temporary things can never satisfy eternal longings. "He has made everything beautiful and appropriate in its time. He has also planted eternity [a sense of divine purpose] in the human heart [a mysterious longing which nothing under the sun can satisfy, except God]—yet man cannot find out (comprehend, grasp) what God has done (His overall plan) from the beginning to the end" (Ecclesiastes 3:11 AMP).

Listening higher will take you higher into all that the Lord has for you. As you listen more, you'll start to live life like you never imagined you could. You'll start to live a spiritual life that can still walk on the surface of this planet. You'll become a vessel of God, and sometimes, a mouthpiece for what He would have you say.

Listening higher will be listening more to everything that the Lord has for you. This is not meant to make you higher but to keep you lower before God and the souls He wants you to serve. The more you hear God, the less you can stand tall in your pride. His voice will drop you to your knees and keep you there as long as He is talking.

Prayer

Lord, open my ears so that I hear You, and give me a heart that can understand all that You tell me. Teach me to be quiet and still before You so that I hear Your voice and go where You're leading me.

Challenge

Pick at least one day per week in which you devote time to listening to the Lord. Later, make this a daily time, but try doing it once a week to start. Consider what you might ask Him, then write that down. Be determined to go into this prayer session without any requests, only a commitment to hear what the Lord would tell you. Afterward, write down everything you heard, whether it was audible or a quiet message in your heart. Then pray that the Lord would confirm it. Learn to pray with your ears wide open and your mouth closed shut. If you don't hear anything after your first try, or even your hundredth, just keep persisting in your prayer time. Stop thinking it happened all at once for others. You've no idea how long they had to press in.

Going further

Our problem with listening to the Lord is that most of us don't really want to do what He asks of us. Rather, we want Him to do what we ask of Him. Lose the idea that you know better than God. Be willing in your heart to do whatever the Lord asks of you. Sometimes people will counsel you to do differently than what the Lord told you. Never allow the best of intentions in others to overrule a word from the Lord. Be obedient to His calling and let the chips fall where they will. *You cannot be led by the Spirit while holding on to the expectations of man.* As Paul once testified, "I did not immediately confer with flesh and blood" (Galatians 1:16 NKJV).

34

The
Narrow Path

*The Christian faith is not the easy
way out but the hard way in.*

The Lord Jesus taught us, "Enter through the narrow gate. For wide is the gate and broad and easy to travel is the path that leads the way to destruction and eternal loss, and there are many who enter through it. But small is the gate and narrow and difficult to travel is the path that leads the way to [everlasting] life, and there are few who find it."
–Matthew 7:13-14 AMP

As you grow higher in your faith, the path will become narrower. It's often the difficulties we face that show us we're on the right path.

There are many paths we can walk on, but none so eternally important as the narrow path for growing higher in our faith. The narrow path is the only path that will lead you straight to heaven. This is the path we must find and stay on, so that we'll live with Jesus forever and ever. It's the path we're to follow here on earth, the path that prepares us for all we might have in heaven.

The Christian life is not an easy road, but it is the right road. "As for God, His way is perfect" (Psalm 18:30 NKJV).

The narrow path isn't hard to find if you're willing to let Yeshua HaMashiach (Jesus the Messiah) show you. So few will find it, because it's only the few who seek after it. Many say they desire to go to heaven, but they're seeking only for a heaven of their own design, and not God's holy presence. Though Christians know about the narrow path, many still prefer the wide road where they can go their own way.

If your journey is easy, you might be on the wrong road. "A highway shall be there, and a road, and it shall be called the Highway of Holiness. The unclean shall not pass over it, but it shall be for others. Whoever walks the road, although a fool, shall not go astray" (Isaiah 35:8 NKJV).

The narrow path is a hard path because it requires that we surrender ourselves to the Lord. It's much easier for us to strive than to surrender. The hardest thing we can ever do in this life is to surrender ourselves to Yahweh Sabaoth (the LORD of angelic armies). The greater your surrender, the further you'll go on the narrow path. The farther you go, the less you'll have in which you can stand back and say, "This is mine."

There's not an easy way out when you're pressing into the narrow way.

The reason so many Christians fall away is that they were told a lie about the Christian life being easy. It's not easy. Father God, following You isn't the easy path, but the right path. The way may be difficult, but the destination is to die for. "Dear brothers, is your life full of difficulties and temptations? Then be happy, for when the way is rough, your patience has a chance to grow. So let it grow, and don't try to squirm out of your problems. For when your patience is finally in full bloom, then you will be ready for anything, strong in character, full and complete" (James 1:2-4 TLB).

The narrow path isn't reserved for only those who seemingly deserve it from man's perspective. The narrow gate is open, and the narrow path is available to anyone who chooses to be on it. The right to be on it is never by your credentials, but only by your faith that it's Christ alone who can get you there. The Holy Spirit can guide you every step of the way once you're willing to listen to Him.

You cannot be too bad to get into heaven, nor good enough to stay out of hell—by Christ alone will you be saved. "'Nor is there salvation in any other, for there is no other name [besides Jesus of Nazareth] under heaven given among men by which we must be saved'" (Acts 4:12 NKJV).

The path to heaven is narrow, not because it's so hard for us to get there, but because so few of us are willing to follow the Lord Jesus.

The narrow path never has anything on it that doesn't belong in heaven. But beyond the edges of the path are many temptations that will try to lead you astray. The secret to staying on the path is in listening and adhering to the Holy Spirit, who can guide you so that you remain on it. Keep your eyes focused on Jesus, and keep your ears open to the guidance of the Holy Spirit.

If you're led by the Holy Spirit, the path you're on will show it. "If you go the wrong way—to the right or to the left—you will hear a voice behind you. It will say, 'This is the right way. You should go this way.'" (Isaiah 30:21 ICB).

The narrow path is not achieved in your ability to be obedient but in your willingness to let the Lord Jesus Christ help you. Nobody can be obedient apart from the inward working of Yahweh Mekoddishkem (the Lord who sanctifies you), as He gives you the power to overcome. Legalism is never the answer, because it relies only upon yourself, and you're not strong enough to keep the law on your own. Grace covers your sin, but the Holy Spirit gives you power over sin.

Legalism is the letter of the Law, dead ink on paper. Obedience is the Spirit of the Law—Christ in you. "But now we have been delivered from the law...so that we should serve in the newness of the Spirit and not in the oldness of the letter" (Romans 7:6 NKJV).

The narrow path is narrow not to limit how many can walk on it, but because of the limited options for how to walk down it. The Lord doesn't give us a hundred ways to find salvation, only one, that we might be willing to take it. The narrow path takes away a thousand wrong choices and replaces them with the single right choice that you should walk in. Being narrow is not closed-minded, but right-minded with the things of El Hanan (the gracious God).

Only the Lord Jesus can say, "My way or the highway." "Yeshua said, 'I AM the Way—and the Truth and the Life; no one comes to the Father except through me'" (John 14:6 CJB).

The narrow path doesn't allow man the wiggle room to choose how he might walk down it. The more wiggle room you have in your faith, the less likely it is that you're actually on the narrow path. Stop looking for the exceptions to the rules, and start seeking the Lord's help in following them. Be satisfied to never get your way so long as you're following the Lord's way in how you live.

It's more important for a train to stay on the rails than to go faster. The same is true with your faith. "'The LORD your God is testing you to know whether you love the LORD your God with all your heart and mind and all your soul [your entire being]'" (Deuteronomy 13:3 AMP).

You may not like the fact that Yahweh Go'el (the LORD our redeemer) provided only one narrow path to heaven. But we should all be eternally grateful that He has provided a path at all. Christ died on the cross so that you can live for eternity with no more pain or suffering. When you press on to follow Jesus, you're on the narrow path. You'll be walking on that glorious narrow path to heaven, a journey that makes you more like Christ each day.

With Christianity, you're either all in, or you're not. "Then Yeshua said to his disciples, 'Those who want to come with me must say no to the things they want, pick up their crosses, and follow me'" (Matthew 16:24 NOG).

When I was young, my father and I used to go hiking in the woods and backpacking in the mountains. One trip we took was up to Yosemite in California, so we could hike up to the top of Half Dome. Driving there, we were on freeways with many lanes, but as we went into the mountainous area, it became two-way narrow roads. When we set out on foot from the trailhead, it was a wide trail, and we could walk side by side on it. But the trail became very narrow as it wound its way up to the steeper parts of the mountain. The higher we went, the narrower the path became.

The higher you climb up the mountain, the narrower the path will become. "Who may ascend the mountain of the Lord? Who may stand in His holy place? The one who has clean hands and a pure heart, who has not set his mind on what is false, and who has not sworn deceitfully. He will receive blessing from the Lord, and righteousness from the God of his salvation. Such is the generation of those who seek Him, who seek the face of the God of Jacob" (Psalm 24:3-6 HCSB).

As we ascend higher, this narrowing of the path is as true in natural mountains as it is in the spiritual ascension that El Elyon (God Most High) has for us. The higher we go, the less wiggle room we have in a faith where we're called to go so much higher. Most will say they want to ascend higher, but their desire for this fades when they discover all that it will cost them. The cost is not measured in things or in suffering as much as in giving up the right to yourself. Spiritual ascension requires that you surrender yourself, and that's where most will stop and go no further.

The only way to ascend spiritually is to kneel down in the natural. "'He must increase, but I must decrease'" (John 3:30 NKJV). *As hard as you try, you cannot have the "more" without becoming the "less."*

When you climb natural mountains, you pack as little as possible. You take only what you need, so the weight you're carrying doesn't keep you from ascending higher. Spiritual ascension is the same, where we must let go of the past and the natural things that hinder us from going higher. When we're traveling higher in the spiritual realm, every natural weight will hinder how high we can go. A man or woman is most blessed when they discover how little they really need in their flesh, and how much they're satisfied with nothing more than the Holy Spirit dwelling within them.

You can go further if you travel light. "Throw all your anxieties upon him, because he cares about you" (1 Peter 5:7 CJB).

The narrow path is the right path because it focuses us on exactly where we should be going. When you have your focus right, you'll have your mind at peace with everything you see before you. El Yeshuati (the God of my salvation) is waiting for you to discover the higher levels of this blessed path. This path begins here on earth and extends right into heaven. You'll find the path when you look for it, and you'll walk the path when you step onto it. After that, all you have to do is make a choice to let the Lord help you go higher.

What you think about has you. "'You will keep him in perfect peace, whose mind is stayed on You, because he trusts in You'" (Isaiah 26:3 NKJV).

Prayer

Lord Jesus, help me find the narrow path and step into it, so my life goes exactly the way You intend. Help my ears to listen to the Holy Spirit as He leads me into higher levels on the narrow path.

Challenge

Write down a list of current things or activities in your life that have no place on the narrow path of the Lord. Ask the Lord to bring to your mind those things that don't have His stamp of approval. Be honest with yourself, because you can be sure that God knows already anyway. Now pray to the Lord to help you be delivered from each of these things. Don't stop praying about these each day, until the entire list is crossed off. Buckle in, Christian; this journey is just getting started.

Going further

You need to get to a point in your life where you'll finally throw your reasonable human arguments out the door and plop your life right into the hands of Jesus. When you stop making excuses for not surrendering to Christ, He will completely have you. Commit in your heart right now that today is that day. Stop putting off for tomorrow what you should have done years ago. You said you gave your life to Jesus—so now, finally, just do it. *Either Jesus is at the center of your life, or you are.* "You have been raised to life with Christ. Now set your heart on what is in heaven, where Christ rules at God's right side" (Colossians 3:1 CEV).

35

Under the Anointing

If you want to walk in the anointed life,
be prepared to let go of the life you lived before.

Then Samuel took the horn of oil and anointed him in the
midst of his brothers. And the Spirit of the LORD rushed upon
David from that day forward. – 1 Samuel 16:13 ESV

To go higher in our faith, we must first be willing to go lower.
We must get lower to get under the anointing from the Lord.

It's not how many you reach, but who you move. What matters is that you do what God asks you to do. There's nothing you cannot do with help from Jesus, but barely a thing you can accomplish without Him. The harder you try, and the prouder you are, the less you can do for the kingdom. If you want to grow higher in your faith, you must get under the anointing. The anointing is not something you do but something the Lord will do to you. It cannot be gained, only received.

The anointing is meant to consecrate you from the world, not to make you part of it. "'You shall put the holy garments on Aaron, and anoint him and consecrate him, that he may minister to Me as priest'" (Exodus 40:13 NKJV).

The only qualification required for being under the anointing is to bow down low before Yahweh Qadosh (the Holy One). He'll reign supreme over you only when you surrender yourself beneath Him. Your pride stands between you and God, and your pride must be dealt with before you can serve Him any higher.

Where you lack sanctification, you'll lack the anointing. "God has chosen you from the beginning for salvation through the sanctifying work of the Spirit [that sets you apart for God's purpose] and by your faith in the truth [of God's word that leads you to spiritual maturity]" (2 Thessalonians 2:13 AMP).

Too many seek the anointing for attention, and in so doing, they create the barrier of pride that prohibits them from serving Yeshua (Jesus) effectively in the kingdom. When you think yourself high, you're not. To the degree that you want to be seen, you're wrong. Pride has no place in the throne room of heaven; it belongs only in the pits of hell.

You cannot be under the anointing so long as you refuse to kneel down. "Oh come, let us worship and bow down; let us kneel before the Lord, our Maker!" (Psalm 95:6 ESV).

The anointing goes only to those who are willing. If the Lord Jesus Christ were to take us by force, we wouldn't be His lovers, only His captives. Jesus wants us to love Him not just to gain something, but to give up everything, so that nothing means more to us than He does. If you're not willing to let your faith cost you something, just admit that, and sit down. Then pray that the Lord will change you.

Everyone wants the anointing until they find out what it will cost them. Our Lord Jesus taught, "I tell you for certain that a grain of wheat that falls on the ground will never be more than one grain unless it dies. But if it dies, it will produce lots of wheat" (John 12:24 CEV).

The anointing is never meant to lift a man or woman above others; it is meant to make them a utensil for a time in the hands of El Chay (the living God). When the utensil is done, the Lord will set it down. The utensil must wait to be picked up again to bring glory to God and be a blessing to the kingdom. Your willingness to sit down will determine how often He'll pick you up and use you again.

Never seek the anointing to be seen, only to serve. Never extend the anointing past the close of His purposes, just sit down and be thankful He used you for a time. Let your tears be your thanks, and let your kneeling be your praise, that God might someday choose to use you once again.

You won't walk in your anointing until you first sit in His presence. "But you have an anointing from the Holy One [you have been set apart, specially gifted and prepared by the Holy Spirit], and all of you know [the truth because He teaches us, illuminates our minds, and guards us from error]" (1 John 2:20 AMP).

Nobody can stand tall under the anointing while having the power of El Shaddai (God Almighty) poured out upon them. The more we come under the anointing, the smaller we feel before our heavenly Father. In this place of humility, where pride is no longer a hindrance, the Lord can accomplish the most.

You can't be under the anointing until you get over yourself. "'Blessed [spiritually prosperous, happy, to be admired] are the poor in spirit [those devoid of spiritual arrogance, those who regard themselves as insignificant], for theirs is the kingdom of heaven [both now and forever]'" (Matthew 5:3 AMP).

When once you're under the anointing, the favor of the Lord will pour down from the reservoirs of heaven. Whatever you need in order to serve Him at that moment will be yours. Angels will be beside you, and the Holy Spirit within you, and nothing on earth will be able to stand against you.

The anointing stays on you only so long as the fullness of the Holy Spirit remains in you. "The Spirit of the LORD came upon David from that day forward.... But the Spirit of the LORD departed from Saul" (1 Samuel 16:13-14 NKJV).

When you fall under the anointing, the presence of Christ Jesus will overwhelm you. A rushing of wind will go through you. Spiritual power will flow within you, then pour out of you. Words will spill out from heaven and overflow through you onto those around you.

I've found that being under the anointing is one of the greatest experiences a Christian can ever hope to have while here on earth. Sometimes, we can have spiritual experiences without any special deep presence within us. But under the anointing, you'll feel the heavy presence of Ruach Ha'Kodesh (the Holy Spirit) upon you, in you, and through you. You'll get so filled with the Holy Spirit that often, it will push tears right out of you. You'll barely be able to remain standing.

Your anointing isn't your calling, but it will establish the degree to which you're able to fulfill the office for which you're called. You're called to something, then you're anointed to do it. "But the anointing that you received from him abides in you, and you have no need that anyone should teach you. But as his anointing teaches you about everything, and is true, and is no lie—just as it has taught you, abide in him" (1 John 2:27 ESV).

You can walk in a perpetual anointed life, but when you're under the deeper anointing—the heavy presence—this will be only for special times. You can be under the deeper anointing once a year or every day; the choice will be both yours and the Lord's. Your choice is to place yourself where you can be put under the anointing. The Lord's choice will be whether to do it and to what degree. All you have to do is ask Him, then let Him pour into you the richness and fullness of the Holy Spirit.

I will tell you how I often prepare myself, but don't try making this a process for yourself. It's merely an example of how the Lord has led me to place myself where I'm ready for His deeper anointing.

First and foremost, I confess any sin, known or not, and then receive His forgiveness and His cleansing so I can be cleansed within and covered in the righteousness of Christ.

The washing precedes the anointing. The Lord said, "Then I washed you in water; yes, I thoroughly washed off your blood, and I anointed you with oil" (Ezekiel 16:9 NKJV).

I then separate myself from the world and join myself to the Lord Jesus. Even if I'm in a crowded worship meeting, I'll isolate myself so that the natural will not disrupt the spiritual experience I am longing to have. I'll most often sit on the ground so I'm bowed low before the Lord. Then I'll start to pray and worship and adore the Lord for who He is and all He has done. Praising Him places you in His presence.

The best way to start this is to have spiritual music to soak in and usher in the presence of the Holy Spirit. The type of music will vary depending on your heart and what moves you. The test will be if the music is preparing you to be in His presence, because that's where the anointing will happen.

The anointed life is not determined by what you take hold of, but by what you let go of. We should be "always carrying about in the body the dying of the Lord Jesus [crucifying ourselves with Him, dying to self], that the life of Jesus also may be manifested in our body" (2 Corinthians 4:10 NKJV).

I'll anoint myself with oil, touching next to my eyes, on my ears, under my nose, on my lips, and on the tip of my tongue. As I'm anointing myself, I pray that the Lord will open my spiritual eyes, spiritual ears, and spiritual nose, so that I'm sensing in the Spirit. I'll pray that every word that comes from my tongue and through my lips will be anointed and holy.

I continue to anoint myself, putting oil on each side of the back of my neck and praying that the Holy Spirit will be upon me. Then I anoint the palms of my hands and rub them together, praying that the works that I do will be pleasing to the Lord. The oil represents the Holy Spirit, and my actions represent my surrender to the Lord Jesus.

The reason you want the anointing determines the degree of your anointing. If you seek to be seen, you've set your sights on the limit of man. But when you're under God's limits, the praise of men will never matter. "He poured some of the anointing oil on Aaron's head and anointed and consecrated him" (Leviticus 8:12 HCSB). *Where you lack consecration, you lack anointing.*

When we anoint ourselves, or others, or where we live, or where we worship, this is an expression of setting apart and making these things holy. It symbolizes the presence of the Holy Spirit and the power and protection He brings to everything we touch with the oil. We're called out in Holy Scripture to do this, and we must understand that when we do what the Lord commands, the Lord will bless it.

I don't have a timetable in mind for when I fall under the deeper anointing. I never want to rush God, because when I do, He won't act on my lack of patience. Instead, I just sit and pray and let Yahweh Sabaoth (the LORD of angelic armies) decide what He's going to do and when. The deeper anointing doesn't always come like a light switch, but more like a rising tide, until finally I'm all in. And when I'm there, I never want to leave. But we have to return, and it's up to God when we will.

Never chase the anointing, but seek to live a life worthy of the anointing. "With this in mind, we always pray that our God will make you worthy of his call. We also pray that through his power he will help you accomplish every good desire and help you do everything your faith produces" (2 Thessalonians 1:11 NOG).

When you're under the anointing, others who are spiritually enlightened will know you are. You, too, will see others when they're under the anointing. When you've been deep under the anointing, you'll recognize it when others are there as well. When you're under the deep anointing, you'll hear God's voice more clearly and discern His will with greater precision. This is where you can serve Him higher, all for His glory.

Sometimes, I've been so heavy under the anointing that I remained in it late into the evening while ministering, and still later that night when falling asleep. I would lie down in the darkness on my bed, and I could still see a glow above me. Being under the anointing became such an important part of my ministry that I could barely serve without it. The more you lean on the power of El Elyon (God Most High), the less you'll rely on your own strength.

The weight of glory cannot be measured on the scales of man. "For our momentary, light affliction is producing for us an eternal weight of glory far beyond all comparison" (2 Corinthians 4:17 NASB).

This need for the anointing in order to serve Him is something I've carried over from prison ministry to the writing ministry. My ministering just moved from the spoken word to the written word. I always need God for anything I might do for Him. Sometimes, I'll agonize over a single word to write. I'll roll around in my head topics and ideas, and nothing will come from them. I'll pour over things I've written before, and nothing will jump out at me. But once I get myself broken before God, I can get under the anointing, and the river flows.

The thing that breaks the anointing is when the natural invades the spiritual. The greater the anointing, the more resistant it is to the natural. But at some point, the anointing will eventually subside. This often comes about when someone unspiritual—even if they're saved—starts having a conversation with me on the natural level. This is why ministers will isolate from people before giving a message, so that their preaching can be done while under the anointing.

If you can explain everything that happens in your life, you're missing out on the supernatural from God. "Even Simon himself believed; and after being baptized, he continued on with Philip, and as he observed signs and great miracles taking place, he was repeatedly amazed" (Acts 8:13 NASB).

The anointing is for you. The anointing will help you know God and serve God like you never have before. It's a supernatural experience given to you supernaturally by God. I can never hope to explain it completely, but you'll know all about it the moment you get there. Pray to the Lord that He will shower this blessing on you this day.

Prayer

Holy Spirit, I long to have You reigning over my life so that I'm under the anointing. Fill me up and pour right through me, so that I'm useful in the kingdom. Help me have my attitude rightfully bowed low, so that You can take me higher.

Challenge

If you don't already have anointing oil, get some. Make it your first priority to anoint the windows and doors of the place where you live, and ask the Lord to consecrate that place to be holy. Anoint your devices and media players so that they're set apart as holy. Then anoint yourself, and ask the Lord to consecrate you from the world and then to Him, so your life is His own utensil that He can use for the kingdom. Anoint yourself regularly. When you pray for others, ask them if you can anoint them first. There's something special that happens with the anointing.

Going further

Set aside time before you minister to others or go to a worship service. Make it a time of soaking in His presence. Find a spot you can call holy ground—a place for you to meet with God. Put on music that moves your heart. Posture yourself lower before the Lord, on the ground, or wherever you can comfortably bow lower before Him. Anoint yourself with oil. Ask the Lord to fill you with His Holy Spirit. Pray for Him to make His presence manifest in that moment. If you have Spirit-filled friends, get together with them to do this. It's often when we're together that we get the greatest movement of God. Don't be in a rush, and don't give up trying. It will never be by your striving, but by your patient resting and trusting in all that He can do. *The greater the yielding to the Holy Spirit, the greater the filling of the Holy Spirit.* "Therefore do not be foolish and thoughtless, but understand and firmly grasp what the will of the Lord is.... Be filled with the [Holy] Spirit and constantly guided by Him" (Ephesians 5:17-18 AMP). *You cannot fill a cup until it's first empty.*

36

The Remnant

*Minister to the masses, but be
joined only to the remnant.*

There has also come to be at the present time a remnant
according to God's gracious choice. – Romans 11:5 NASB

To go higher in your faith will require that you get
nearer to the Lord. To get nearer to God will require
you to get further from the crowd.

I n our churches today, we have three categories of people. The first is those who are unsaved and are only going through the motions, but have not yet given their life to Jesus. They're Christians in name only. Most of these people think they're saved, but their life proves otherwise. My fear is that there are more people in this category than we dare to consider.

The second category is those who are saved but who aren't progressing in their faith. They may attend Bible studies and read books to increase their knowledge, but there's no power of the Holy Spirit working within them. They may get into heaven, but they won't accomplish much here on earth before they get there. What regret many Christians will have when they arrive in heaven by the skin of their teeth and receive no rewards when they get there.

The third category is those blessed few who go on with El Olam (the eternal God) and grow higher in their faith. They're the remnant within the church, the ones set apart by God to be more, so that they could do more for the purposes born out of heaven. They'll likely be unpopular and not known by very many, but their names are known in the throne room of heaven.

The remnant is that small and often strange group of believers who don't fit into the popular cliques in the church. They don't march in the formations of tradition or popularity conjured up by the religious elite of our day. To be in the remnant requires that you don't fit in with the crowd. The remnant is often made up of misfits and loners and those deemed too foolish to be used by the Lord. These are the very ones the Lord can do the most with.

Many are called, few will listen, and only the remnant will respond. Be the remnant. Dare to believe He can use you—and He will. "For the gifts and the calling of God are irrevocable" (Romans 11:29 NKJV).

The remnant lives by the Word of God over the word of man. They're like the Bereans who make sure that what they hear preached lines up with what the Father has already spoken through His prophets and apostles long ago. They don't take at face value the many claims of man, but make sure they hold fast to the truths of God.

They're not easily tricked by the fallacious and emotionally charged words tossed around all too often in our churches today. Rather, they hold fast to sound reasoning and are guided by the Spirit of the Lord. They'll listen to people but be led by the Holy Spirit. They're determined to walk in the will of God even if it means being ostracized by the religious elites of our day. Jesus never let anyone deter Him from following where the Father took Him, and neither should we.

While many argue that there's no longer spiritual power for the believers of our day, the remnant yet walks in this power. Jesus said, "You will receive power when the Holy Spirit comes into your life" (Acts 1:8 NLV).

The remnant is more interested in living a doctrine than arguing a doctrine. They understand that Jesus Christ will measure them by what they've done and not by what they know. They don't get distracted by the divisions in the church but instead seek to live in unity with other believers. They'd rather anoint and pray over the sick for healing until the miracle comes, rather than argue about whether God does miracles in our day.

God is more interested in your living a doctrine than in your ability to argue it. "Stay away from foolish and stupid arguments. You know that these arguments grow into bigger arguments. As a servant of the Lord, you must not argue. You must be kind to everyone. You must be a good teacher, and you must be patient" (2 Timothy 2:23-24 ERV).

The remnant isn't those who are the most righteous, but those who are the most forgiven. They don't pretend to be great before men, but bow down in their lowliness before Yahweh Hesed (the LORD of faithful love). They see themselves more clearly because they ask the Lord to show them. There are many popular people in the church who may seem more holy than those in the remnant, but the lives of these popular people are often a stench in the nostrils of God. It's not what we appear to men that matters, but what God can see within us.

The most righteous person isn't the one who has sinned the least but the one who has been forgiven the most. Jesus told the story, "The Pharisee stood and prayed thus with himself, 'God, I thank You that I am not like other men....' And the tax collector, standing afar off, would not so much as raise his eyes to heaven, but beat his breast, saying, 'God, be merciful to me a sinner!' I tell you, this man [the sinner] went down to his house justified rather than the other" (Luke 18:11,13-15 NKJV).

Those in the remnant aren't the strongest but the weakest, and that's why God can work in them. They don't stand tall but fall down at the feet of Yeshua HaMashiach (Jesus the Messiah), where they can be filled with the all-powerful Holy Spirit. They're not full of themselves but emptied out, then filled with the fullness of God. They know they can do nothing of their own power, and it's from there that the power of God is released right through them.

When you rely upon God, you're not limited by you. "Even young people grow tired and become weary, and young men will stumble and fall. Yet, the strength of those who wait with hope in the LORD will be renewed. They will soar on wings like eagles. They will run and won't become weary. They will walk and won't grow tired" (Isaiah 40:30-31 GW).

In the remnant, they may not have a high position noticed by men, but they have a lowly position that pleases the Lord. They may not get many likes on social media posts, but they're noticed in the courts of heaven. The lowest seat on earth is the highest place you can be in heaven. When the Father chose regular people like Moses, Gideon, David, Mary Magdalene, and Paul, it wasn't for what they could bring to the table; it was because they came to the table empty-handed. God's best is reserved for man's worst.

The work of a great saint isn't in what is seen but in the roots grown in the dark places with God. "'And the remnant who have escaped of the house of Judah shall again take root downward, and bear fruit upward'" (Isaiah 37:31 NKJV).

The remnant may not be the smartest by the standards of men, but they're considered wise by the measure of the Lord. Wisdom from God isn't in what we have, but in what we are. The remnant seeks to learn more so they'll be more in the will of God. Their knowledge isn't used to lift them higher over others but to lead them in how they can please the Lord. Holy wisdom is that which always brings glory to El Elyon (God Most High).

The measure of God's wisdom in you is the degree to which the world thinks you the fool. "Let no one deceive himself. If anyone among you seems to be wise in this age, let him become a fool that he may become wise. For the wisdom of this world is foolishness with God. For it is written, 'He catches the wise in their own craftiness'" (1 Corinthians 3:18-19 NKJV).

The remnant isn't an elite club for the few, but a humble group that few are willing to belong to. To be in the remnant, there's not a class or college you must go to, but a humble position you must bow to. To belong to the remnant means that you must belong to God, and you no longer belong to yourself. The higher faith is the lower place that's found in the remnant. You cannot climb up to a position that's lower; you can only bow down to it.

If you cannot find the remnant, be the remnant. The reason you don't fit in (with the popular crowd) may be that you don't belong. "God paid a great price for you. So use your body to honor God" (1 Corinthians 6:20 CEV).

We must each make the choice to be in the remnant. The remnant is as much a place as it is a people. To get to this place, you must leave where you are and vow that you'll never return. It's a place of sacrifice, and that sacrifice is yourself. You'll gain in this transaction, because you trade your lower life for His higher life that fills you. Nobody who trades their life for the life of Jesus Christ ever wants their old life back.

There's a whole new life for you when once you've given it to God. "Present your bodies as a living sacrifice, holy and acceptable to God, which is your spiritual worship. Do not be conformed to this world, but be transformed by the renewal of your mind, that by testing you may discern what is the will of God, what is good and acceptable and perfect" (Romans 12:1-2 ESV).

I've been greatly blessed in my life to meet some special men and women of God who are part of the remnant here on earth. I met one at a hospital who was a dear friend of my mother. Her name is Melissa Hunt, and she is safely home with the Lord now. But back on that day, she was coming there to pray over my mother. They both went to the same church where my brother-in-law was the pastor. I met this woman in the hallway as she slowly walked along, rolling a large canister of oxygen; she had battled a lifelong condition that made it extremely hard to breathe.

Difficult circumstances don't determine our hearts; they reveal our hearts. "They...laid many stripes on them...threw them into...the inner prison.... But at midnight Paul and Silas were praying and singing hymns" (Acts 16:23-25 NKJV).

The moment I met her, I felt the Holy Spirit upon her. I've felt this with others as well, and I'll instantly know that Yahweh 'Ori (the Lord our light) is near them. She spoke very softly, each word carefully selected. I could see that her body was very frail, but her inner spirit was strong. There was a strength and a power within her that wasn't limited by the physical limitations of her body. When someone like this prays, they speak with God as if He were very near them because He is. She may not have been known by many people, but the Father knew exactly who she was.

We are meant to be near to the Lord, and prayer is the means by which we get there. "The Lord is near to all who call upon Him" (Psalm 145:18 NKJV).

I remember another dear soul I often saw when I was ministering in the prisons. He was part of another ministry that I would meet up with when I went to weekend prison events. He led a group of Hispanic men. He and I couldn't talk much to each other, because neither of us knew the other's language. But the Holy Spirit can translate a common language for us all. Outside the prison, this man was a street preacher ministering to the broken and the lost. Oh, how much this man must have been pleasing the Lord with everything he was doing! He did not pastor a big church, but God had a special role for him in the kingdom.

How you treat the least reveals the most. "'And the King will answer and say to them, "Truly I say to you, to the extent that you did it for one of the least of these brothers or sisters of Mine, you did it for Me"'" (Matthew 25:40 NASB).

Every time I met this man, the presence of Ruach Ha'Kodesh (the Holy Spirit) would increase ever higher. When you're under the anointing and meet another who is also under the anointing, there's a multiplication that takes place in the presence of the Holy Spirit. It's hardly explainable, but readily attainable—because all you must do is be there. It's the most incredible experience in the world to have the Holy Spirit at such a heightened level that you can hardly remain standing. No one can experience such a thing and ever forget it.

"And when they had prayed, the place where they were assembled together was shaken; and they were all filled with the Holy Spirit, and they spoke the word of God with boldness" (Acts 4:31 NKJV). *You know you're praying in the Spirit when even the building can't sit still.*

Be willing to be nothing before men so you can be everything for Yahweh Hoseenu (the LORD our maker) and all He is doing. If you want to be part of the remnant, you must abandon the idea that you'll be something before the masses. Be willing to let God take you where He chooses and use you for the kingdom in even the lowliest of ways. Be the least on earth, and you'll find that's exactly where heaven will help you the most.

Prayer

Father God, I want to be part of the remnant that's dedicated to You and given over to Your kingdom. Help me put away every ounce of my old person and take hold of the new person that You can help me become. Help me do this with all my determination.

Challenge

In every church I've gone to, in every ministry I've been part of, and in every part of the country where I've visited, I've found that there is a remnant. Sometimes, it has taken me a long time to find the remnant, but it's always there. You'll rarely find it among the popular or the proud; rather, it's hidden in the fringes, where they're pleasing to the Lord. Pray to the Lord to help you become the remnant and to find the remnant. Then trust Him on this journey.

Going further

Once you're in the remnant, even if you're the only one, then the Lord wants you to help other people find the remnant as well. This is different from evangelism, where we try to save the lost and introduce them to the Lord. It's reaching out to others who have faith but aren't yet going further with the Lord. You cannot convince someone that they need to go further, but you can find some who are ready to go further. These are the willing few who haven't yet found the way to go higher. Let your life be a light to those looking to go higher in their faith. *Be an example to others and leave the rest to God.* "For he raised us from the dead along with Christ and seated us with him in the heavenly realms because we are united with Christ Jesus. So God can point to us in all future ages as examples of the incredible wealth of his grace and kindness toward us, as shown in all he has done for us who are united with Christ Jesus" (Ephesians 2:6-7 NLT).

37

Ascension

*God has created us to
live higher than we do.*

"For I am Yahweh your God, so you must consecrate
yourselves and be holy because I am holy."
–Leviticus 11:44 HCSB

If you want a higher faith, you'll have to ascend higher
than where you are now. If you ask the Lord,
He will help you.

You can live a life higher than you are right now. You may be backsliding, flatlining, or barely growing in your faith, but that can change the moment you really want to change and are willing to let the Lord help you. All things are possible with our faith when we rely upon our God, in whom all things are possible.

Nothing is impossible for God, and it's to that height we should pray to. "But Jesus looked at them and said, 'With men it is impossible, but not with God; for with God all things are possible'" (Mark 10:27 NKJV).

You can start to make better choices than you have before. You can be faced with two choices, one which is easy and one which is right—and you'll make the right choice no matter what it might cost you. The greatest thing you'll learn is that making the right choices each day brings to your life an eternal reward that will last forever.

The sum of your life is all the choices you make. "'But if you refuse to serve the LORD, then choose today whom you will serve.... But as for me and my family, we will serve the LORD'" (Joshua 24:15 NLT).

When you stop striving in your power and start yielding to the Holy Spirit's power, your life will be changed forever. When you simply become weak before Him, He'll become strong in you, and you'll be able to accomplish more, because it's Him doing it in you.

Some people spend a lifetime striving to become what God can do for them in a day. "'Then the Spirit of the LORD will come upon you, and you will prophesy with them and be turned into another man'" (1 Samuel 10:6 NKJV).

You can be on good ground, from which good fruit can come from your life. You can produce wonderful fruit that's beneficial to those around you. As your life flourishes more, it will nourish more of everyone around you. Your life can be God's vessel to a dark and needy world.

The evidence of Christ in you is Christ through you. Yeshua HaMashiach (Jesus the Messiah) told us, "I am the vine, you are the branches; the one who remains in Me, and I in him bears much fruit, for apart from Me you can do nothing" (John 15:5 NASB).

When you surrender to Yahweh Sabaoth (the LORD of angelic armies), He will give you the victory in Christ that you've only dreamed you could have. This is a victory in His ability so there will be nothing you can be prideful about in achieving it. You'll only be grateful for His great mercy.

The secret of the victorious Christian life is that it's yours not to accomplish, but to surrender to. "But thanks be to God, who gives us the victory through our Lord Jesus Christ" (1 Corinthians 15:57 NKJV).

You can have a higher faith because God on high can lift you there. It's a life that's lowly and humble in the natural, but at the same time, high and lifted in the spiritual. The lower you're willing to go, the higher the Lord will lift you up.

To go higher in your faith, you must become lower in yourself. "Therefore humble yourselves [demote, lower yourselves in your own estimation] under the mighty hand of God, that in due time He may exalt you" (1 Peter 5:6 AMPC).

You can be as high in your faith as you want to be. You can be as close to Yahweh Shammah (the LORD is there) as you want to be. You can be as holy as you want to be. The only question is: Are you willing to pay the price? It's a small price on the scales of heaven. The price is the right to yourself.

If you want to be near to the Lord, it's up to you to make the first move. "Draw near to God and He will draw near to you" (James 4:8 NKJV).

When you're faced with choices here on earth, there are implications from the vantage point of heaven. You can go for higher ground and please the Lord, or you can do as you please, serving yourself. We'll take to heaven only those things we've done that are pleasing to the Lord here on earth.

Begin on good ground, then go for higher ground. "But you are a chosen race, a royal priesthood, a consecrated nation, a [special] people for God's own possession, so that you may proclaim the excellencies [the wonderful deeds and virtues and perfections] of Him who called you out of darkness into His marvelous light" (1 Peter 2:9 AMP).

In everything you do, go for higher ground. Ask God to help you. Let Yahweh Ezer (the Lord our helper) help you. Choose to desire to live a life pleasing to the Lord Jesus. Put your choices before the Lord Jesus Christ and ask Him to help you make them. When we ask with the right motives, the Lord answers and gives us the right direction.

You won't have to try so hard if you'll just pray for God to help you. "'There is no one like the God of Israel. He rides across the heavens to help you, across the skies in majestic splendor'" (Deuteronomy 33:26 NLT).

In my faith journey, I've experienced periods of drought with seemingly no ascension in my faith at all. I seemed to be walking on the flattest desert floor one could imagine, yet going nowhere, even though I was checking all the boxes and doing all the right things. This is real life. Don't let anyone tell you that their faith journey has been nothing but ascension at rapid rates; with things going so easy like that, how would a person be trained up by God? No, that's not the process God uses. We all must have our time in the wilderness. That's where He's preparing us for all that He'll have us become.

God has to send you back into the wilderness before you're ready to receive the promise. "'And you shall remember the whole way that the Lord your God has led you these forty years in the wilderness, that he might humble you, testing you to know what was in your heart, whether you would keep his commandments or not'" (Deuteronomy 8:2 ESV).

There are other times when I'm on the mountaintop and seeing visions one after the next, and it feels like I'm swimming in miracles. It's as if God is answering my every prayer and removing every obstacle standing before me. I'll be walking so deeply in the Spirit that I can feel the Holy Spirit moving in and through me. When I'm ministering to others, I will hear the Lord so clearly giving me what to say, and with confidence, I minister these words to them. These are the most blessed times, but they're short-lived, because the Lord will have us do most of our work and spend most of our time in the valley down below. The mountaintops are to inspire us to do the work down below. We're not meant to live on the mountaintop, only to visit there from time to time.

The height of your faith is measured not on the mountaintop, but on the valley floor below. The mountains may get the first rain, but the valleys are where the waters flow to. "Yes, even if I walk through the valley of the shadow of death, I will not be afraid of anything, because You are with me. You have a walking stick with which to guide and one with which to help. These comfort me" (Psalm 23:4 NLV).

Most often, I find myself in the valley, with the elevation rising before me as I approach the mountain up ahead. It's a slow and steady pace as the Lord leads me along a narrowing path that leads me to the higher faith. This is a greatly blessed place to be as a believer—not out in the wilderness, where sometimes we feel far from God, and not up on the mountaintop, where we only want to be with God and not be bothered with the work He would have us do. But the valley is where we're needed and where Adonai (the Lord) will use us if we're willing to be used by Him.

The lower the valley you're in, the higher the mountains that rise before you. "Who may climb the mountain of the LORD? Who may stand in his holy place? Only those whose hands and hearts are pure, who do not worship idols and never tell lies. They will receive the LORD's blessing and have a right relationship with God their savior" (Psalm 24:3-5 NLT).

Ascension is not done in one day and is not done in every area of your life at one time. Ascension is often painful and tiring, yet when you see how each step takes you higher, there's nothing you want more than to keep going. A slower ascension is better, because you can remain humble in yourself, which gives you that firm foundation that you'll not fall from a place higher than you're ready to be. We must grow in stages, and we must ascend over time so we can be strong yet humble for each new level we get to.

You cannot ascend spiritual mountains burdened by your natural self. "That you put off, concerning your former conduct, the old man which grows corrupt according to the deceitful lusts, and be renewed in the spirit of your mind, and that you put on the new man which was created according to God, in true righteousness and holiness" (Ephesians 4:22-24 NKJV).

Ascension never places us above others, because true spiritual ascension lowers us before Yahweh Tsidkenu (the LORD our righteousness) and His other children. Nobody standing tall with natural pride can ascend higher in the spiritual realm before God. Spiritual ascension brings us closer to God on high only because we're willing to go lower in ourselves. The lower we bow ourselves, the higher we can ascend. Be patient, because it always takes time to go to the next level.

The only way to ascend spiritually is to kneel down in the natural. "'He must become greater; I must become less'" (John 3:30 NIV).

Ascension is the path of humility and of sober self-reflection as we come to see just how much we need to be forgiven. The closer we are to the light, the brighter it shines, and the more it will show us the intricate details of our flaws. Yet in the light, we'll find something greater than we imagined—His mercy overflowing, and His grace so deep we can never reach the end. The more you ascend, the more you come to realize just how wonderful Yahweh 'Ori (the LORD our light) truly is. The closer we get to heaven, the further we are from the world and all the fleeting empty pleasures it has to offer.

It takes all the courage we can muster each day to dare look at the real person who stares back at us in the mirror. I always know a man or a woman who has done this, because they stop being so critical of others. "The LORD is

close to the brokenhearted and saves those who are crushed in spirit"
(Psalm 34:18 NIV).

Wherever you are in your faith, seek something higher. It's not by
your abilities or qualifications that you can ascend, but only by your
surrender and willingness to let Him help you. The higher we ascend,
the narrower the path will become. The narrow path is the only way
we can get there. We need it to be narrow, so that as we ascend to
higher levels we're careful to remain humble and obedient while we
get ever closer to the Lord.

*The hindrance to growing in your faith is the plans you make to do so.
You cannot ascend spiritual mountains walking on natural paths.* "'Don't
be afraid, for I am with you. Don't be discouraged, for I am your God.
I will strengthen you and help you. I will hold you up with my victorious right hand'" (Isaiah 41:10 NLT).

Prayer

Father God, help me ascend ever higher in my faith for no
other reason than my wanting to be near You. Keep me
humble along the way, and show me that only by Your
strength can I ever hope to ascend higher.

Challenge

List out reasons why you want to ascend higher spiritually. Be brutally
honest with yourself, knowing that God already knows. Stop thinking
you'll be disqualified for having a wrong motive, and just realize that
the Lord wants only to help those who are honest before Him with
their shortcomings. Mark each reason that would not pass the test
from Jesus Christ as a good reason to grow higher. Pray that the Lord
Jesus will help you overcome those wrong desires.

Going further

Begin your ascension. How do you do that? One step at a time. Choose today to begin, then start to make choices that will help you along on your journey. Say yes to God and no to the world whenever there's a choice between the two. Get down on your knees, and you'll be making an upward motion in your faith. Don't tell one soul on this earth what you're doing; just keep it between you and God. Pray each day that He will help you, then keep track of all the ways that He does. God always answers prayers that are in His will, so long as you're willing to obey His leading. *It takes God's power both to get you in His will and to keep you there.* "Yes, it is God who is working in you. He helps you want to do what pleases him, and he gives you the power to do it" (Philippians 2:13 ERV).

38

Seven Levels of
Overcoming

The Holy Spirit convicts you of sin,
then helps you overcome it.

Jesus promised us, "When the Helper (the Holy Spirit) comes, He will show the world the truth about sin. He will show the world about being right with God. And He will show the world what it is to be guilty. He will show the world about sin, because they do not put their trust in Me [Jesus]." – John 16:8-9 NLV

As you grow higher in your faith, you'll find that it's Yahweh Chereb (the LORD the sword) who is helping you overcome all the obstacles that stand before you.

I always ask the Lord what to preach or write about. He always gives me direction. I wait and wait until He does. Several years ago, Yahweh Qadosh (the Holy One) led me to preach a message on holiness. The Lord's great call for us all is to live holy lives. I had spent a few days preparing this message. The day I was going to preach the message, I was in prayer, and the Holy Spirit brought to my mind this question: Why should we preach to live holy lives? Then the Lord gave me the phrase "he who overcomes." This phrase is in the book of Revelation, and so I searched for all the places it was written. It is included as a message to each of the seven churches in Revelation chapters 2 and 3.

The Holy Spirit is so precious in bringing to our remembrance the things of the Lord. Then He brings greater revelation. We can sometimes be a little clever in our planning, but He can always be revelatory in His surprises. As I read those verses in Revelation about overcoming, I immediately saw something I hadn't seen before, and it became the crescendo of the message I preached that evening. We can discover some things in the Word with our clever little minds, or through the discoveries of others, but it takes the Holy Spirit of El Elyon (God Most High) to bring us a revelation we haven't seen before.

The secret to revelation in God's Word is that it cannot be found by you, only revealed to you. Revelation comes not by the efforts of man, but by the power of God. The Lord cannot reveal a new thing until you first have eyes to see it. Pray to the Lord, "Open my eyes that I may see wonderful things in your law" (Psalm 119:18 NIV).

I'm convinced that the effort of a saint preaching a thousand words produces so little when compared to a single word spoken by the power of Ruach Ha'Kodesh (the Holy Spirit). If we spent more time seeking power from the Holy Spirit, we would see more change in those we speak to. We spend too much time operating in our own power and not enough time kneeling broken before God so He can pour out His strength and wisdom through us.

The problem with most sermons is that they're born out of the tomb of men's offices and not from the life of the Holy Spirit within them. "And when they had prayed, the place where they were meeting together was shaken [a sign of God's presence]; and they were all filled with the Holy Spirit and began to speak the word of God with boldness and courage" (Acts 4:31 AMP).

In Revelation 2–3, Yeshua HaMashiach (Jesus the Messiah) is giving a word to the seven churches. For each church, the Lord praised the church where it was praiseworthy, admonished it where this was needed, then called each one to overcome. We must remember this when we're being disciplined by the Lord—it's not to put us down but to raise us up to who we're supposed to be. We must learn to let His words to these churches be the words we hear from Him regularly over our own lives.

Jesus rebuked His disciples not to put them down, but to draw them up. Jesus said, "I correct and punish those whom I love. So be eager to do right. Change your hearts and lives" (Revelation 3:19 ICB).

As the Holy Spirit led me, I focused on the verses for each of the seven churches that mentioned what would happen if they overcame some obstacle specific to that church. As I was reading through these seven verses, it was the answer to my question about why we should teach about living holy lives. What's the benefit of overcoming in this life we're in? Why shouldn't we just simply rest in His grace instead of desiring to be holy? The answer is this: Yahweh Hashopet (the Lord our judge) commands us to be holy, period.

Jesus didn't just come to save you from your sin but to give you the power (with the Holy Spirit) to overcome your sin. "He saved us through the washing that made us new people. He saved us by making us new through the Holy Spirit" (Titus 3:5 ERV).

Consider that everything you do has eternal implications for all that you'll have in heaven. How you live now will impact you for all eternity. It's never wrong to seek to live a more holy life, but it's a dangerous thing to be taught a grace message that would encourage otherwise. We're saved by grace to then be sanctified by the Holy Spirit, so that by His power within us we live a holy life.

The Lord Jesus taught, "Therefore you shall be perfect, just as your Father in heaven is perfect" (Matthew 5:48 NKJV). Jesus always means what He says. It matters what you do. Seek to live holy lives.

Father God promised to put His Spirit within us, enabling us to live holy lives. "I will put my Spirit inside you and cause you to live by my laws, respect my rulings and obey them" (Ezekiel 36:27 CJB). The only ones who preach that we don't need to strive to live holy lives are the ones who serve the devil. We're not saved by our works, but the result of salvation will be our works.

We must lose the idea that living holy lives is like a light switch, where either we are or we're not, and there's no in-between. The higher faith is where holiness is found, and the path there is with levels of progression. We mustn't get discouraged along the way in how we're failing, but simply fall to our knees and pray that Yahweh Raah (the LORD is my shepherd) will take us higher. Progression in spiritual matters comes from your natural surrender and a sincere willingness in your heart to be changed by Him. Never give up on your journey, because the Lord will surely never give up in trying to help you.

The following paragraphs are what the Lord led me to preach on that evening many years ago, as He revealed to me the seven levels of overcoming.

Overcoming, Level One: To the first church, Jesus said, "To him who overcomes I will give to eat from the tree of life, which is in the midst of the Paradise of God" (Revelation 2:7 NKJV). Level one is salvation, leading to your eternal life in heaven. This is free; all you must do is accept Jesus as your Lord. This is more than simply going to the altar once and calling yourself a Christian. This is *being* a Christian. If you do nothing else in your life, make sure you get this right. Get right with God and give your life to Christ so He can make you into something new. Stop trying to get away with what you can and only hope you make it to heaven. If you gave your life to Christ, live a life that proves it.

Overcoming, Level Two: To the second church, Jesus said, "He who overcomes shall not be hurt by the second death" (Revelation 2:11 NKJV). Level two is higher: you get salvation, which prevents the second death, the spiritual death. And you don't get hurt; you have good works that pass through the fire of judgment, and so you reach a higher level in heaven. There are some who'll get to heaven by the skin of their teeth, and all their self-promoting deeds on earth will be worth nothing as they enter heaven. They'll regret having given up so much in heaven for such little gain they thought they were getting on earth. It's not what man sees on the outside that Jesus Christ will measure, but the motives on the inside. What you do matters, and why you do it matters infinitely more. The genuineness of your life will someday be revealed. What will your life show? It's never too late to change.

Overcoming, Level Three: To the third church, Jesus said, "To him who overcomes I will give some of the hidden manna to eat. And I will give him a white stone, and on the stone a new name written which no one knows except him who receives it" (Revelation 2:17 NKJV). Level three is higher—you have intimacy with the Lord, sharing in the manna and being rewarded with a new heavenly name that describes your faith and your purpose. You're nearer to the Lord. We're not meant to barely make it into heaven, but to arrive at a higher level in our faith so the Lord will bless us. The greatest blessing is to be nearer to the Lord, and that's as true here on earth as it will be in heaven. What are you holding on to that doesn't belong in His presence?

Overcoming, Level Four: To the fourth church, Jesus said, "And he who overcomes, and keeps My works until the end, to him I will give power over the nations" (Revelation 2:26 NKJV). Level four is higher: because of your great faithfulness to do what the Lord directed you to do on earth, you're being entrusted to be a ruler for Christ in heaven. You not only are nearer to the Lord, but you're trusted by Him. He knows you'll follow His commands, and so He places you in a greater position of trust. You have a position of authority given by the Lord Himself. The Lord will test you in the littlest things on earth to see if He can trust you with the bigger things in heaven. What matters is not how big the things are that you do on earth, but whether you're doing what He led you to do. It's not enough that you trust the Lord, but can He trust you?

Overcoming, Level Five: To the fifth church, Jesus said, "He who overcomes shall be clothed in white garments, and I will not blot out his name from the Book of Life; but I will confess his name before My Father and before His angels" (Revelation 3:5 NKJV). Level five is higher. Because of your devotion and holiness, you're being brought closer to the Father and presented before the angelic armies in heaven. Jesus will tell our Father of your faithfulness and devotion while you were on earth. You may think all you do goes unnoticed, but Christ is watching, and Christ will testify of your hidden deeds here on earth. Keep pressing into all you're doing, in your prayers and your actions, because the Lord sees it all. Are you living a life of faithfulness that Jesus can see?

Overcoming, Level Six: To the sixth church, Jesus said, "He who overcomes, I will make him a pillar in the temple of My God, and he shall go out no more" (Revelation 3:12 NKJV). Level six is still higher. Because of your higher walk on earth and your faithfulness to the Word, you're now serving in the holiest of temples in heaven. You not only get nearer to the Lord, but you stay there with Him. The Lord won't measure you by whatever high position you had in the church here on earth but on how lowly and humble you were before Him and before others. The higher faith is the lower posture that allows the Lord to work through you. Are you living a life of humility?

Overcoming, Level Seven: To the seventh church, Jesus said, "To him who overcomes I will grant to sit with Me on My throne, as

I also overcame and sat down with My Father on His throne" (Revelation 3:21 NKJV). This is the highest level, in which the Lord has you sitting right next to Him. What a glorious thing we should hope for—to be sitting so near to our Lord Jesus! This is completeness. This is the perfection of our faith. This is the highest faith. When Jesus is the highest in our life, we'll be the highest in our faith. Never think it takes a great saint to make it there, but a humble one who has given their life completely to the Lord. Have you surrendered all to Jesus Christ in your life?

Let us pray for one another that we "stand perfect and complete in all the will of God" (Colossians 4:12 NKJV). You don't reach the higher levels by your effort, but by surrendering yourself to the Lord, so the Spirit of Christ will reign in you.

Prayer

Lord Jesus, help me overcome every obstacle that stands between me and You. Help me have the strength and the willpower to press upward in my faith so that it grows higher every day. Let me not be complacent with where I am, but always yield to You so I can go higher.

Challenge

Write down the things in your life that the Lord has helped you to overcome. Consider how you once thought you'd never be able to overcome these things. Now, write down the next list, which is all those areas of your life where you haven't yet overcome. You might even be thinking these are things you cannot overcome—and you're right, at least so long as you're trying on your own. For each thing, pray to the Lord that He will help you overcome it. As you grow higher in your faith, you'll cross off all these things on your list. But then there's a whole other level you'll discover that needs to be overcome. Christian, get your boots on; it's going to be a journey.

Going further

Consider the day when you'll go to heaven. You'll be judged by your deeds and rewarded based on what you've done. Pray to the Lord right now and ask Him to show you what you need to stop doing and what you need to start doing. Don't worry about the logistics of how these things will happen; just let the Lord judge you now versus waiting for later. Then ask yourself, based on the eternal consequences of what you do here on earth, if you're ready to let the Lord change you. If your answer of yes is sincere, He'll start changing you this very day. Speak life, and God will give it to you. *Your words lay down the path that you'll walk down.* "A man's stomach will be satisfied with the fruit of his mouth; he will be satisfied with the consequence of his words. Death and life are in the power of the tongue, and those who love it and indulge it will eat its fruit and bear the consequences of their words" (Proverbs 18:20-21 AMP).

39

Heaven

Whatever doesn't belong in heaven
doesn't belong in you.

Since, then, you have been raised with Christ, set your hearts on
things above, where Christ is, seated at the right hand of God.
Set your minds on things above, not on earthly things.
—Colossians 3:1-2 NIV

As you go higher in your faith, you will reach into heaven
and bring those things from above into your life and
into the lives of those around you.

Throughout Scripture, we find progression as the theme for how our faith should grow ever higher. There may be times when we flatline and perhaps even backslide. These are the times that Yahweh Mekoddishkem (the Lord who sanctifies you) uses to teach us and to help us get back on our feet and go even higher. Never despair in your failures, but press ahead, knowing the Lord will come and help you.

Stop thinking you've fallen from grace when you've landed right in the middle of it. "Let us then fearlessly and confidently and boldly draw near to the throne of grace (the throne of God's unmerited favor to us sinners), that we may receive mercy [for our failures] and find grace to help in good time for every need [appropriate help and well-timed help, coming just when we need it]" (Hebrews 4:16 AMPC).

The higher faith is a greater intimacy between you and the Lord Jesus Christ. This intimacy was portrayed in the natural with the marriage between a man and a woman. It's an example for us in progressing in our faith and our intimacy with the Lord Jesus. Before the natural marriage, the couple came to know each other, and then grew in their love for one another. They held hands and felt time standing still, and a kiss on the cheek felt like a dream coming true. Their relationship grew ever more intimate with each passing day.

Marriage is the earthly natural pattern for your heavenly spiritual relationship with the Lord Jesus Christ. It's the most intimate union with no natural bloodlines, one that establishes a spiritual bond never meant to be broken. "And hasn't he made [them] one [flesh] in order to have spiritual blood-relatives?.... Take heed to your spirit, and don't break faith with the wife of your youth" (Malachi 2:15 CJB).

The higher faith is the spiritual reflection of the natural marriage here on earth. It's the heavenly marriage between the groom, Yeshua HaMashiach (Jesus the Messiah) in heaven, and His bride, those faithful few here on earth. The spiritual intimacy with the Lord Jesus is infinitely deeper than the physical intimacy we have in our earthly marriages. It's a spiritual bond that's always perfectly pure and holy. It goes deep into the spiritual realm, and lasts forever. The natural is always a dim reflection of the spiritual.

There's always preparation before the marriage. The bride must get herself ready for the groom. "The [Holy] Spirit and the bride (the church, believers) say, 'Come.' And let the one who hears say, 'Come.' And let the one who is thirsty come; let the one who wishes take and drink the water of life without cost. He who testifies and affirms these things says, 'Yes, I am coming quickly.' Amen. Come, Lord Jesus" (Revelation 22:17,20 AMP).

Another progression of faith is with the design of the Tabernacle. The Tabernacle is an image of the levels of intimacy with the Lord. The outer court was for those who knew about the Lord but had not yet met Him up close. The inner court, or the Holy Place, was where the table of showbread was found, which represented the person of Jesus Christ, the bread of life. The Holy Place is also where the lampstand was found, representing the Holy Spirit. In the Holy Place, your intimacy with the Lord Jesus and the Holy Spirit is greater and deeper than ever before.

Drawing near to the Lord is an act of the heart and not of the mind, because intimacy is founded on love. "'Then I will give them a heart to know Me, that I am the LORD; and they shall be My people, and I will be their God, for they shall return to Me with their whole heart'" (Jeremiah 24:7 NKJV).

A veil separated the Holy Place from the Holy of Holies, which is where the presence of the Father was found. Here, in the heavenly Tabernacle, Jesus stepped in to sprinkle His precious blood on the mercy seat so we could live forever. This is where the Ark of the Covenant was kept secure, and the tablets of the Law of God were kept within. The tablets are the treasure of God's love letter to mankind, kept for all eternity. Those who enter the Holy of Holies have entered the most intimate place of all.

His perfect mercy covers the law you could never fulfill. The Lord said, "You shall put the mercy seat on top of the ark, and in the ark you shall put the Testimony [the law] that I will give you" (Exodus 25:21 NKJV). *Notice where mercy sits in relation to the Law—the mercy seat covers the Law.*

You can either be under the law or under the mercy of Jesus, His own blood sprinkled onto His mercy seat. "But Christ came.... With His own blood He entered the Most Holy Place once for all" (Hebrews 9:11-12 NKJV).

Another example of progressing in faith is found in the Beatitudes found in Matthew 5. The Beatitudes are the ladder of faith we should aspire to climb. Each beatitude takes us higher and nearer to the Lord. We start out by coming to Him as paupers, poor in ourselves and relying completely on Him. And the final level is that we gladly receive persecution, knowing it's there so that we'll always be nearest to our Lord. To the degree the world is against us, we know we're closer to Him.

The more clearly you see yourself, the more clearly you see God. The Lord Jesus taught, "Blessed are the poor in spirit, for theirs is the kingdom of heaven" (Matthew 5:3 NKJV).

We must remember that our destination is heaven, and in heaven our journey will be told. We're not meant to live a half-baked and meager Christian life on earth but to live each day with the thought of heaven on our minds in choosing all that we do. Heaven is more real than your life right now because it's not distorted by the deceptions of your heart. Let the Lord Jesus show you what it means to be in heaven, and you'll surely live a different kind of life here on earth.

Look forward to heaven more than you fear the things inbetween. "But we are looking forward to God's promise of new heavens and a new earth afterwards, where there will be only goodness" (2 Peter 3:13 TLB).

When our eyes are fixed on heaven, we'll stop worrying so much about what we look like here on earth. Natural looks will blind us from spiritual truths. Natural appearances are a deception of what's really true. As we progress higher in our faith, our looks will take a lower importance in our lives. We must remember that in God's eyes, we're all beautiful. He designed you, and you can be sure He is well pleased with what He has made.

What you see as flaws in yourself are the beauty marks of God. "You made all the delicate, inner parts of my body and knit me together in my mother's womb. Thank you for making me so wonderfully complex! Your workmanship is marvelous—how well I know it. You watched me as I was being formed in utter seclusion, as I was woven together in the dark of the womb" (Psalm 139:13-15 NLT).

You're so beautiful to Yahweh Hoseenu (the LORD our maker). He designed you, formed you, and shaped you into who you are today. I pray that you'll learn to see yourself as God sees you. He sees His own image reflected in you. Don't look at your natural image but at your spiritual one, so you can see what El Roi (the God who sees me) is looking at. So long as you focus on your natural looks, your true image won't change. "But we all...are being transformed into the same image from glory to glory, just as by the Spirit of the Lord" (2 Corinthians 3:18 NKJV).

Don't agonize over what you look like; but who you are. Stop trying to please man and instead seek to please God. You're not called to become like the image of man, but of Christ. "For whom He foreknew, He also predestined to be conformed to the image of His Son" (Romans 8:29 NKJV).

I had a vision one night that I was in heaven. The vision lasted only a minute or two, as best as I could measure time while in eternity. It was so perfectly light there, a supernatural light, a glory light—not blinding or glaring, but a light so complete that no shadows could form and no darkness could be present.

There was a large open fire in a giant bowl-shaped structure. The bowl was at least ten feet tall and twenty feet across or more. The bowl was filled with orange flames that illuminated the surrounding courtyard with color. I remember thinking that I didn't expect there to be fire in heaven, yet we know that fire reveals what is true and good.

Next to the large bowl of fire were large vase-like objects that were also at least ten feet tall, each with a diameter of about seven feet. I was very near one of them.

These large vases were made with a metal-like substance having a color like pure-white gold mixed with silver. The color was so brilliant, I couldn't begin to describe it. The vases appeared to be perfectly clear, though I couldn't see through them because they had reflective surfaces. The material of these vases seemed to be liquid, with an appearance of being wet yet held together. The surfaces were perfectly polished so that every reflection could be seen. There was not a single scratch or blemish on the surface.

Then, in a split second, it happened—I saw one glimpse of myself in my reflection off the vase. At that moment, I saw myself as I'm seen in heaven by El Yeshuati (the God of my salvation). I was beautiful and pure. I was loved and at peace. I was perfect in His eyes. I was a treasure in His heart. There was nothing imperfect or ugly in me anymore. It was me in heaven.

"For our citizenship is in heaven, from which we also eagerly wait for the Savior, the Lord Jesus Christ, who will transform our lowly body that it may be conformed to His glorious body" (Philippians 3:20-21 NKJV).

It was a single moment within a vision that pointed to an eternal reality in heaven. What matters is not how I see myself on earth, but my reflection in heaven that shows how Christ Jesus will see me forever. That's what El Hanan (the gracious God) has in store for you and me. Don't miss out on the plot for your life story, which is you in heaven.

You're an eternal creature, designed in the image of God. "So God created man in His own image; in the image of God He created him; male and female He created them" (Genesis 1:27 NKJV).

The more of Christ Jesus there is in you, the more His image will be seen in you. "We shall also bear the image of the heavenly Man" (1 Corinthians 15:49 NKJV).

You're an image bearer, and that image is Jesus. "Put on the new man who is renewed in knowledge according to the image of Him who created him" (Colossians 3:10 NKJV).

The progression of our faith to something higher is nothing less than being transformed into the likeness of Jesus Christ. Not that you'll look exactly like Him, but you'll be more like Him. Not that you'll rise to His position, but He will raise you up higher toward His likeness, His holiness, His love, His humility, and His everlasting compassion for others. The higher faith is being filled up higher with the likeness of Christ forming within you.

The Lord wants more for you than you're yet taking hold of. "Not that I have already obtained it [this goal of being Christlike] or have already been made perfect, but I actively press on so that I may take hold of that [perfection] for which Christ Jesus took hold of me and made me His own" (Philippians 3:12 AMP).

Never forget that someday you'll be in heaven. You'll see your reflection there, and El Rachum (the God of compassion and mercy) will show you exactly how He sees you. You'll see what you'll look like forever. Perhaps He'll give you a brief preview as He did for me. Or perhaps He is building up an even greater faith in you that you won't even have to see, and yet you'll still believe. Let God take you higher, and let Him choose the path in which He'll get you there.

Prayer

Father God, someday I'll be in heaven, and everything will become so much clearer. Help me now to understand more, so that I live a life here on earth that's pleasing to You. I want to be with You in heaven, but I will faithfully serve You until then here on earth.

Challenge

There are two extremes with our self-image. Either we think we're so much better than we really are, or we think too little of ourselves, not realizing how much the Lord values us. What the Father wants from us is to be satisfied with the value He has placed on us, in which He loved us so much that He sent His Son to die for us. Write down those things about you that you think the Lord loves about you. When you finish this list, read these verses: "How precious are your thoughts about me, O God. They cannot be numbered! I can't even count them; they outnumber the grains of sand!" (Psalm 139:17-18 NLT).

Going further

Write down what you think heaven will be like. Write down the names of the people you pray will be there—people whose salvation you pray for with all your heart. Write down other things that you pray the Lord will give you when you get to heaven, like healing or deliverance or anything that you think would be wonderful. (I've prayed that all my animals will be there.) Now consider that your heavenly Father loves you eternally and infinitely and has higher plans for you than you have yet to imagine. *The closer you get to heaven, the less you worry about the things of this world.* "'He will wipe every tear from their eyes, and there will be no more death or sorrow or crying or pain. All these things are gone forever'" (Revelation 21:4 NLT).

40

The Higher Faith

The higher your faith, the more humble you'll be.

For thus says the High and Lofty One who inhabits eternity, whose name is Holy: "I dwell in the high and holy place, with him who has a contrite and humble spirit." —Isaiah 57:15 NKJV

As you go higher in your faith, you'll find out how wonderful it is when Yahweh Shammah (the LORD is there) fills you with His presence, and your life becomes blessed in ways you never imagined.

When I was starting out in my Christian life, I used to think the higher faith would entail living a higher life of holiness and having a higher knowledge of the things of God. But what I found is that the higher faith is something far greater than our individual holiness and far deeper than our intellectual understanding of the things of God.

You cannot go mining for spiritual truth using the tools of your natural mind. Intellectualism can be an obstacle to spiritual understanding. The wisdom of man is foolishness to God, and the wisdom of God is foolishness to man. "But people who aren't spiritual can't receive these truths from God's Spirit. It all sounds foolish to them and they can't understand it, for only those who are spiritual can understand what the Spirit means" (1 Corinthians 2:14 NLT).

This doesn't mean we shouldn't be sanctified as we progress in our faith, because a man or woman given over to Yeshua HaMashiach (Jesus the Messiah) will be formed by Him into something more holy. But that's not the higher faith; it's merely a byproduct of what happens to us as we're ascending in our faith. If we make our personal holiness the goal, our goal has more to do with us than it does with Jesus. As we climb that self-righteous ladder, we'll begin to swell with pride and start judging those who we think are far below us. But if we keep our eyes on Jesus, His life in us will result in His holiness through us. Jesus is the higher faith.

The higher faith is always counter to the desires of the flesh. "But I say, walk by the Spirit, and you will not carry out the desire of the flesh. For the desire of the flesh is against the Spirit, and the Spirit against the flesh; for these are in opposition to one another, in order to keep you from doing whatever you want" (Galatians 5:16-17 NASB).

We should be growing in wisdom so that we not only know how to live, but also live what we know, and then teach others to do the same. Learning doctrines is never the goal, only a stepping stone toward living them out. It's better to know a little and live a lot than to know it all and live out very little. The higher faith doesn't require a higher intellect, but it does require a surrendered heart before El Shaddai (God Almighty). We must learn that the higher faith is measured by what we do and not by what we know.

The carnal Christian argues doctrines, whereas the spiritual Christian lives them. "But avoid foolish disputes, genealogies, contentions, and strivings about the law; for they are unprofitable and useless" (Titus 3:9 NKJV).

I used to see those that were highest in the church and imagined that they were highest in the faith. While that can sometimes be true, it's often far from true. Sadly, the same methods used to succeed in the world are the same methods used to succeed in many churches, and that's why we find so much worldliness in many church leaders. We must use heavenly methods to reach spiritual heights. If we want to have Christians growing higher in their faith, we need leaders who can help lead the way.

We don't need a new way but to return to the old. To solve twenty-first-century problems, we need the Holy Spirit power that the first-century church experienced. "And they chose Stephen, a man full of faith and the Holy Spirit" (Acts 6:5 NKJV).

The higher faith is not elusive, but is clearly held up for all to see in Holy Scripture. It's spoken of in a hundred ways in terms that are easily understood, yet most of us pass them by without even looking.

The higher faith is not complicated and is readily available to anyone wanting to walk in it. Jesus didn't pick the best—He equipped the least with the best. Don't worry about your position in the world or the church, for El Elyon (God Most High) can bring you higher in your faith regardless of how low others perceive you to be.

The Lord doesn't make you higher—He takes you higher. "Whoever exalts himself [with haughtiness and empty pride] shall be humbled (brought low), and whoever humbles himself [whoever has a modest opinion of himself and behaves accordingly] shall be raised to honor" (Matthew 23:12 AMPC).

The higher faith will put us in a place of greater revelation, but the revelations are not the higher faith. The higher faith isn't necessarily knowing the highest things, but simply living a faith in lowliness and simplicity with a genuine love toward others. As we live a lower life before God, He'll entrust us with higher things. We can be so blessed in receiving revelations so long as we don't worship them. Instead, we should worship the Lord in lowliness and humility and thank Him for all He has shown us.

Lowliness is godliness in its highest form. "Live in harmony with one another. Do not be haughty, but associate with the lowly. Never be wise in your own sight" (Romans 12:16 ESV).

The higher faith loves El Yeshuatenu (the God of our salvation) and loves others. The higher faith treats people with kindness and respect. It has compassion for those who are hurting and tries to understand those who are unkind to us. The higher faith means we have a higher respect and love for all humanity, both the saved and the lost. The higher faith thinks of self the least and of others the most.

The Christian faith is not complicated—people are. Just love others. "If you love others, you have done all that the Law demands" (Romans 13:8 CEV).

The higher faith is more interested in winning souls than in winning arguments. It's willing to be seen as weak by others so long as it's living right before God. In the higher faith, pride has melted away and revealed a meekness and humility that can be fully appreciated only in heaven. The world will mock such a soul as this, but God is smiling down upon them.

I would rather win a soul than an argument. "Give no offense...just as I also please all men in all things, not seeking my own profit, but the profit of many, that they may be saved" (1 Corinthians 10:32-33 NKJV).

The higher faith wants to spend more time with Yahweh Qadosh (the Holy One) and waste less time on the things of this world. There'll be a realization of the profit in giving, and of the loss when we selfishly horde. Pouring out will come naturally, because it's being done supernaturally. Scarcity will no longer be a worry, because the abundance of God is always more than we need.

Givers always have plenty, and takers never have enough. "One who gives to the poor will never lack anything, but one who shuts his eyes will have many curses" (Proverbs 28:27 NASB).

The higher faith discovers that mountaintop experiences are more about filling up for the journey than they are about being a final destination. The mountaintops are where we see the Lord Jesus in His glory, but the valleys below are where we serve Him for the kingdom. In the higher faith, we'll run down the mountain into the valley to serve the Lord Jesus with the same eager anticipation as when we were climbing up the mountain to go see Him.

The life of a saint is not having more mountaintop experiences, but bringing more mountaintop experiences into the valley they live in. You cannot always bring people to Jesus, so bring Jesus to the people. You cannot illuminate the darkness if you remain only in the light. "Make your light shine, so others will see the good you do and will praise your Father in heaven" (Matthew 5:16 CEV). The message you preach is the life you live. Live a holy life.

One attribute of someone with the higher faith is the presence of humility and gentleness as they speak with you. They have a higher knowledge, yet have a genuine desire to hear what your thoughts are. They don't look for opportunities to correct you or teach down to you. You'll learn invaluable lessons from such special souls as these, because the way they are is the lesson they teach.

You won't have a higher faith so long as your goal is to elevate yourself. "Humble yourselves [with an attitude of repentance and insignificance] in the presence of the Lord, and He will exalt you [He will lift you up, He will give you purpose]" (James 4:10 AMP).

Another attribute of someone with the higher faith is their measure of selflessness. As you get to know them, you find they're more interested in getting to know you than in putting themselves on display to be seen by you. Though they walk so high, they kneel so low as they come alongside you. They never look down on you, and yet they're always lifting you higher. You won't feel small sitting next to them, though you'll sense how high they really are.

The higher your faith, the less you'll look down on others. "Don't do anything from selfish ambition or from a cheap desire to boast, but be humble toward one another, always considering others better than yourselves" (Philippians 2:3 GNT).

In my life, I've been highly blessed to meet some of God's special servants who have walked in the higher faith. They modeled for me what a higher faith means. I've met far too many of these godly saints to list them all here, so I'll select a few precious souls who've gone on before us to heaven, where they're now with the Lord.

Don't be surprised that the higher faith from heaven has a lower standing here on earth. "Since you were brought back to life with Christ, focus on the things that are above—where Christ holds the highest position. Keep your mind on things above, not on worldly things" (Colossians 3:1-2 NOG).

One person I knew who exemplified the higher faith was Chaplain Jon Wetterholm. He was a hospital chaplain who touched lives everywhere he went. I met him in a Bible study group and immediately felt the genuineness of his spirit. As I grew spiritually, I came to see that Jon was walking at a higher level than most Christians I'd met. Yet Jon was as humble and kind to me as anyone has ever been. His wisdom flowed out with the words he spoke, but was made more evident in the way he listened to me. Jon spoke to me as a friend. The higher your faith, the less you'll talk down to others.

Jon had always wanted a Harley-Davidson motorcycle. Because of this, he was always quite interested to hear about my adventures on my Harley. I remember telling him one day how I had to sin to get to a prison ministry on time while riding my motorcycle. He put his arm around me, and with sparkling eyes, he asked me, "And just how fast were you sinning?" Oh, how I love it when Christians show me grace! I sure miss him.

The more you accept people as they are, the greater your influence will be to change them. "In your hearts honor Christ the Lord as holy, always being prepared to make a defense to anyone who asks you for a reason for the hope that is in you; yet do it with gentleness and respect" (1 Peter 3:15 ESV).

Another man who walked in a higher faith was Dennis Swick. He had been a missionary in Spain until he was diagnosed with brain cancer, and they sent him back home for treatment. He never returned to Spain, but praise God, back home, he helped to start a Spanish church. I also met Dennis at a Bible study group. We're so blessed when we gather with other believers.

Dennis had an incredible mind, yet you knew it only if you were ready to be poured into by him. Though he was so smart, he had a simple understanding of the things of God. He never tried to teach down to you; he came alongside you and shared in your faith journey. I was so moved by the fact that his faith was unwavering while his health declined. He told me he knew all too well that God could heal him, and that was enough.

As brilliant as Dennis was, he never acted like it. As we talked about a subject, he would ask me what I thought, then quietly listen to me. I didn't know much, but what I was learning from him was what I needed to know, which was how to minister to people instead of trying to impress them. Dennis was genuine, and that's an attribute found in anyone walking in the higher faith.

The higher faith has more to do with your attitude than your intellect. "Let your gentle spirit [your graciousness, unselfishness, mercy, tolerance, and patience] be known to all people. The Lord is near" (Philippians 4:5 AMP).

With Jon and Dennis, I was learning from men who had an incredible knowledge of theology but walked in the simple path of godly men. They're both in heaven now, having completed their tasks from God here on earth. I'm certain they'll be recognized in heaven for their genuine and simple higher faith that God longs for us all to have. The higher faith is not to be puffed up, but to lift Him up. When walking in the higher faith, we don't try to impress people, but our humility will make an enduring impression upon them. Heaven welcomes such souls as these. Your heavenly Father wants you to be one of these precious souls.

Praise God that He won't always heal us, that we'll perish and go to heaven. "For this world is not our home; we are looking forward to our everlasting home in heaven" (Hebrews 13:14 TLB).

Don't make your faith more complicated than this: Love God and love others. That's the highest faith we can have, and the highest faith that Yahweh Ezer (the LORD our helper) will help us get to, if only we're willing to let Him. Nothing on earth and no power in heaven will satisfy your eternal soul except Jesus Christ alone. When that is true in your life, people will see it.

Keep your faith simple. Love God and love others. "'Teacher, which commandment is the greatest in Moses' Teachings?' Yeshua answered him, '"Love the Lord your God with all your heart, with all your soul, and with all your mind." This is the greatest and most important commandment. The second is like it: "Love your neighbor as you love yourself"'" (Matthew 22:36-39 NOG).

The higher faith is when you see just how high Jesus Christ is and surrender yourself to Him. When you fill your life with Him, that's when you find the highest faith. It is yours not to gain, but to surrender to. My prayer is that you'll surrender to Jesus Christ. The Lord Jesus is praying for you right now. All you have to do is take one step into the higher faith, then keep going, and keep trusting Him to help you along the way.

The higher faith is not from knowing more but trusting more. "Trust in Him at all times, you people; pour out your heart before Him; God is a refuge for us" (Psalm 62:8 NKJV).

Prayer

Lord Jesus, help me walk in a humble and simple faith that seeks only to love You deeper and to love other people genuinely. Show me where I'm off, and help me get on track, so my life will be a blessing to those around me.

Challenge

Write out a declaration for your life, signing over to the Lord the right to yourself. This will be your declaration of dependence (not independence), where you're letting go once and for all, throwing caution to the wind, and giving your whole life to Jesus. In this declaration, commit yourself completely to the Lord so His life will reign in yours, with your life as a sacrifice to Him. Be daring enough to pin this declaration up where others in your life can see it. And be daring enough to actually do it.

Going further

Growing higher in your faith is not a one-and-done experience but an ever-progressing change in your life. Be brutally honest with yourself about who you really are and where you really are. If you can do this, the Lord will continue to change you. Make it your pledge to remain pliable in the hands of the Almighty God. Know that you'll never reach the end of what God can do for you, and that's why He has reserved all eternity in which to work on you. With His help, you can reach the higher faith.

There's nothing impossible for God—not even you.

"'Nothing is impossible for God!'" (Luke 1:37 CEV).

Conclusion

Child of God, the Lord wants to take you so much higher. I encourage you to be patient along the way, but to never become complacent with where you are. It doesn't matter whether other people know that you're progressing, but if you are progressing, this will be impossible for you to hide. The greatest thing you can do for the Lord is to give Him your life in which He can reign. When Christ fills a man or woman, they'll be serving the Lord to the fullest.

[God's best for you is found when you're living your best for God.]
Let us not become weary in doing good, for at the proper time we will reap a harvest if we do not give up. – Galatians 6:9 NIV

Don't mistake this book as being a singular track of progressing from chapter one all the way to chapter forty, and once you've made it to the end, you're finally done. Your faith journey will never be done. The process may progress in the manner described in this book, but that will be only the first round for the believer willing to go on with God. Then it will all begin again, at a deeper level, and the process will begin anew in the life of a saint. The Lord will plop you back down in chapter one. Then it must all begin anew at an entirely new level. Let the Lord take you from level to level, knowing He'll never steer you down the wrong way.

When it comes to growing higher in your faith, there's no conclusion. "Grow [spiritually mature] in the grace and knowledge of our Lord and Savior Jesus Christ. To Him be glory (honor, majesty, splendor), both now and to the day of eternity. Amen" (2 Peter 3:18 AMP).

For leaders in the church, there's no greater thing you can do for those you lead than to live a higher faith. Make it your passion to grow higher in your faith each day. Don't worry what people might say. You answer to God. If you want to draw people higher, *you* must be higher. What you teach is not as important as what you live—especially the life you live when nobody's watching.

To teach the higher faith, you must live the higher faith. "And you your-self must be an example to them by doing good works of every kind. Let everything you do reflect the integrity and seriousness of your teaching. Teach the truth so that your teaching can't be criticized. Then those who oppose us will be ashamed and have nothing bad to say about us" (Titus 2:7-8 NLT).

If you aren't one of the leaders in your church, you're still called to be a leader in God's kingdom. From wherever you are, lead from there. Live your life so that whoever is following you will be going in the right direction. What you do matters, and what you do now will someday be your legacy. Build good legacies. Live higher in your faith, and your life will be a blessing to those around you.

Child of God, my heartfelt prayer is that you'll grow higher in your faith. It's a journey like no other, and the Lord will be your prize. You'll never regret living a life that grows higher in the faith, and you'll be a blessing to all those around you. There isn't one other thing on this earth of greater importance to a soul than growing higher in faith. Make this the heartbeat of your life, and you'll be living higher in everything you do.

"The LORD bless you and keep you;
The LORD make His face shine upon you,
And be gracious to you;
The LORD lift up His countenance upon you,
And give you peace."
(Numbers 6:24-26 NKJV)

Blessings to you always,
Paul Balius

Acknowledgments

My lovely bride, Mary Balius, you are the most gentle and sweetest woman I have ever known. The Lord blessed me with you and for that I am forever grateful.

My parents, Herbert and Patricia Balius, who have been my model for godly living and the greatest intercessors for my ministry.

My children and grandchildren, who are such a blessing to me and inspire me to be better than I am. In the order I met you, Sarah, Trevor, Annie, Duyen, Erik, Emily, and Ellie.

Thomas Womack, who has blessed me with his masterful work in editing this book and my other books as well. I'm so blessed I met him. *BookOx.com*

Tamara Dever from TLC Book Design, I am eternally grateful for your patience, your guidance, and sharing pictures of your dogs with me. *TLCBookDesign.com*

Monica Thomas from TLC Book Design, you always amaze me with your creativity and attention to detail. I am so blessed to have you helping me!

Misti Moyer referred by TLC Book Design, I was absolutely blessed by the proofreading work you performed. Your godly discernment was a blessing to me. *MistiMoyer.com*

I want to thank the many precious souls who have poured into my life and blessed me with their friendship, counsel, and prayers. I could never name everyone here, but your names are written on my heart and spoken in my prayers.

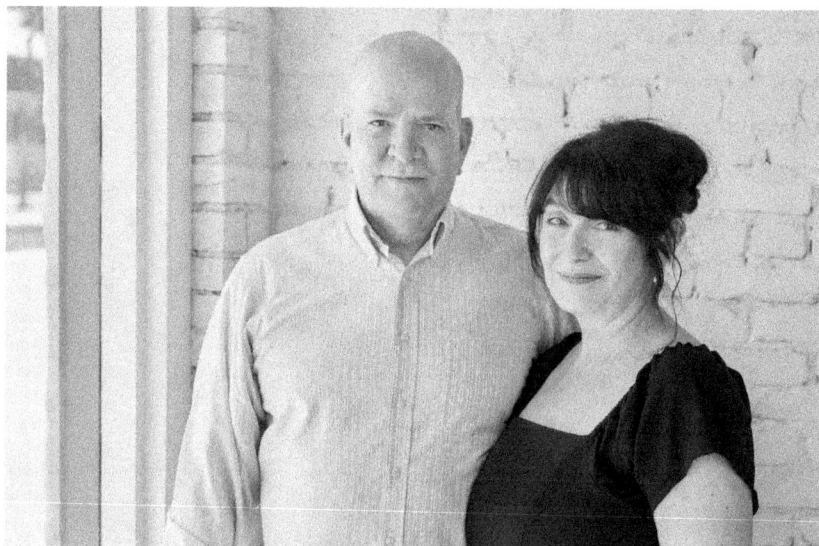

About the Author

Paul Balius is an author and teacher devoted to helping God's children grow in their faith. Paul spent fourteen years in prison ministry, the last seven teaching and preaching in several prisons. The Lord called Paul out of the prisons and into solitude, where he could begin writing for the kingdom.

Over the last several years, Paul has written thousands of devotions and hundreds of blogs. He is publishing books in the hope of reaching even one. His passion is to help people to unlock the mystery of the power of God into their life. Paul believes there is nothing impossible for God, not even you. Paul and his wife, Mary, currently reside in Orange, California.

Hehasyou.org
Facebook.com/Hehasyou

Other
Books by
Paul Balius

Do you sense that you were meant for something more?

You were meant for something more, and the something more is nothing less than being filled with the Spirit of God.

Do you long to walk in a higher faith with a deeper sense of the presence of the Holy Spirit?

Do you long to hear the voice of the Lord speaking into your life?

Do you long to have spiritual gifts that you might serve God with them?

In *The Promise of the Holy Spirit*, you will learn:

- ❖ About the promises of God for you.
- ❖ Coming to know the Holy Spirit.
- ❖ Being filled with the Holy Spirit.
- ❖ Being changed by the Holy Spirit.
- ❖ How to hear the Holy Spirit.
- ❖ Being led by the Holy Spirit.
- ❖ How to receive prophetic words.
- ❖ Discovering your spiritual gifts.
- ❖ How to reach a higher faith.

Are you ready to go to the next level in your faith? Get your copy of *The Promise of the Holy Spirit* and take hold of all that God has in store for you.

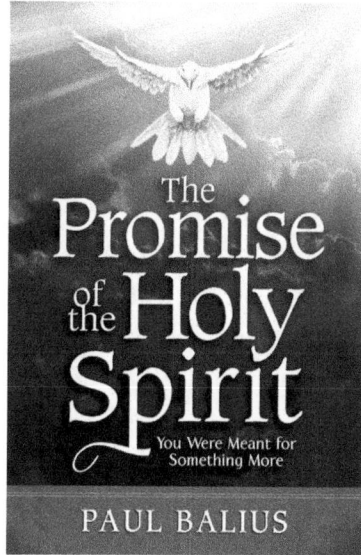

Have you ever felt like your faith is not that strong and your prayers don't seem to reach heaven?

Wouldn't you love to have a faith to get help from God with some impossible situation in your life?

In the book, *If You Can Believe*, you can learn how to have a faith that can move mountains!

In the book *If You Can Believe*, you will learn:

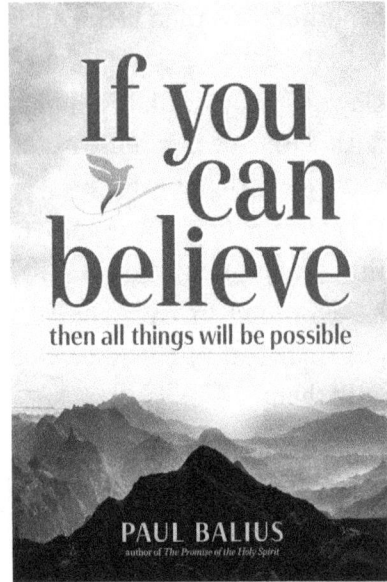

then all things will be possible

PAUL BALIUS
author of *The Promise of the Holy Spirit*

Available in hardcover, paperback, and ebook. 6 x 9 / 218 pages

❖ That you can have a faith so that all things are possible.

❖ The incredible power that comes through believing.

❖ The ways that God teaches you to believe even more.

❖ How to believe for that miracle you need.

❖ Having faith even when God says no.

❖ Overcoming all your doubts and fears.

❖ How to have a faith that can move mountains.

If you can believe, then the impossible will become possible! Get your copy of *If You Can Believe* and take hold of all that God has in store for you.

www.ingramcontent.com/pod-product-compliance
Lightning Source LLC
LaVergne TN
LVHW051451080426
835509LV00017B/1731